Income, Inequality, and Poverty during the Transition from Planned to Market Economy

WORLD BANK

REGIONAL AND

SECTORAL STUDIES

Income, Inequality, and Poverty

during the Transition

from Planned to

Market Economy

BRANKO MILANOVIC

The World Bank
Washington, D.C.

The World Bank Regional and Sectoral Studies series provides an outlet for work that
is relatively focused in its subject matter or geographic coverage and that contributes
to the intellectual foundations of development operations and policy formulation.
Some sources cited in this publication may be informal documents that are not readily
available.

Branko Milanovic is principal economist in the World Bank's Development Research
Group.

Cover design by Sam Ferro and Sherry Holmberg. The graphic shows that the
decline in Russia's gross domestic product (GDP) during the transition (1987 to
1995) was even greater than that of the United States during the Great Depression (1927 to 1935). U.S. GDP in 1927 and Russia's GDP in 1987 = 100.
Photograph: church in Tula, Russia, by Jan Pakulski.

Library of Congress Cataloging-in-Publication Data

Milanovíc, Branko. 1957–
    Income, inequality, and poverty during the transition from planned to
market economy / Branko Milanovíc.
       p. cm. — (World Bank regional and sectoral studies)
    Includes bibliographical references.
    ISBN 0-8213-3994-X
    1. Income distribution—Europe, Eastern. 2. Income distribution—
Former Soviet republics. 3. Poverty—Europe, Eastern. 4. Poverty—
Former Soviet republics. 5. Europe, Eastern—Economic
conditions—1989– 6. Former Soviet republics—Economic conditions.
    I. Title. II. Series.
    HC244.Z9I547   1997
    339.2'0947—dc21

                  96-32776
                  CIP

Contents

Appendices

Country Data Sheets   195

References   221

Indices   233

Tables

Figures

Preface

This is a book about income, inequality, and poverty during the remarkable period of collapse of Communism and the "construction" of capitalism in eighteen formerly socialist countries. It covers a period of almost ten years, from the time of the early Gorbachevian reforms of 1987–88 to approximately 1996. The book was made possible by two almost simultaneous revolutions that took place in the late 1980s. The first, of course, was the collapse of Communism. The second was the opening up of information on income, inequality, and poverty, even in countries (such as the former Soviet Union) where for the better part of the last seventy years such information had been treated as a state secret.

This is indeed a period of great turmoil—comparable with the period that followed both World Wars. It is the period of dramatic declines in income, the reappearance of diseases long forgotten, growing poverty and unemployment, and great uncertainty. But it is also a period when great fortunes are being made, consumer goods of incomparably better quality are becoming available for many, and people have the opportunity to control and radically alter their lives. Unlike during some previous episodes of turmoil, we now have relatively reliable and up-to-date information that allows us to follow and analyze the developments. The goal of this book is precisely this: to describe what happened during the transition in eighteen countries —from the Czech Republic in the West to Kazakhstan and Russia in the East. Specifically, the book will examine what happened to the real incomes of the population, to the inequality with which incomes and expenditures are distributed, and to poverty. It will also attempt to find out why these changes occurred.

A word about the data used in this book. All data on incomes and expenditures come from household budget surveys. Most of these surveys are conducted regularly (on an annual or quarterly basis) by national statistical offices, while some are done by independent non-governmental organizations, often in an *ad hoc* fashion. The surveys are of uneven quality. Some—for example, the regular, official surveys conducted in most Central European countries—are of a quality comparable with surveys conducted in advanced market economies. Because the quality of these surveys has remained unchanged or has improved during the transition, they allow us to measure the impact of the transition relatively well. But in some other countries, the quality of surveys has not improved, and their reliability may have deteriorated as circumstances changed. For example, while the surveys may have once offered a more or less accurate picture of households employed in the state sector, the decline in the size of that sector has significantly reduced the importance of that information.

These are only some of the problems peculiar to transition economies. Other data problems, common to surveys everywhere—such as inadequate coverage of the very rich and very poor, differing concepts of income, and differences in survey periods—further complicate the analysis undertaken here. The interested reader can consult appendix 1, where issues related to limitations of the data are discussed at length.

The book has its origin in the encouragement I received from Alan Gelb of the World Bank. The book would not have been possible without the large and varied data sources the World Bank has collected and developed during the past seven years of work on the transition economies. In particular, I benefited greatly from Jeni Klugman's and Jeanine Braithwaite's early work on poverty in Russia, recently published by the World Bank as *Poverty in Russia: Public Policy and Private Responses*.

I am grateful to the many colleagues, in the World Bank and elsewhere, who helped me locate necessary data, or who gave me the benefit of their advice. In particular, I am grateful to Jeanine Braithwaite, Mark Foley, and Jeni Klugman, who generously allowed me to use their Russian data. I am also grateful to Anna Ivanova, Nanak Kakwani, Alberto Martini, and Paolo Roberti, who provided me with data for Belarus; Jiří Večernik and Thesia Garner (Czech and Slovak Republics); Christiaan Grootaert, Gi-Taik Oh, and Zsuzsa Ferge (Hungary); Helen Jensen and Edmunds Vaskis (Lithuania and Latvia); Carlos Cavalcanti (Estonia); Mansoora Rashid (Romania); Jan Rutkowski and Irena Topińska (Poland); Tom Hopengartner (Ukraine); Milan Vodopivec and Irena Krizman (Slovenia); Neeta Sirur (Bulgaria); Michael Mills (Kyrgyz Republic); and Timothy Heleniak (countries of the former Soviet Union).

The book also benefited from the comments of Martha de Melo, Clara Else, Zsuzsa Ferge, Alan Gelb, Carol Graham, Christiaan Grootaert, Emmanuel Jimenez, Jeni Klugman, Janos Kornai, Mark Kramer, Kathie Krumm, Robert Liebenthal, Costas Michalopoulos, Aleksandra Pošarac, Martin Schrenk, and Maciej Żukowski. I am also thankful to the six anonymous reviewers who read the draft manuscript and contributed valuable comments and suggestions.

Parts of this book were presented at seminars sponsored by various organizations: the Economic Development Institute of the World Bank in Washington, D.C., Harvard University, the Council of Europe in Strasbourg, the Institute of Labor and Social Policy in Warsaw, the European Center in Vienna, and the 1995 meetings of the American Economic Association in San Francisco. I am also grateful for the fine research assistance provided by Yvonne Ying and Nadia Soboleva. Rachel Cantor did an excellent editing job. Virginia Hitchcock ensured the consistency of the style and editing. Vicky Hilliard and Kristi Stoner worked hard to put in shape the text, tables, and graphs: it was not an easy book to produce.

—————

To my mother, who has survived it all:
monarchy, capitalism, and Nazism;
Communism, socialism, and nationalism.

—————

1

The Tectonic Changes

June 4, 1989, was an eventful day. In Tehran, Imam Khomeini died. In Beijing, tanks rolled in to suppress student demonstrations. In Poland, the first freely contested election ever under a Communist regime took place.[1]

Political Developments: The New States

In June 1989, Communist regimes in Europe (including the U.S.S.R.) ruled more than 24 million square kilometers of territory, or 17 percent of the world's land area, and about 420 million people, or approximately 9 percent of the world's population. These people lived in the Soviet Union, six smaller Communist countries in Eastern Europe that were allied to the Soviet Union, and two independent Communist states (Yugoslavia and Albania).[2] In no country was organized opposition tolerated,[3] and in no country had genuine multiparty and free elections been held after 1947.[4]

Eight years after 1989—at the time of this writing—the landscape has entirely changed. In all these countries, competitive elections have taken place, even if these elections have not always been fair and transparent. In all these countries, except a few (Armenia, Azerbaijan, Kazakhstan, Tajikistan, Turkmenistan, and Uzbekistan), all kinds of political parties exist.[5]

---

1. Although the election was freely contested, the number of seats for the lower house of Parliament was predetermined, giving Communists almost 50 percent of the seats regardless of the outcome of balloting. The first entirely free elections in Eastern Europe were held in March 1990 in Slovenia and Hungary.
2. Mongolia is not included in the analysis.
3. Technically, Bulgaria, the German Democratic Republic, and Poland were multiparty states. Elections were held with predetermined seat allocations, however, and the so-called opposition parties functioned as faithful allies of the ruling Communist party. Yet, in a historic twist, it was the defection of the two "faithful" allied parties after the June 1989 Polish elections that allowed non-Communists to form the government.
4. The last free election in any of these countries was the Hungarian election in August 1947.
5. Turkmenistan had only a single-candidate election for Parliament (in December 1994). The president's term was simply extended by a referendum. In Uzbekistan, Birlik and Elk opposition groups are banned and their leaders exiled. In Kazakhstan, parliamentary elections in December 1995 featured almost no opposition parties, but a collection of government-sponsored parties, while the president's term was extended by referendum. In Azerbaijan, the president was elected in September 1993 with 99 percent of the vote and virtually no opponents. In February 1996, three major opposition parties were banned. In Armenia, the major opposition party Dashnak was suspended in December 1994. In Tajikistan, a collection of opposition groups and the government are at war.

The three Communist federations—Czechoslovakia, the Soviet Union, and Yugoslavia—have disintegrated, spawning in their stead a total of twenty-two countries. The number of countries in the world thus rose by approximately 15 percent. One Communist country (the German Democratic Republic) disappeared. Only five of the former European Communist countries (Albania, Bulgaria, Hungary, Poland, and Romania) have remained within the same borders. Approximately 345 million are now citizens of countries that did not exist prior to 1992. Forty-three million people in the former U.S.S.R. and 1.5 million in the former Yugoslavia now find themselves living outside their ethnic republics.[6]

As figure 1.1 shows, the number of countries in Europe is now greater than it has been in the last 140 years—even slightly greater than it was in 1860 before the Italian and German unifications. The difference now is that while in 1860 the West was segmented (Italy in three states and Germany in twenty-one), Eastern and Central Europe were largely unified under the Habsburg, Ottoman, and Russian Empires.[7]

Figure 1.1. *Number of Independent States in Europe, 1860–1995*

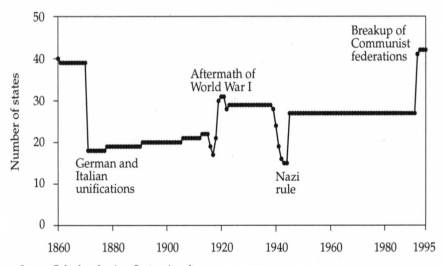

Source: Calculated using *Centennia* software program.

---

6. The number for Yugoslavia does not include Bosnia and Herzegovina, the only republic of twenty-three in the U.S.S.R., Czechoslovakia, and Yugoslavia not to have had a "titular" nationality.

7. The Habsburg empire spun off six countries: Austria, Croatia, the Czech Republic, Hungary, Slovakia, and Slovenia. Also, parts of the Empire were, at different times, taken over by Italy, Poland, Romania, and Yugoslavia. The Russian empire spun off twelve European countries: Armenia, Azerbaijan, Belarus, Estonia, Finland, Georgia, Moldova, Latvia, Lithuania, Poland, Russia, and Ukraine. The Ottoman empire spun off three countries: Albania, Bosnia, and Bulgaria.

The current emergence of new countries implied huge needs for institutional build-up, since many republics (particularly in the former Soviet Union) had underdeveloped national institutions and little experience running their own affairs. They are all practically "new" countries in the sense that they either had almost no experience with self-government or were never independent.[8] Of the seventeen countries born out of the ruins of the three Communist federations (not including Central Asian countries), five had not been independent states during the last two centuries: Bosnia, the Czech Republic, Macedonia, Moldova, and Slovenia. Five (Armenia, Azerbaijan, Belarus, Georgia, and Ukraine) were independent for three years or less during the turmoil of the Russian civil war that followed the 1917 Revolution. Two countries (Croatia and Slovakia) were independent for a brief period of four to five years during the Nazi rule over Europe. The three Baltic states had approximately twenty years of independent existence between the two World Wars. Serbia was independent for about sixty years, from about 1860 until 1915, before it merged into Yugoslavia in 1918.[9] And, finally, Russia, the big exception, went through practically all the stages: an Empire, a Soviet Republic, and now, as the Russian Federation, an independent democratic country. Excluding Russia, however, the average duration of independence for the other "new" countries was less than nine years over a 200-year period from the French Revolution until 1990.

In addition to the increase in the number of recognized countries, a number of states not recognized internationally have appeared—a new phenomenon in Europe. In virtually all countries with civil strife (see table 1.1), regions have in their turn declared independence. Often such regions control their own territory, a fact which in the past was sufficient to ensure them international recognition. Such self-declared independent states include the Transdnestrian Republic in Moldova, Chechnya in the Russian Federation, South Ossetia and Abkhazia in Georgia, Nagorno-Karabakh in Azerbaijan, and Kosovo in Yugoslavia. It is revealing that all regions, except the Transdnestrian Republic, enjoyed the status of autonomous republic in the U.S.S.R. or of province in the former Yugoslavia—a status one step below that of a republic.[10] The fissure along republican boundaries that rendered asunder the three Communist federations is apparently continuing at the next level of administrative organization.

---

8. Independence and self-governance are not necessarily the same thing: Hungary, for example, was self-governing in the Austro-Hungarian Empire but was not independent.

9. Montenegro, interestingly enough, had more experience of independence than any other country (except, obviously, Russia). Both Montenegro and Serbia, as well as Bulgaria and Romania, were officially recognized as independent states at the 1878 Berlin congress.

10. Transdnestria was "added" to Moldova (then called Besarabia) when Besarabia was annexed by the Soviet Union in 1940.

Table 1.1. Countries at War or under Economic Blockade, 1991–96

Country	War on its territory (pre-war population) in millions)	Estimated dead (in thousands)	Estimated internally displaced persons (DP) and refugees (in millions)	Percentage decline in GDP between 1987 and 1996	Economic sanctions
Armenia	No (3.2)	0	DPs: 0.376 Ref.: n.a.	58	Azeri and Turkish blockade
Azerbaijan	Yes (7.2)	15	DPs: 0.9 Ref.: n.a.	66	No
Bosnia	Yes (4.4)	250	DPs: 2.7 Refs.: 0.6	70[a]	No
Croatia	Yes (4.8)	20	DPs: 0.187 Refs.: 0.4	47	No
Georgia[c]	Yes (5.5)	11	DPs: 0.28 Refs.: n.a.	67	Yes
Macedonia	No (2.1)	0	n.a.	47	Greek blockade[d]
Moldova	Yes (4.3)	1	DPs: 0.015 Refs.: n.a.	61	No
Russia	Yes (148.2)	100[e]	DPs: 1.4 Refs.: 0.3	38	No
Tajikistan	Yes (5.2)	50	DPs: n.a. Refs.: 0.1	70	No
Yugoslavia	No (10.4)	0.2	DPs: 0.65 Refs.: 0.2	41	UN sanctions[b]
Total	7 countries with wars; 48 million people[g]	≈450	≈8[f]	40	

n.a. = not available.

a. Estimate.

b. Imposed in May 1992; suspended in November 1995.

c. Includes two conflicts: in Abkhazia and Southern Ossetia.

d. Lifted in September 1995.

e. Casualties in Chechnya.

f. The numbers cannot be added because of double-counting: out-refugees of one country are in-refugees of another.

g. Excluding Russia.

Source: Data on refugees in Bosnia and Croatia are from UN High Commissioner for Refugees, August 1995 (reported in *Nasa Borba,* August 20, 1995). For Federal Republic of Yugoslavia, from the census of refugees in April-June 1996. For countries of the former Soviet Union, from *International Migration Bulletin,* No. 6, May 1995 (data at the end of 1994) and Heleniak (1997). Sources for casualties: Tajikistan: Akchurin (1995); Azerbaijan: *The Economist,* November 13, 1993, p. 61; Croatia and Bosnia: Zimonjic-Peric (1995); Russia: *RFE/RL Daily Service* April 1994; Moldova, Georgia and Azerbaijan: Gurr (1994).

War and civil strife have affected approximately 50 million people in the war-torn countries profiled in table 1.1. Almost half a million people have been killed and about 8 million (or approximately 15 percent of the countries' population excluding Russia) have become refugees or displaced persons, fleeing either persecution and war or leaving the newly independent states where they are minorities for the relative safety of their "mother countries." As shown in table 1.1, 4 million refugees and displaced people are from the territory of the former Yugoslavia (or almost 20 percent of the former Yugoslavia's population); 1.5 million are from the Transcaucasian countries; and 1.5 million are from the Russian Federation. Those in war-torn countries who have not been killed, maimed, or injured, or who have not become refugees, have experienced plummeting standard of living. Best available estimates suggest that nowhere has real per capita income decreased by less than one-third. Major economic and social dislocations, of a size unseen since the Second World War and its aftermath, are clearly underway.

By the end of 1997, only the bloodiest of these conflicts, the Bosnian had been resolved. The intensity of all the conflicts, however, was less by the end of 1997 than it had been one or two years before.[11]

Political instability has also been accompanied by coups, successful and unsuccessful popular uprisings, and assassination attempts. A bloody coup against Georgia's first democratically elected president brought Georgia's former Communist party boss back to power. Later, Shevardnadze himself was the target of a failed assassination attempt. Similarly, a creeping coup against Azerbaijan's first elected president brought Azerbaijan's former Communist leader, Haidar Aliyev, to power. Aliyev himself later faced an unsuccessful coup. In Russia, the president dissolved Parliament, and the Parliament responded by attempting an armed rebellion. The president bombed the deputies out of the Parliament building. Macedonia's first president narrowly escaped an assassination attempt. The results of Armenia's presidential elections were so contested that the re-elected president had to call in tanks and troops against his opponents. In Serbia, the ruling Socialists refused to accept electoral defeat until three months of peaceful demonstrations and international pressure obliged them to do so. In Albania, after the fraud-marked parliamentary elections and collapse of a score of government-sponsored pyramid schemes, the country plunged into anarchy. In Tajikistan, an assassination attempt on the president failed but left several people dead.

The building of new democratic institutions is also hampered by the paucity of democratic traditions in virtually all transition countries.[12] If democ-

---

11. The Abkhaz-Georgian, Nagorno-Karabakh, Chechen, and Transdnestrian conflicts are in the cease-fire stage; war in Tajikistan is much less intense.

12. For a historical overview of political developments in Eastern Europe, see Polonsky (1975) and Walters (1988). For Hungary, see Sugar, Hanak, and Frank, eds. (1990). For Bulgaria, see McIntyre (1988). For the Baltic countries, see von Rauch (1974). For Transcaucasia, see Goldenberg (1994). Very useful is also a beautiful historical atlas with the text by Magocsi (1993).

racy is defined as (a) universal and secret (male) suffrage[13] with competitive party elections, from which no important parties are banned; and (b) a government responsible to a parliament or to a democratically elected president, then the longest pre-1990 democratic tradition is that of the Czech Republic and Slovakia, which have twenty-three years of experience (1918–38 and 1945–48). Romania and Serbia each have about twenty years of (checkered) experience with democracy,[14] followed by Latvia and Estonia each with about thirteen years (1920–33). Several countries had only a few years of experience with democracy: Bulgaria during 1919–23 and 1926–35, Lithuania during 1920–26, Poland during 1922–26, and Armenia, Azerbaijan, and Georgia during their brief periods of independence. All other countries under discussion here have had no democratic experience at all—only a few democratic episodes, such as the period from March to November 1917 when Russia was ruled by the provisional government, or Hungary between 1945 and 1947. During the entire period following World War I, when universal franchise became the norm in many Western countries, and until 1990, countries in Eastern Europe and the former Soviet Union had an average of nine years of democratic experience, and no country had lived in a democratic system for more than twenty-five years.

Social Costs

The total value of goods and services produced by the vast area covered by the transition economies, extending from the Baltic and the Adriatic in the West to the Northern Pacific in the East, has declined since the transition started by at least one-quarter in real terms. Expressed in dollars, the decline has been even steeper, as many local currencies have depreciated. In 1989, the value of this area's output, assessed at realistic (that is, *not* official) exchange rates, was about US$1.2 trillion, or virtually the same as the gross domestic product (GDP) of the Federal Republic of Germany, and three times that of China.[15] The average annual per capita income was about $3,000. In 1996, transition economies (exclud-

---

13. Democracy is defined in this restricted way in order to identify discrimination based on social class and income, not gender.

14. Romania, from 1919 to 1938, and Serbia from 1903 to 1914, and then (as part of Yugoslavia) from 1919 to 1929. (Obviously, other successor states of the former Yugoslavia also experienced democracy between 1919 and 1929.) However, in both Romania and Yugoslavia, there were problems. The respective prerogatives of the kings and parliaments were not clearly spelled so that governments sometimes depended more on kings than on parliaments (for example, Romania under Carol II during 1930–38, and Yugoslavia under Alexander I during 1919–29). Not surprisingly, both kings (Alexander in 1929 and Carol in 1938) eventually suspended the constitution and assumed full power. Also, fraud was massive during several Romanian elections and two large parties were banned in Yugoslavia (the Communists after 1921 and the Croat Peasant Party briefly in 1925).

15. All data are from various years of the *World Bank Atlas*. All dollar amounts are current U.S. dollars.

ing eastern Germany) produced goods and services valued at approximately $880 billion, or only 40 percent of the united Germany's GDP and just 20 percent more than China's GDP. The GDP of the Netherlands is equal to that of the Russian Federation; the GDP of Finland is equal to that of Poland; and the GDP of Hong Kong, China, is greater than the GDP of Ukraine. The region's average GDP per capita has declined to about $2,000. After the Great Depression of 1929–33, this decline represents the largest peacetime contraction of world output.

At the same time, poverty has increased substantially in the region. While it was estimated that, in 1989, the number of people living on less than $4 per day (at international prices) was 14 million (out of a population of approximately 360 million), it is now estimated that more than 140 million people live below the same poverty line.[16] (See chapter 5 for the calculations and the discussion.) Social transfers, and free health care and education, once taken for granted, are now rapidly shrinking. Mortality and morbidity, particularly in the countries of the former Soviet Union, have increased substantially in some cases, without peace-time precedent (Heleniak 1995). Unemployment, almost nonexistent (except in the former Yugoslavia) before the transition, affected more than 15 million people by 1996 and is still rising.

On a more positive note, the economic landscape is rapidly changing for the better. In all the countries studied here, state ownership is being replaced by private ownership (see table 1.2). While in 1989, only Hungary, Poland, and Yugoslavia were members of the International Monetary Fund (IMF), and none of them had a convertible currency, by 1996, thirteen of eighteen countries shown in table 1.2 had convertible currencies. As an indicator of monetary stabilization, by 1996, triple-digit inflation was present in only two countries (Bulgaria and Turkmenistan), and in several countries (the Czech Republic, Slovakia, and Slovenia), inflation was reduced to single-digit levels.

Such massive dislocations—the creation of new states, civil wars, and declines in GDP—have had huge social costs. Conceptually, we can divide these costs into three categories.

First, costs associated with decreases in output due to systemic changes (that is, the transition to market economy) and to macroeconomic stabilization. These costs are expressed in lower incomes, higher inequality, and greater poverty.

Second, job-loss costs associated with the transition. Job-loss is sometimes accompanied by poverty but not always. Unemployment is a distinct issue from poverty.

Third, costs associated with civil strife. These are costs of lives lost, people becoming refugees, and destruction of property.

In this book we shall deal only with the first type of costs. The second (unemployment) will be discussed only to the extent that it affects poverty

---

16. This calculation does not include the countries at war or with civil strife listed in table 1.1. (Russia is included though.)

Table 1.2. Speed of Reforms in Selected Countries, 1992–96

Country	Estimated privatized state assets (percent)	Non-state sector share in total employment (percent)	Share of retail trade sales in private hands (percent)	Current account (exchange rate) convertibility	Explicit producer subsidies (percent of GDP)	CPI inflation in 1996
Belarus	Slow 13 (95)	28 (96)	39 (96)	No	9 (92)	40
Bulgaria	Slow	59 (95)	69 (94)	No	2 (93)	310
Czech Republic	Fast 60 (end 94)	57 (95)	66 (93)	Yes	2 (95)	9
Estonia	Fast 85 (end 94)		54 (93)	Yes	<1 (94)	15
Hungary	Medium 49 (end 94)	54 (95)	48 (93)	Yes	2 (95)	20
Kazakhstan	Medium 8 (92)	37 (95)	78 (96)	Yes	5 (93)	29
Kyrgyz Republic	Medium 35 (93)	67 (95)	80 (96)	Yes		35
Latvia	Fast 50 (mid-95)	66 (95)	83 (97)	Yes	<1 (94)	13
Lithuania	Fast 55 (end 94)	63 (95)	82 (95)	Yes	1 (95)	13
Moldova	Slow	66 (95)	64 (96)	Yes	1 (95)	15

Country	Estimated privatized state assets (percent)	Non-state sector share in total employment (percent)	Share of retail trade sales in private hands (percent)	Current account (exchange rate) convertibility	Explicit producer subsidies (percent of GDP)	CPI inflation in 1996
Poland	Medium 35 (93)	64 (96)	83 (91)	Yes	1 (95)	19
Romania	Slow 8 (94)	56 (95)	74 (95)	No	6 (93)	57
Russia	Fast 70 (end 94)	63 (96)	73 (96)	Yes	7 (93)	22
Slovakia	Medium	21 (92)	94 (96)	Yes	5 (92)	6
Slovenia	Slow	28 (94)		Yes	>1 (92)	9
Turkmenistan	Slow	52 (95)	66 (96)	No	9 (93)	100
Ukraine	Slow 1 (93)	33 (95)	76 (96)	Yes	4 (96)	40
Uzbekistan	Slow	63 (95)	74 (96)	No		86

Note: Areas are shaded if a variable takes the value at least equal or "better" than "fast" for privatized state assets, 40 percent for non-state share in total employment, 50 percent for share of private retail trade, "yes" for current account convertibility, "less than 5 percent" for producer subsidies, and "less than 20 percent" for inflation. All data in parentheses refer to the year.
Source: See appendix 7.

Figure 1.2. *A Map of Europe and Central Asia*

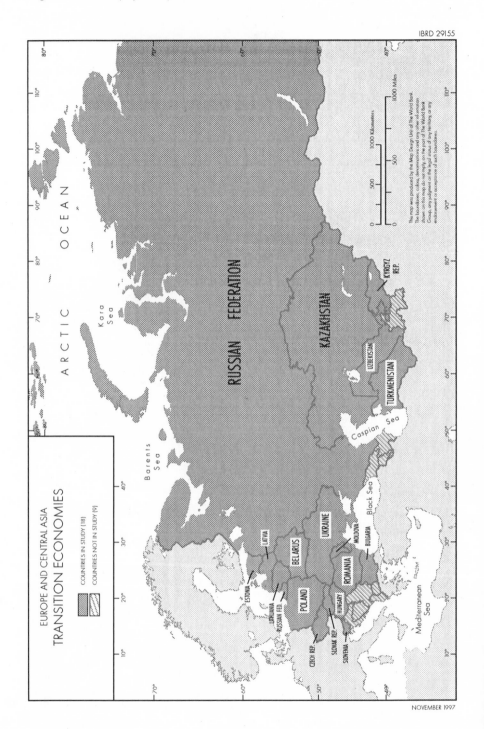

IBRD 29155

EUROPE AND CENTRAL ASIA
TRANSITION ECONOMIES

COUNTRIES IN STUDY [18]
COUNTRIES NOT IN STUDY [9]

This map was produced by the Map Design Unit of The World Bank. The boundaries, colors, denominations and any other information shown on this map do not imply, on the part of The World Bank Group, any judgment on the legal status of any territory, or any endorsement or acceptance of such boundaries.

1000 Miles
1000 Kilometers

ARCTIC OCEAN

Kara Sea

Barents Sea

RUSSIAN FEDERATION

KAZAKHSTAN

KYRGYZ REP.

UZBEKISTAN

TURKMENISTAN

Caspian Sea

Black Sea

Mediterranean Sea

LATVIA

ESTONIA

LITHUANIA

RUSSIAN FED.

POLAND

CZECH REP.

SLOVAK REP.

SLOVENIA

HUNGARY

BELARUS

UKRAINE

MOLDOVA

ROMANIA

BULGARIA

NOVEMBER 1997

10

and inequality. The third type is not, properly speaking, a cost of economic transition, but rather the cost of nation-building and the creation of a "new world order." Responsibility for the latter cost lies with politicians, not economists.

In this book, the topics of income, inequality, and poverty shall be discussed only in reference to the countries listed in table 1.2, that is, the eighteen countries unaffected by military conflict.[17] They are shown in figure 1.2.

The organization of the rest of the book is as follows. Chapter 2 will review the key features of income composition, income inequality, and social policy in the former system. Chapter 3 will look at what happened to the population's real income—its size and composition—during the transition. Chapter 4 will analyze the inequality with which income and expenditures are distributed and the change in the relative position of different social groups during the transition. Chapter 5 will assess what happened to poverty under the twin impact of declining income and growing inequality. Chapter 6 discusses social policy issues related to the transition. Chapter 7 presents a brief look at what might lie ahead.

---

17. The only exception is Russia, which had a limited military conflict on its territory, but is obviously too important not to include.

2

The Way It Was

Income Composition and Inequality

The defining characteristic of socialist countries was state ownership of the means of production. Though this ownership took various forms—direct state ownership, "social" ownership, or some form of collective ownership—and though the management rights of the state varied—from direct allocative central planning to bureaucratic interference in decentralized decision-making—the role of the state was undeniably major. On average, 90 percent of the labor force was employed by the state as compared to members of the Organisation for Economic Co-operation and Development (OECD), where an average of 21 percent was so employed (see table 2.1). On the household level, the role of the state was reflected in the fact that most income was received through the mediation of the state: through wages paid to employees working in state-owned enterprises (SOEs) (including farms) or in government; pensions paid out of state-administered funds or directly out of the budget; and family allowances, scholarships, etc. Only in countries with private agriculture (Poland, Yugoslavia, and, more recently, Bulgaria and Hungary) were private sources of income of some importance. In other countries, private income was

Table 2.1. *State Employment as a Proportion of the Labor Force, 1988*
(percent)

Country	Share
Socialist average	*90.0*
Czechoslovakia	98.8
U.S.S.R.	96.3
Romania	95.2
German Democratic Republic	94.7
Hungary	93.9
Bulgaria	91.5
Yugoslavia	78.9
Poland	70.4
OECD average	*21.2*

Note: All averages are unweighted. Czechoslovakia, Poland, and Romania, 1989; German Democratic Republic, 1987. The state sector includes the government, social services run by the state (health and education), and state-owned enterprises (SOEs), including agricultural cooperatives (*kolkhozes* in the U.S.S.R.). "Social sector" in Yugoslavia is treated as a state sector. OECD data from the late 1970s and mid-1980s.
Source: Milanovic (1994a, appendix 1).

minimal and limited to income from small-scale agricultural plots, self-consumption, gifts or remittances, moonlighting, and black market activities.

Table 2.2 shows the composition of household income in socialist countries before the transition. Countries are arranged, from left to right, in the order of the increasing importance of private sources in total gross income.[1] At one end of the spectrum is Czechoslovakia, where an almost total "socialization" of agriculture and severe restrictions on non-agricultural private business meant that only a small fraction (5 percent) of total income was not received through state mediation. In the Soviet Union, approximately 14.4 percent of gross income was derived from private sources. In Bulgaria, Hungary, Yugoslavia, and Poland, the private income share was greater than 20 percent.

Labor income—virtually all of it derived from the state—ranged from 53 percent of total gross income (in Poland) to 72 percent (in the U.S.S.R.). Social transfers ranged between 13 percent (Yugoslavia and the U.S.S.R.) and 25 percent (Czechoslovakia) of gross income.

Table 2.2. *Composition of Income in Socialist Economies, 1988–89*
(gross income=100)

Income source	Czecho-slovakia	U.S.S.R.	Bulgaria	Hungary	Yugoslavia	Poland
Primary income	72.9	78.8	71.2	71.7	83.1	78.2
Labor income	69.5	72.0	56.5	55.0	62.2	53.0
Self-employment income	3.4	6.8	14.7	14.0	20.9	25.2
Property income	n.a.	n.a.	n.a.	2.7	n.a.	n.a.
Social transfers	25.4	13.6	21.2	22.4	13.3	20.7
Pensions	16.5	8.0	16.6	13.4	12.1	14.3
Child benefits	5.6	1.2	2.3	6.0	1.2	5.2
Other cash transfers	3.3	4.4	2.3	3.0	0.0	1.2
Other income[a]	1.7	7.6	7.6	6.0	3.6	1.1
Gross income	100.0	100.0	100.0	100.0	100.0	100.0
Personal taxes	14.2	*n.a.*	*n.a.*	16.5	1.2	1.6
Direct taxes	0.0	n.a.	n.a.	10.7	1.2	1.6
Payroll tax (employee)[b]	14.2	0.0	0.0	5.8	0.0	0.0
Memo: Private income[c]	5.1	14.4	22.3	22.7	24.5	26.3

n.a. = not available.

a. Includes private transfers (gifts, alimony, remittances), insurance and lottery receipts, and rental income (if not included in property income).

b. Except in Hungary and Czechoslovakia, the entire payroll tax was paid by enterprises.

c. Equal to self-employment income, property income, and other income.

Source: Czechoslovakia: *Microcensus 1988.* Poland, Bulgaria and Yugoslavia: 1989 Household Budget Surveys; Hungary: 1989 Income Survey; U.S.S.R.: 1988 Family Budget Survey.

---

1. The entire wage income is here allocated to the state sector. This is only a very slight exaggeration because the private sector (outside of self-employment) was minimal.

Table 2.3. *Composition of Gross Income in Socialist, Market, and Developing Countries, 1980s*
(percent)

	Socialist countries	Market countries	Developing countries
Primary income	77	85	90
Labor income	63	64	35
Self-employment income	13	14	48
Property income	1	5	6 [a]
Occupational (private) pensions	0	2	0
Social transfers	19	14	3
Pensions	13	12	2
Child benefits	4	1	0
Other cash transfers	2	1	0
Other income [b]	6	1	7
Gross income	100	100	100
Total taxes	34	38	n.a.
Direct taxes	3	20	n.a.
Payroll tax (employee)	7	5	n.a.
Payroll tax (employer) [c]	24	13	n.a.
GDP in '000 $PPP (1988, per capita)	5.5	14.0	1.8 [d]

Note and Source: All averages are unweighted. Socialist is the average of the countries listed in table 2.2. Market economies are the following eleven OECD countries: Australia, Canada, France, West Germany, Israel, New Zealand, Norway, Spain, Sweden, the United Kingdom, and the United States. All of the data are from 1979-81, with the exception of Australia and New Zealand (1985–86) and Spain (1988). The source for the first seven countries is LIS data reported in O'Higgins, Schmaus, and Stevenson (1989, p. 107); New Zealand and Australia from Saunders, Stott, and Hobbes (1991); France from Sologoub (1988, p.5); Spain calculated from INE (1989, pp. 366-67). Developing countries are represented by Côte d'Ivoire, Ghana, Jordan, Peru, Madagascar, and Vietnam with sources respectively Kozel (1991, p.15), Boateng and others (1992, p. 22), World Bank (1993, p. 33), World Bank (1994), World Bank (1996c, p. 22), and Vietnam State Planning Committee General Statistical Office (1994, p. 218).
  n.a. = not available.
  a. Includes inputed rent.
  b. Includes private transfers (gifts, alimony, remittances), insurance and lottery receipts.
  c. Estimate based on 40 percent enterprise-paid payroll in socialist countries and 20 percent in market economies.
  d. Excludes Vietnam.

Features specific to socialism are more apparent when the average income composition for former socialist countries is contrasted with income composition of developed market economies and of developing countries (see table 2.3). There are three such features.

1. The share of primary income, that is, income that results from economic activity (labor, capital, entrepreneurship), was smaller in socialist than in market economies or developing countries. This is a reflection of three phenomena: (a) virtual absence of property incomes; (b) absence of occupational pensions (which are considered part of primary income); and (c) greater importance of income redistribution,

whether via the state (social transfers in socialist countries represented 19 percent of gross income as compared with 14 percent in market economies) or privately (6 percent in socialist countries as compared with 1 percent in market economies).[2]

2. Much lower direct taxation under socialism (personal income taxes plus employee-paid payroll tax): 10 percent of gross income as compared with 25 percent for market economies. Total payroll taxes were high, however (between 40 and 50 percent of net wages), and the overall tax burden was not much different from that found in market economies.

3. Child benefits were more important in socialist countries than in market economies (4 percent of gross income as compared with 1 percent).

In addition, the following regularities ("stylized facts") regarding the distribution of income in socialist countries are generally accepted.

4. Overall income distribution was more egalitarian than in most market economies even after allowing for (a) fringe benefits and various forms of implicit income received by the *nomenklatura* and (b) direct subsidies.[3] The distribution of direct subsidies generally favored the poorer segments of the population.[4] Element (a) pulled income inequality up while element (b) pulled income inequality down. When both *nomenklatura* benefits and subsidies were added to measured income, overall inequality did not change much. The Gini coefficient was in the range of 23 to 26[5] or slightly above that of very egalitarian Nordic countries, but definitely below inequality in other OECD countries, or other countries at similar level of development.[6]

---

2. Most of other income is private transfers.

3. There are numerous studies comparing income inequality in socialism and capitalism. I will cite only a few: Atkinson and Micklewright (1992), which present the most detailed study of inequality and poverty in Central Europe (Czechoslovakia, Hungary, and Poland) and Russia during the post-War period. Phelps-Brown (1988) and Morrisson (1984) contrast East and West European income distribution. Muller and others (1991) compare the German Democratic Republic and the Federal Republic of Germany. Bergson's (1984) excellent review of inequality in the Soviet Union, with its extensive bibliography, is a classic in the field. Good comparative studies of several socialist countries include Asselain (1987), Kende (1987), Debroy (1986), and Flakierski (1986, 1989, 1993).

4. See Milanovic (1994, pp. 193–95), where results of several studies of East European countries are discussed. For the German Democratic Republic, see Bird, Frick, and Wagner (1995, p. 6), who show that the simultaneous inclusion of consumer subsidies and benefits for the *nomenklatura* leaves the calculated Gini coefficient unchanged. For discussion of Czechoslovakia, see Hiršl, Rusnok, and Fassman (1995, p. 2).

5. Except in Yugoslavia, where it was greater because of huge regional differences in average income. For the exact values of the Gini before the transition, see table 4.1.

6. In the work on the Kuznets' curve, it was standard practice to introduce a dummy variable for socialist countries. The dummy variable was always found significant and negative. That is, socialism was found to reduce inequality below its expected level (see, for example, Ahluwalia (1976) and Kaelble and Thomas (1991)).

5. Cash social transfers were distributed almost equally per head in socialist countries in contrast to some market economies where such transfers were more focused on the poor.[7] As shown in figure 2.1, the absolute amounts of cash transfers in Czechoslovakia, Hungary, and Poland
were approximately equal for the poor and the rich (a value of 1 indicates that the share of the decile in the total amount of transfers was 10
percent; a value of 2 indicates that the decile of recipients received 20
percent of transfers, and so on). The concentration coefficient of cash
transfers was thus very close to zero in socialist economies.[8, 9]

The approximate equality of cash transfers per capita regardless of the recipients' position in income distribution was the outcome of two separate
distributions: pensions, and other cash transfers, among which family allowances were the most important. [10]

Pensions tended to be slightly pro-rich in absolute terms. The positive correlation between recipients' positions in income distribution and their level
of pensions was stronger in countries where pensions were relatively high
(that is, where the average-pension-to-average-wage ratio was greater than

---

7. Market economies differ greatly in terms of concentration of cash transfers. Differences in results are driven by differences in (a) how pensions are administered (for
example, whether the pension system is mostly state-financed, in which case pensions
are a part of social transfers, or differently, occupational and other private pension schemes
are important), and (b) the relative position of pensioners (whether they are relatively
well off or not). Thus, while some countries (for example, Australia, Finland, and Switzerland) target social transfers on the poor (so that the concentration coefficients of social
transfers is around -10), other countries (Belgium, Germany, and Sweden) have strongly
positive concentration coefficients for transfers showing that there is a positive correlation between disposable income and the amount of received social transfers. For the definition of the concentration coefficient, see footnote 9 below. (Data on market economies
are derived from the LIS data base, and cover the late 1980s to the early 1990s; see Milanovic
1995c, table 2.)

8. The discussion of the distributional incidence of transfers (stylized fact 5) and
taxes (stylized fact 8 below) is based on Milanovic (1994, p. 178) and Milanovic (1995).
Using an equivalent scale rather than a per capita measure (for example, assigning less
weight to children than to adults) would tend to place families with children higher, and
pensioners lower, in the income-distribution scale. Because pensions account for a bulk
of cash social transfers, the distributional impact of cash transfers might then become
more pro-poor.

9. The concentration coefficient shows the concentration (or cumulative percentage) of an income source (for example, social transfers or wages), when recipients are
ranked by amount of disposable income. The coefficient ranges from -1 (or -100 if expressed in percentages as is done here), when the entire income source is received by the
poorest (by income) recipient; through 0, when all recipients receive the same amount; to
+100 when the entire income source is received by the richest recipients. A concentration
coefficient's negative (or positive) value shows that a given source is negatively (or positively) correlated with overall income.

10. Family allowances include all family-related transfers: birth grants, maternity
pay, regular monthly family allowances, and so on.

Figure 2.1. *Distribution of Social Cash Transfers by Income Decile*

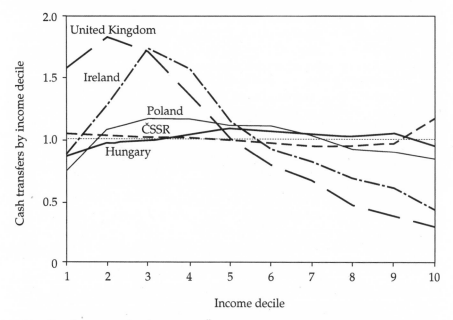

Income decile

Note: Equal per capita distribution = 1. ČSSR = Czechoslovak Socialist Republic.
Source: Milanovic (1995, p. 495).

50 percent) as in Eastern Europe. In the late 1980s, pension concentration coefficients ranged between +5 and +10 in Eastern Europe (see the concentration curves for Czechoslovakia and Hungary in figure 2.2, which just barely depart—to the right—from the line of perfect equality).[11] By contrast, in the Soviet Union, where the pension-wage ratio was smaller, pensioners belonged to lower income groups, and the concentration coefficient was strongly negative (see data for Russia in figure 2.2). Transfers other than pensions were mildly pro-poor with concentration coefficients ranging between -5 and -15. Most progressivity of non-pension transfers was due to family allowances and other family-related transfers (for example, child care and maternity allowances). Thus, the mildly pro-rich or neutral pensions and the mildly pro-poor family allowances combined to produce a basically flat distribution of

---

11. The concentration curve shows the cumulative percentage of income source (on the y axis) against the cumulative percentage of recipients (on the x axis). An income source is said to be pro-poor in absolute terms, if its absolute amount declines with increases in income (for example, social assistance). Such a source is associated with a negative concentration coefficient and a concentration curve that lies above the 45-degree line (for example, see pensions for the Russian Republic in figure 2.2). The opposite is true for a source that is pro-rich in absolute terms.

Figure 2.2. *Concentration Curve for Pensions in Hungary, Czechoslovakia, and the Russian Republic, 1988–89*

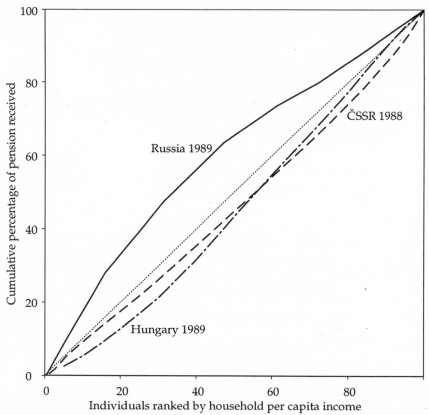

Note: ČSSR = Czechoslovak Socialist Republic.
Source: Milanovic (1995, table 1).

social transfers—social transfers were paid more or less equally across the entire income spectrum.

6. In countries where private sector incomes were low, the share of private sector incomes in gross income was broadly flat across income distribution. In countries with private agriculture, where private incomes were more important, the share of private income in gross income exhibited an inverted U-shaped pattern—being high in relation to overall income at the low and high end of income distribution. This meant that most "private-oriented" households were either poor agricultural households (often living barely above the subsistence level) or very successful, even if not very numerous, private businesses (see Milanovic 1991, and Marnie and Micklewright 1993, figure 5).

7. There is some debate regarding inequality of wage distribution. According to some (for example, Atkinson and Micklewright 1992, chap-

ter 4; Phelps-Brown 1988, pp. 39–51; and Lydall 1968, pp. 152–62), wage distribution in socialist countries was more egalitarian than in market economies. [12] According to others (for example, Redor 1992), the differences between the two distributions were not systemic—that is, they could be explained by elements other than the difference in the economic system, such as the size of the country, enterprise concentration, and participation rates (although the latter two can be regarded as system induced). Most authors, however, agree that the difference between average pay of non-manual and manual workers was less in socialist countries than it was in market economies and that returns to education were therefore less (see Redor 1992, pp. 60ff.; Rutkowski 1996; and Jackman and Rutkowski 1994).[13]

8. Direct taxation was proportional to wages because most direct taxes were paid as proportional payroll taxes. Progressive direct taxes were minimal and no country had a personal income tax system similar to systems common in the West.[14] Taxes had virtually no redistributive effect: if, on average, direct taxes were proportional to wages, which were not distributed much differently from overall income, it follows that tax distribution was close to the distribution of income—taxes, in other words, were proportional (or "flat," to use the current terminology) rather than progressive (Milanovic 1994, pp. 184–86).

These eight regularities ("stylized facts") define the distribution of income in socialist countries relatively well. But what was the logic of the system that engendered such distribution?

Ideological Underpinnings

According to socialist ideology, most of the population was supposed to work in the state sector. To have people employed by the state was both a statement of the ideological objective and a means. The objective was to speed up realization of a "developed socialism" characterized by a predominance of the state sector. The means for achieving this objective was fast economic growth, which in turn meant fast growth of the state sector, because the state sector was (not unlike in Schumpeter's *Capitalism, Socialism and Democracy*) regarded as more efficient than the private sector. It is worth remembering that the time when Communists came to power was in many countries the epoch of the "big is beautiful." The state sector was also considered to be the

---

12. For example, Phelps-Brown (1988) notes the absence of the Paretian right-end tail (that is, highest earnings) in socialist wage distributions.

13. Redor (1992, p. 63) finds that the difference between average manual and non-manual wage explained between 17 and 30 percent of the overall wage inequality in the Federal Republic of Germany and France and practically none in Eastern Europe.

14. In 1988 Hungary became the first to introduce a real personal income tax system.

best vehicle for transferring the labor force from agriculture to industry and from rural to urban areas (particularly since socialism won mostly in agrarian countries).

In consequence, the state sector was to be developed, while the private sector was to be allowed to wither away, or was, at best, to be tolerated. [15] High participation rates for both men and women were to be encouraged, as work in the state sector was also a way to be usefully integrated into society. High participation of women was needed both to speed up growth (by utilizing all labor resources) and as a proof of the equality of the sexes, an early Communist objective. High participation rates combined with a generally pro-children stance (as reflected in free health care and education) resulted also in a heavy emphasis on family allowances, the size of which, in relation to wages, could be several times greater than in market economies (see table 2.4). Family allowances also introduced an element of reward "according to needs"—a harbinger of distribution as it should be, according to Marx, in a developed Communist society.

Ideological views on wage distribution were ambivalent. On the one hand, socialist ideology is against wide differences in income; on the other hand, people should be paid according to their contribution, at least in theory, which means that differences in abilities and effort should be recognized. Marx's dictum that under socialism, workers are paid according to their work (as opposed to "communism," where workers should be paid according to their needs), as well as the influence of Taylorism on the early Bolshevik practice, meant that wage differences were not only to be tolerated, but accepted. [16] *Uravnilovka*, or leveling, had, from the early days of Soviet Communism, acquired a negative ideological connotation.

Manual labor was, in general, preferred to non-manual labor: small differences in wage between manual and non-manual labor reflected this ideological preference. The preference itself had roots in the crude (and actually mistaken) interpretation of Marx's concept of "productive" and "unproductive" labor, and in the *nomenklatura's* belief that manual workers represented the "salt of the earth" for the Communist party and were politically more reliable than intellectuals. [17]

---

15. Incidentally, this view resulted in a desire to statistically demonstrate the progress of socialization by contrasting the shares of the state and private sectors. This explains why such statistics are more readily available in formerly socialist countries than they are in market economies.

16. Taylorism remained quite alive well into the 1970s. Redor (1992, p. 159) points out that in the late 1970s, piece-rate pay was much more common in Eastern Europe and the Soviet Union than it was in OECD economies. About 50 percent of industrial workers in socialist countries were paid according to the piece-rate system. Corresponding percentages in the West ranged from 5 percent in Belgium, to 12 percent in France, to 22 percent in West Germany.

17. A high percentage of Communist leaders were workers or came from a working-class background. Often they were skilled (metal) workers rather than less-skilled (say, textile) workers. Examples include Brezhnev in the U.S.S.R., Tito in Yugoslavia, Kádar in Hungary, and Novotný in Czechoslovakia.

Table 2.4. *Family Allowance for Two Children as Percentage of Average Earnings,*
1988

Country	Percentage of average earnings
Hungary	24.9
Bulgaria	20.0
Czechoslovakia	19.6
Poland	17.0
Austria	16.9
Belgium	10.7
Netherlands	9.0
United Kingdom	8.2
France	6.5
Italy	5.4
United States [a]	0.0

Note: Does not include tax deductions available for families with children (important in the United States and France) and thus underestimates the amount of family benefits in the market economies.
a. No universal child allowance.
Source: Sipos (1994).

Finally, individual accumulation of wealth was frowned upon for ideological and pragmatic reasons. Ideologically, Communists were against big differences in wealth. Large wealth inevitably "overflows" into the production process: initially such wealth may be used for personal consumption (for example, for purchasing a house and a car), but eventually it will be used to obtain ownership of the "means of production" complete with hired labor, an outcome which is obviously antithetical to socialism. On pragmatic grounds, Communists were also against private wealth because wealth provides "an island of liberty" for those who have it. The rich can become independent from imposed political obedience. Thus, Communist authorities preferred collective consumption and income-in-kind to cash rewards. Collective consumption (for example, state-sponsored sanatoria and kindergartens, or free vacations) and income-in-kind (for example, plush houses for the *nomenklatura*) have the advantage that they appear more "collectivistic," they cannot be accumulated, and they can easily be withdrawn if one fails to toe the political line.

From the above tenets, the shapes of "ideal" socialist income distribution emerge. Most income is earned in the state sector (pensions received after retirement are an extension of state-sector employment); high participation rates obtain; unemployment is non-existent; family allowances are relatively high; wages are compressed with low pay in intellectual professions; collective consumption and income-in-kind are important; and wealth accumulation is minimal. Actual income distributions in socialist countries came reasonably close to this ideal. Actual income distributions, therefore, did not evolve by accident: they were logical extensions of the ideological premises of Communism, which, conveniently, often coincided with the political interests of Communist rulers.

3

Income

Changes in income are the most decisive factor influencing poverty. This is especially true when income declines are as great as those found in Eastern Europe and the former Soviet Union. Changes in income distribution, as a factor influencing poverty, then take a second place.

The Post-Communist Great Depression

Incomes

Table 3.1 shows the average (weighted) change in the officially recorded GDP during 1987–96. [1] In Eastern Europe as a whole, growth fell from about 2 percent in 1987 and 1988 to slightly above zero percent in 1989. In 1990, the average growth rate was strongly negative (-8.2 percent). The decline reached its maximum in 1991 (-14.7 percent). Eventually, in the 1994–96 period, Eastern Europe grew at the rate of about 4 percent per year, and growth spread to almost all countries in the region. [2] In 1996, overall GDP in Eastern Europe was approximately 80 percent of its 1987 level. The trend in the former Soviet Union was similar to that in Eastern Europe with about a year, at first, and then apparently longer time lag. The Soviet GDP continued to grow until 1989. [3] It shrank by 2.5 percent in 1990 and by 6.5 percent in 1991, and in 1992 it fell precipitously by 16 percent. In the following two years, the region's GDP experienced a double-digit decline. The combined GDP of countries that composed the former U.S.S.R. was in 1996 approximately 60 percent of its 1987 level.

---

1. The officially recorded decline in GDP almost certainly exaggerates the actual decline (see the section, *The effect on population incomes: how level and composition of income changed*, below). It is nonetheless necessary to begin with official measures—which in the further text will be adjusted (to the extent possible). The year 1987 is used for comparison purposes because it was a year before serious reforms were initiated and because economic levels reached by socialist countries in 1987—while not likely to improve by much— could have been sustained for a prolonged period.

2. In 1994 and 1995, only the Former Yugoslav Republic of Macedonia experienced negative growth, as did Bulgaria in 1996.

3. According to the alternative calculations of Khanin (1992), however, the Soviet GDP had begun to decline already by the second half of 1988 (yielding zero growth for the year as a whole), and in 1989 it shrank by 2 percent. For a critique of Khanin's methodology, see Kudrov (1995, 1996). For a general discussion of Russian post-Soviet macroeconomic data, see Bloem, Cotterell, and Gigantes (1995) and Koen (1996).

Figure 3.1. *Distribution of Countries' Growth Rates in Eastern Europe, 1987–96*

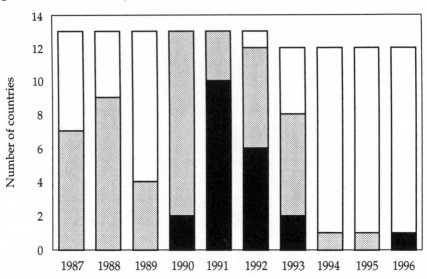

Figure 3.2. *Distribution of Countries' Growth Rates in the Former Soviet Union, 1987–96*

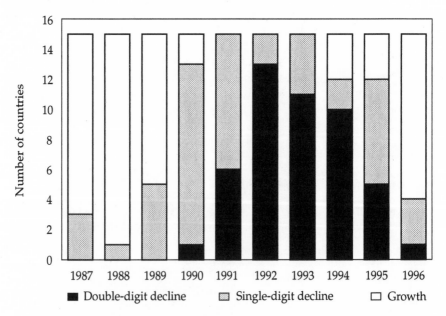

Note: The Czech Republic, the Slovak Republic, and all republics of the former Yugoslavia and Soviet Union are shown here as separate countries. German Democratic Republic is not included. Bosnia and Herzegovina is not included after 1992.

Table 3.1. GDP Growth Rates in Eastern Europe and the Former Soviet Union,
1987–96
(percent per annum)

Region	1987	1988	1989	1990	1991	1992	1993	1994	1995	1996
Eastern Europe	1.9	1.6	0.5	-8.2	-14.7	-8.1	-1.9	4.1	5.5	3.6
Former Soviet Union	2.4	5.2	2.7	-2.5	-6.5	-16.1	-10.1	-14.0	-5.2	-4.7
Total	2.3	4.0	1.9	-3.7	-8.6	-14.3	-8.1	-9.2	-1.9	-2.0

Note: Eastern Europe includes the German Democratic Republic until 1989.
Source: Official government statistics. Data for the Soviet Union are official statistics except for
Russia where the revised official GDP statistics published by the World Bank and Government
of the Russian Federation (1995) are used also for the period before the Soviet Union's breakup.
There are minimal differences between these statistics and PlanEcon statistics or the data
published by World Bank Socio-economic Data Division (1992).

How widespread, deep, and long-lasting was the post-Communist depression? Depression is defined as involving at least two years of continuous
GDP decline. According to this definition, all transition economies experienced a depression after 1990; no country experienced fewer than three years
of consecutive GDP decline.

Both the GDP decline and its subsequent recovery affected all the countries in
the region (figures 3.1 and 3.2). In 1987, most socialist countries recorded growth
rates of between 2 and 3 percent per year, and only Albania, Armenia, Georgia,
Tajikistan, and the former Yugoslavia had negative growth.[4] The situation did
not change much in 1988 and 1989. By 1990, however, all East European countries and all republics of the former Soviet Union (except two: Uzbekistan and
Turkmenistan) were in a decline. For three years, during 1990–92, in a remarkable unison, the GDPs of almost all twenty-eight countries dropped, with the
GDP of more than half the countries shrinking more than 10 percent annually.
Only one country (Poland) posted positive, if minimal, growth (1.5 percent) in
1992. By 1993, half the East European countries (Albania, Poland, Romania, and
Slovenia) were growing again, and by 1994 and 1995, almost all were. In the
former Soviet Union, however, the decline was still universal in 1993. Three
countries turned the corner in 1994 (Armenia, Latvia, and Lithuania), and by
1996, nine of fifteen countries were growing again, although the largest countries (the Russian Federation and Ukraine) continued to post negative growth
rates.

The depth of the depression is best assessed by comparing it to the 1929–33
Great Depression. Figure 3.3 shows the GDPs of Russia and Poland, and the
United States and Germany. Data on Poland and Russia are presented because of the size of these countries (combined, they produce almost one-half
the output of all transition economies) and because of the radicalism of their
reforms. For Poland and Russia, the base year is 1987; for Germany and the

---

4. The then-republics of Czechoslovakia, the U.S.S.R., and Yugoslavia are considered separate countries here for the sake of comparison.

Figure 3.3. *Real GDP in Poland and Russia (1987–95); and in the United States and Germany (1927–35)*

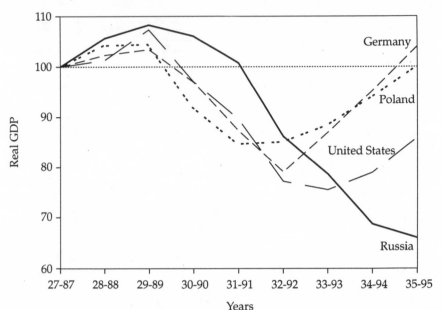

Note: 1927 = 100 for the United States and Germany; 1987 = 100 for Poland and Russia.
Source: The Great Depression data, unless noted otherwise, are from Fozouni, Gelb, and Schrenk (1992).

United States, the most hard-hit countries during the Great Depression, the base year is 1927. For all countries, peak output is reached in the third year following the base year. If Russia is compared with Germany and the United States, it emerges that initially, the decline was steeper in Germany and, particularly, in the United States.[5] By the third year of depression (1932 and 1992), GDPs in the United States and Germany were approximately 20 percent below pre-depression levels; in Russia, the GDP was 14 percent below. Then, the situation reversed. In 1933, Germany grew quickly, at a rate of approximately 10 percent per year, and the U.S. GDP declined, although by very little, while Russia's GDP continued its plunge, in both 1993 and 1994 by 9 and 13 percent, respectively. Thus, by 1935, Germany was above its base GDP level, the United States was approximately 15 percent below, while Russia in 1995 was 34 percent below its base level. In other words, the post-Communist depression in Russia is deeper than the Great Depression was in the United States and Germany. The depres-

---

5. Throughout, revised GDP statistics for the Russian Federation published jointly by the World Bank and Government of the Russian Federation (1995) are used. The revised GDP is approximately 6 to 7 percent higher for the period 1991–93 than that recorded by earlier official statistics. There is virtually no difference between the two sets of numbers for 1990 and 1994 (see World Bank and Government of the Russian Federation, 1995, p. 94).

sion in Poland, although deeper during the first two years (1990–91), was not as severe as the depressions in the other three countries. The Polish trough, reached in 1991, was approximately 15 percent below the base level. Moreover, as already mentioned, Poland was the first transition economy to emerge from the depression: in 1995, its GDP had returned to its 1987 level.

Russia had experienced another major GDP decline in 1917–21, during the Revolution and Civil War, when its GDP declined by approximately one-half (according to Block [1976] as quoted in Sokoloff [1993]). The decline of 1917–21 represented a fall of approximately 60 percent from the pre-War level (see table 3.2). The current post-Communist depression is about half as severe. During both crises, agricultural output, not surprisingly, contracted less than industrial output.

The duration of the depression is also important. A longer depression probably has a more deleterious effect on welfare than a shorter depression, even if the overall decline is the same. The same conclusions can be drawn from the permanent income hypothesis. A short, even if sharp, decline in income is treated as transitory because it does not affect long-term income or consumption. A drawn-out depression, on the other hand, reduces people's perception of their long-term income and consumption, possibly by even more than the actual decline, because they may expect decreases to continue. Thus, for example, the GDP in the United States dropped in 1938 by about 5 percent to quickly recover the following year. Understandably, no one talks of 1938 with nearly the same awe with which people still refer to the Great Depression. In terms of duration, the post-Communist depression appears as bleak as or worse than the 1929–33 Depression. Most transition countries have experienced between three and four years of successive GDP declines, and some have experienced five (Romania, 1988–92; Estonia, 1990–94) or six years (Hungary, 1988–93; Slovenia, 1987–92;[6] and Belarus,

Table 3.2. *Russia's Output Decline after the Dissolution of the Czarist Empire and after the Dissolution of the U.S.S.R.*

Year	GDP		Industrial output		Agricultural output	
	1913=100	*1987=100*	*1913=100*	*1987=100*	*1913=100*	*1987=100*
1917 or 1991	75	101	77	97	100	97
1919 or 1992	54	86	26	79	88	87
1920 or 1993	45	79	18	66	62	84
1921 or 1994	38	69	n.a.	52	n.a.	77
1922 or 1995	n.a.	66	n.a.	51	n.a.	70

n.a. = not available.

Source: 1913–22: GDP from Sokoloff (1993); industrial output (only large-scale) and agricultural output (only cereal production in Central Russia) from Kritsman (1926), quoted in Pipes (1990, p. 696). 1987–95: World Bank data.

6. Declines in Hungary and Slovenia were, however, small, at least by the standards of other transition economies. War-affected countries are not included here; Azerbaijan, Croatia, and Georgia have each experienced six successive years of GDP decline.

1990–95) or even seven years (Moldova, Russia, and Ukraine, 1990–96) . During the Great Depression, by contrast, GDP decreased for three successive years in Germany, four years in the United States, and six years in France, while the GDPs of the United Kingdom and Italy alternated between growth and decline.

While the effects of the two depressions were similar for the populations concerned (and probably worse for Russians now than for Americans sixty years ago), the impact of the two depressions on the rest of the world was different. In the late 1980s, transition countries accounted for about 6 percent of the world's GDP (at current exchange rates); about 6 percent of world trade, only half of which was not among themselves; and approximately 9 percent of the world's population. The shrinking of their GDPs by a quarter thus reduced the world's GDP by approximately 1.5 percentage points. On the other hand, the major capitalist countries where the Great Depression began (the United States, the United Kingdom, Germany, and France) accounted for more than half the world's output, $\frac{2}{3}$ of world trade, and 70 percent of industrial production (Gazier 1983; Romer 1993, p. 20n). Their combined GDP decline of about 20 percent between 1929 and 1933 meant that the world's GDP shrank as much as one-tenth; world industrial output decreased by one-third (Bairoch 1993, p. 136), and the volume of world trade dropped by 25 percent.[7] Since they were the "core" countries, their links with the rest of the world (via trade and capital flows), and the dependence of the rest of the world on them, was much greater than the dependence of the rest of the world on formerly socialist economies. The Great Depression led to export declines and a sharp deterioration in the terms of trade for African, Asian, and Latin American countries. Some authors hold that the Great Depression signaled the beginning of underdevelopment in the Third World.

Wages and unemployment

One major difference between the Great Depression of 1929–33 and the current post-Communist depression is the way in which wages and employment have adjusted (see figures 3.4 and 3.5). During the Great Depression, wages in all major countries (the United States, the United Kingdom, and Germany) remained stable in real terms. At the same time, unemployment grew from an initial rate of 5 to 10 percent of the labor force in the late 1920s to between 20 and 25 percent (and even more in Germany). The adjustment of the wage bill was thus entirely borne by a quantity adjustment: that is, unemployment went up. The wage bill was cut by between 15 and 20 percent in real terms, falling a few percentage points short of the decline in output. The labor share in GDP

---

7. GDPs in major market economies declined, between the peak and the trough, as follows: the United States by 30 percent (1929–33), Germany by 24 percent (1930–32), France by 17 percent (1930–36), the United Kingdom by 5 percent (1929–32), and Italy by 5 percent (1929–34). Japan's GDP over approximately the same period grew by 20 percent.

Figure 3.4. *Real Wages in Poland and Russia (1987–96); and in the United States, the United Kingdom, and Germany (1927–36)*

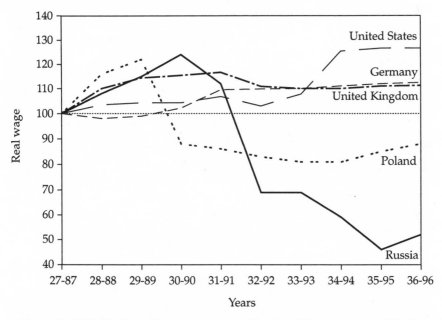

Note: 1927=100 for the United States, Germany, and the United Kingdom. 1987=100 for Poland and Russia.

Source: For the United Kingdom and the United States: Bain and Elsheikh (1976, appendix E). For Germany, James (1986, p. 196) and Pierenkemper (1987). For Poland and Russia, World Bank data.

thus expanded (Fozouni, Gelb, and Schrenk 1992; James 1986, p. 416).

Labor adjustment during the post-Communist depression occurred differently. In Russia and other countries of the former Soviet Union, registered, and even actual unemployment, is very small, while real wages have declined between 40 and 60 percent.[8] This type of wage-bill adjustment is thus exactly the opposite of the adjustment that took place during the Great Depression.

The East European situation lies between these two extremes. Both real wages and employment have decreased. On average, real wages dropped by one-fourth between 1987–88 and 1994, while unemployment grew from zero percent to between 12 and 15 percent of the labor force (except in the Czech Republic, where unemployment is much lower). In no transition economy, except those affected by war, has the severity of unemployment reached Great Depression levels.

The real wage bill was cut by approximately one-third in Eastern Europe

8. In 1995, of all former Soviet republics, only Latvia had a registered unemployment rate of more than 5 percent of the labor force. Registered unemployment in Russia was 3.2 percent, and actual unemployment was estimated at 9 percent.

Figure 3.5. *Unemployment Rates in Hungary, Poland, and Russia (1987–95); and in the United States, the United Kingdom, and Germany (1927–35)*

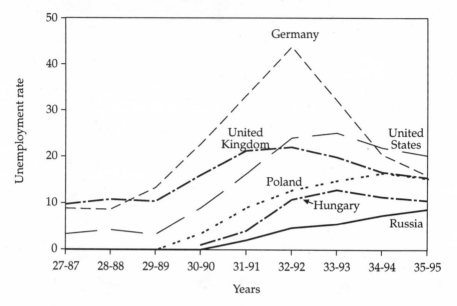

Note: Percent of labor force (annual average).
Source: For the United Kingdom and the United States: Bain and Elsheikh (1976, appendix E). For Germany, Pierenkemper (1987). For transitions economies, World Bank data.

and one-half in countries of the former Soviet Union; both cuts are larger than those experienced by labor in major countries during the Great Depression. Further, in contrast with the Great Depression, the share of labor income in the GDP was reduced in countries of the former Soviet Union, and remained constant in countries of Eastern Europe.

The Effect on Population Incomes: How Level and Composition of Income Changed

Decline in real population income

The decline in real population income provides a better indicator of hardship than an aggregate measure such as GDP. This is so because GDP accounting is faulty and because GDP movements do not always mirror changes in population income and welfare.

Recorded GDP declines in former Communist countries overstate real declines because official accounts err at both ends: by overstating the level of GDP achieved prior to transition and by failing to record fully the growth of the most dynamic sector, that is, the private sector after the transition. Previous GDPs were "padded up," principally for two reasons. First, all levels of the Communist hierarchy had incentive to report better than actual fulfillment of planned targets because their promotions and income depended on target overfulfillment. [9] Second, published GDPs underestimated inflation (and thus overestimated real output) and did not adequately account for the low quality of goods.

On the other hand, the increase in private sector activities since the transition is not fully reflected in macroeconomic statistics. The informal or "shadow" economy is estimated to account for between 10 and 15 percent of recorded GDP in more "orderly" transition economies (for example, the Czech Republic and Hungary) and up to 50 percent in countries affected by war and embargoes (for example, Armenia and the Federal Republic of Yugoslavia). [10] It seems certain that in all transition countries, the share of the informal sector has increased, whether because the absolute size of the sector has expanded or because it had shrunk less than the formal economy has. This increase in the share of the informal sector implies that GDP declines are overstated.

The discrepancy between GDP and welfare in formerly socialist economies existed because some goods produced and recorded as part of the GDP did not contribute much, or anything, to the welfare of the population (such as production of armaments and shoddy goods recorded at higher than market prices). [11] Also, the transition-related declines in gross investments (which have no immediate impact on welfare and were to a large extent wasteful under socialism), in inventories (which tended to be excessively high), and

---

9. The most extreme example of this phenomenon was the hugely falsified cotton harvest results under Uzbekistan's Communist ruler Rashidov in the 1970s and early 1980s.

10. Árvay and Vértes 1994 study of Hungary represents the most detailed study of the informal sector in a transition economy. They estimate that the informal sector not covered by statistics has grown from between 11 and 12 percent of the GDP before the transition to 17 percent in 1993. Kadera (1995) assesses the Czech shadow economy to be 8 to 10 percent of the recorded GDP. Slovak *INFOSTAT* agency estimates Slovak informal economy to be about 12 percent of the recorded GDP in 1995 (Narodna Banka Slovenska, 1996, p. 28). Sadowski and Herer (1996) estimate the Polish informal economy to be 25 percent of the recorded GDP. In Russia, the informal or "shadow" economy was estimated to be 20 percent of the GDP by the chairman of the *Goskomstat* (press conference on December 6, 1994). Croatia's informal economy was estimated to have increased (under very conservative assumptions) from 18 percent of recorded GDP in 1990 to 23 percent in 1995 (Madžarević and Mikulić, 1995). The shadow economy in the Federal Republic of Yugoslavia (Serbia and Montenegro) was estimated to have risen from 32 percent of the official GDP in 1991 to 54 percent in 1993 because of hyperinflation and illegal activities connected with United Nations sanction-busting and the war in Bosnia (see Yugoslav Federal Government 1995).

11. Some argue that official GDPs in socialist countries were necessarily biased upward by the use of arbitrary prices, including higher-than-market prices for inferior goods. This view, however, fails to acknowledge that there were many other products (such as energy, industrial inputs), as well as dwelling rents, and land value that were unrecorded in GDP or assessed at less than market value. Also, the material concept of Net National Product used by all Communist countries yielded estimates that were approximately 20 to 25 percent below the United Nations' System of National Accounts (SNA) concept of gross national product (see Marer 1985, pp. 18–19).

in arms production (in the Soviet Union) had little to do with population welfare. [12]

The problems with estimating population welfare either disappear or are muted if real population income or expenditure is used. Some problems, such as the decline in fixed investments or inventories, then disappear, by definition. Other problems become less acute, because population incomes, and in particular (formal sector) wages and social transfers, are almost fully captured by statistics. Private sector activities, both formal and informal, are better captured by household-level statistics, for example, through household surveys of incomes or expenditures, than they are by GDP statistics. [13] Retail or consumer price indexes also reflect inflation—as it affects consumers—better than GDP deflators do.

Estimates of real population income are derived from two sources: macroeconomic sources (national accounts) and household budget surveys (HBSs). Population income from macroeconomic sources is obtained by adding all money funds received by the population, including cash wages and, sometimes, in-kind fringe benefits; social transfers; entrepreneurial income; dividends; and other sources of income, such as remittances, income from the lease of assets, fees, and honoraria. Estimated home consumption is then added to this figure. HBS income is defined in the same way as it is in macroeconomic statistics, but it is obtained through regular household interviews and then extrapolated to the level of the population. In some HBSs, an attempt is made to account for the differential response of various population groups and to correct for income underreporting. Almost all HBSs also include estimated consumption-in-kind. [14]

Another way to assess what happened to population welfare is to look at real expenditures. Expenditures are also collected by most HBSs and are often considered a more reliable measure than income. The reason for this is that while people may be reluctant to share information about their

---

12. According to Winiecki (1991), at least two components of the registered output decline do not matter to population welfare. One part of the decrease was purely a statistical artifact because of the earlier practice of padding output figures to show fulfillment of plan targets. The second part of the decline was due to behavioral changes among enterprises and, to some extent, individuals. For example, better availability of goods, higher interest rates, and harder budget constraint led enterprises to reduce inventory stocks, which in socialist economies were inordinately high. The drawing-down of inventories produced a short-term output decline, but in reality it represented an adjustment to market conditions. Thus, the first component is fictitious, and the second, while involving a real decline in output, had no effect on population welfare.

13. There are numerous problems associated with household surveys in transition economies, however (see appendix 1).

14. Consumption-in-kind is an important source of income in transition economies. It includes not only own consumption, but also a portion of small-scale production that may be sold. The latter is not, strictly speaking, consumption-in-kind, but is often treated as such because households that sell a portion of their output may not do so regularly or may not be willing to report such sales as commercial activity.

income with interviewers whom they assume to be agents of the government, they may be less wary when asked to give information about expenditures. Results from eleven countries do, on average, confirm that HBS expenditures tend to be higher than HBS incomes: in six cases, expenditures are more than 20 percent greater than income;[15] in three cases, they are about the same; and in only two cases, income is higher than expenditures (see table 3.3).

Table 3.4 and figure 3.6 show estimated changes during the transition in real per capita GDP and in the two measures (macro and HBS) of population real income.[16] Table 3.4 shows that (unweighted) income declines were the least sharp in Eastern Europe. According to GDP and HBS data, real per capita incomes were, on average, 21 percent and 25 percent smaller, respectively, in 1993–94 than they were in 1988; according to macroeconomic data, they were perhaps 10 percent less. In the Baltics, real incomes seem to have fallen by almost a half, according to the GDP data, and 40 percent according to HBS data. In Moldova and the Slavic republics of the former Soviet Union, the decrease in income was more than one-third, according to GDP data, one-

Table 3.3. *Ratio between Expenditures and Income Reported in Household Budget Surveys*

Country (year of survey)	Mean expenditures:mean income
Eastern Europe	*1.03*
Slovakia (1993)	0.83
Bulgaria (1993)	0.85
Hungary (1993)	1.00
Slovenia (1993)	1.02
Romania (1994)	1.19
Poland (1993)	1.30
Former Soviet Union	*1.58*
Estonia (1995)	1.02
Belarus (1995)	1.21
Russia (1993)	1.23
Ukraine (1995)	2.10
Kyrgyz Republic (1993)	2.32

Note: All regional averages are unweighted. Both income and expenditures are defined on a net (that is, after tax) basis.

Source: For surveys, see appendix 4. See also information on surveys and caveats in appendix 1.

---

15. In two cases (the Kyrgyz Republic and Ukraine), expenditures are more than twice HBS income, suggesting that even HBS income must be hugely underestimated.

16. Success in transition should not be assessed from these figures because they refer to different dates.

Table 3.4. Change in Real per Capita GDP and Real per Capita Population Income between 1988 and 1993
(percent)

Country	Real per capita GDP	Real per capita income (macro data)	Real per capita income (HBS data)
Eastern Europe	-21	-7 [a]	-25
Bulgaria (1989–93)	-27	n.a.	-45
Czech Republic	-18	-7	-12
Hungary (1987–93)	-15	+1	-26
Poland (1987–93)	-12	-11	-26
Romania (1989–94)	-26	-18	-43
Slovakia	-29	-29	-29
Slovenia (1987–93)	-21	+20	+8
Baltics	-49	n.a.	-41
Estonia (1988–94)	-37	n.a.	-37
Latvia (1988–95)	-43	n.a.	-45
Lithuania (1988–94)	-66	-44	-42
Slavic republics	-37	-49	-54
Belarus (1988–95)	-34	-30	-44
Moldova	-39	-67	-67
Russia	-27	-33	-42
Ukraine (1988–95)	-49	-64	-62
Central Asia	-28	-39	-54
Kazakhstan	-26	-57	-61
Kyrgyz Republic	-35	-58	-66
Turkmenistan	-31	-40	-46
Uzbekistan	-20	+1	-43

n.a. = not available.

Note: The end years are 1988 and 1993 unless different years are given between brackets. All regional means are unweighted. To insure comparability among the dates of different data sources, the actual years of comparison for GDP and macroeconomic data are the same as the years for which household surveys are available. Macroeconomic and HBS data for Lithuania do not include consumption-in-kind in 1994; HBS data for Hungary do not include consumption-in-kind in 1993.

a. Does not include Bulgaria.

Source: GDP and macro incomes: World Bank data. HBS incomes: calculated from surveys presented in appendix 4. See also caveats in appendix 1.

half according to macroeconomic data, and more than one-half according to HBSs. Similarly, in Central Asia, GDP declines were smaller than income declines whether measured by macroeconomic data or by HBSs.

It is remarkable that of the sixty-two observations in table 3.4 and figure 3.6 [17] only five show an increase: minimal 1 percent macroeconomic income

17. Sixty-two observations represent three observations for each income concept for eighteen countries *less* three unavailable observations *plus* eleven expenditure observations (shown only in figure 3.6).

Figure 3.6. *Real per Capita GDP and Real per Capita Population Income in 1993–95* (pre-transition = 100)

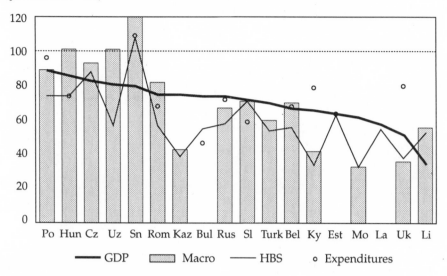

Note: Countries are arranged in ascending order of their GDP decline (Poland has the smallest decline, Lithuania the greatest).
Source: Table 3.4.

increases in Hungary and Uzbekistan, and macroeconomic and HBS income and expenditure increases in Slovenia.

Of interest is the relationship between the two measures of population real income. For most countries where both sources of data are available, HBSs show larger income declines than macroeconomic data do. In Hungary and Romania, the difference amounts to more than one-quarter of initial (that is, pre-transition) income; in Poland, it is 15 percent; and in Russia, it is 9 percent.[18] The correlation coefficient between changes in HBS and macroeconomic income is a high 0.88. HBS income change and macroeconomic income change are less strongly correlated with GDP change: the correlation coefficient is 0.68 for HBS income and GDP, and 0.66 for macroeconomic income and GDP. A stronger correlation between macroeconomic and HBS data is expected because they both measure the same thing: the real income of the population. GDP, of course, includes components other than population income. Perhaps more importantly, during the transition cost-of-living indices used to deflate the HBS and macroeconomic income have moved differently from (often increasing faster than) implicit GDP deflators.

---

18. Note, however, that the large difference between the two measures in Hungary and Lithuania may be explained by non-inclusion of consumption-in-kind in 1993–94.

Table 3.5. *Population Income by Sources in 1987–88 and 1993–94*
(percent of GDP)

Country	Wages 1987–88	Wages 1993–94	Cash social transfers 1987–88	Cash social transfers 1993–94	Non-wage private sector income 1987–88	Non-wage private sector income 1993–94	Social transfers in kind (health and education) 1987–88	Social transfers in kind (health and education) 1993–94	Total 1987–88	Total 1993–94
Eastern Europe	33	32	11	15	10	19	7	9	62	75
Bulgaria	27	25	11	14	9	21	7	11	55	71
Czech Republic	41	32	12	13	4	24	9	12	67	82
Hungary	32	37	13	19	10	14	7	12	63	83
Poland	27	32	9	20	22	25	7	9	65	85
Romania[a]	35	33	9	9	3	14	4	5	52	61
Slovakia	42	31	13	13	4	17	11	6	70	68
Slovenia	28	34	11	16	10	20	7	7	57	77
Baltics	43	35	8	12	9	14	9	8	70	69
Estonia[b]	46	33	9	11	8	10	11	8	73	62
Latvia	38	33	8	14	8	12	8	9	62	69
Lithuania[b]	46	40	8	10	12	18	9	8	76	76
Slavic republics	41	29	8	9	6	16	6	9	61	63
Belarus	40	37	6	8	7	17	7	12	59	74
Moldova	43	23	7	8	8	28	10	12	69	72
Russia	41	26	8	9	5	23	5	7	59	64
Ukraine	42	25	9	12	7	8	7	10	66	55

Note: All regional means are unweighted. Regional means as calculated avoid the rounding off errors.

Definitions: Wages equal income from employment. Social cash transfers equal pensions, family and child allowances, sick leave payments, unemployment benefits, and social assistance. Non-wage private sector income equals income from sales of agricultural products, entrepreneurial income, interest and dividends, income from abroad, gifts, and income (or consumption) in kind. Health and education equals total government expenditures on health and education.

a. 1992–93 instead of 1993–94.
b. Does not include home consumption.
Source: Income of the population as a whole (from macroeconomic sources): World Bank data.

Changing income composition

The composition of population disposable income changed during the transition. Population income can be divided into three categories: (a) wages; (b) cash social transfers; and (c) self-employment, home consumption, property income, private transfers, and other private sector income. The last category can be termed "non-wage private sector" income. It underestimates the true size of private sector income because it omits some informal sector income, as well as wages earned in the private sector. The latter are classified together with other wages. As the transition proceeds, this three-way classification becomes less of an indicator of transformation toward a private property-based economy than it was at the beginning of the transition process. This is because at the beginning of the transition, practically all income from private sector activities was included in the third category. It then served as a good proxy for the size of non-state sector. As privatization expands, however, more private sector income is earned through private sector wages. The three-way classification is thus somewhat biased against faster reformers. In any case, it gives the lower-bound estimate for the size of the private sector.

Table 3.5 illustrates the changing composition of population disposable income. The three types of income, as well as in-kind social transfers (health and education), which are not part of population disposable income, are shown as percentages of (current) market-price GDPs. Not surprisingly, the share of total population income (inclusive of health and education) in GDP increased in most countries between 1987–88 and 1993–94. The accounting explanation for this is that other types of income (for example, gross operating surplus of enterprises, indirect taxes, and inventory build-up) contracted more severely than the GDP did. [19] A more meaningful explanation is that under conditions of rapidly declining GDPs, most governments tried to cushion the population as much as possible from the effects of the depression.

Broad regularities revealed by data in table 3.5 are:

- The (unweighted) share of labor income in the GDP has remained constant in Eastern Europe and has declined in the Slavic republics of the former Soviet Union (by 12 points) and the Baltics (by 8 points).[20]
- The share of social cash transfers in the GDP has risen in all three regions (by between 1 and 4 percentage points of GDP).
- The share of non-wage private sector income in the GDP has increased everywhere: by 9 percentage points of GDP in Eastern Europe, 10 points in the Slavic republics, and 5 points in the Baltics. [21]

---

19. Because GDPs in table 3.5 are at market prices (and not at factor cost), population-income components cannot add up to 100 percent of GDP.

20. Data for the Central Asian republics are not presented because they are not reliable.

21. Private sector data for Estonia and Lithuania do not include consumption-in-kind. Because consumption-in-kind has increased, in real terms probably, and certainly as a share of GDP, the growth of private sector income is underestimated in the Baltics.

- The share of health and education in the GDP has increased by about 2–3 GDP points in Eastern Europe and the Slavic republics of the former Soviet Union.

In all East European countries (except Slovakia) the share of population income in GDP increased. For all these countries combined, the share went from 62 to 75 percent, because of a large increase in private sector income and a smaller increase in social transfers. In the Slavic and Baltic regions of the former Soviet Union, population income share in the GDP remained virtually unchanged.

The situation is, of course, more differentiated at the country level. All transition economies can be divided into three categories, depending on the type of change.

The first category ("the non-compensators") is characterized by a declining share of wages which is not "offset" in any meaningful way, by an increased share of cash social transfers. This particular configuration can be denoted as (- 0 +), where the negative sign, zero, and the positive sign denote a decreased, unchanged, or increased share, respectively, of wages, cash social transfers, and non-wage private sector income. "Non-compensators" include only countries where each $5 in lost wages is accompanied by $1 or less in greater social transfers: the Czech Republic, Estonia, Moldova, Romania, Russia, Slovakia, and Ukraine belong to this group. For example, in Russia, the share of wages decreased by 15 percentage points of GDP while social transfers increased by 1 GDP point.[22]

The second group ("the compensators") consists of countries with a (- + +) configuration, where compensation, in the form of social transfers for lost wages, is more generous. "Compensators" include Belarus, Bulgaria, Latvia, and Lithuania.

The third group ("the populists") has a (+ + +) configuration. In these countries, all sources of population income increased in terms of GDP. "Populist" countries clearly attempted to cushion the population, as much as possible, from the effect of real GDP declines. Only Central European countries (Hungary, Poland, and Slovenia) belong to this group.

Growth of non-wage private sector income

All configurations include a plus sign for non-wage private income, because non-wage private income has risen as a share of GDP in all transition economies. In Eastern Europe, its unweighted share increased from 10 percent of GDP before the transition to 19 percent of GDP in 1993–94; in the Baltics, it went from 9 to 14 percent; in the Slavic republics of the former Soviet Union, it grew from 6 to 16 percent. These figures make clear that Eastern Europe began its transition with a more sizable private sector than did the Soviet Union, particularly so the countries where agriculture was private or semi-private or which exhibited a more

---

22. Interestingly, but perhaps not surprisingly, only countries affected by war and regional tensions (not shown in the table) display the configuration (- - +).

liberal attitude toward the small private sector (Hungary, Poland, and Slovenia). During the transition, however, the share of non-wage private sector income in GDP grew as quickly in the Slavic republics of the former Soviet Union as it did in Eastern Europe. In addition, it is important to recall that the informal sector (which, by definition, is not included in national statistics) is larger in the countries of the former Soviet Union than it is in Eastern Europe. The share of private sector income in the countries of the former Soviet Union is thus more underestimated than it is in Eastern Europe. The most important increase in the share of non-wage private sector income occurred in the Czech Republic and Moldova (an increase of 20 GDP points), Russia (18 points), Slovakia (13 points), and Bulgaria (12 points).

The next chapter will investigate what happened to income distribution during the transition and how it was affected by changes in income composition.

4

Inequality

Income Inequality

Table 4.1 illustrates the change in inequality that has occurred since the beginning of the transition. [1] First, inequality increased in all countries except the Slovak Republic. The average Gini coefficient of disposable (or gross) [2] income rose from 24 to 33. While the first value is equal to the average value of low income-inequality OECD countries (such as the Benelux, the Federal Republic of Germany, and Scandinavia), the second value places transition economies at near the OECD mean, or at about the same level of inequality as Commonwealth countries (for example, Australia, Canada, and the United Kingdom) and Latin European countries (such as Italy and France). [3]

Second, the increase in the Gini coefficient was sharp: over a period of about six years, the average Gini rose by 9 points. This is, on average, $1\frac{1}{2}$ Gini points per year, a rise that is almost three times as fast as the rise recorded in those Western countries where inequality rose most rapidly in the 1980s: United Kingdom, the Netherlands, and United States (Atkinson, Rainwater, and Smeeding 1995, p. 25).

Third, the dispersal of Ginis among transition economies increased. While before the transition, their Gini coefficients (with the exception of Central Asian republics, which were more unequal) lay within a very narrow range between

---

1. Results are based on HBSs presented in appendix 4. A discussion of problems associated with these surveys and biases in estimating inequality is presented in appendix 1.

2. Disposable and gross income in transition countries are not very different because direct personal income taxes are still very small.

3. Atkinson, Rainwater, and Smeeding (1995, p. 16) divide OECD countries into four groups. Very low income-inequality countries, with Ginis between 20 and 22, include Nordic countries (Finland, Sweden, Norway) and Belgium. Low income-inequality countries, with Ginis between 24 and 26 include the Federal Republic of Germany and the Netherlands. Latin Europe (France and Italy) and Commonwealth countries (Australia, Canada, and the United Kingdom) have average levels of income-inequality, or Ginis of between 29 and 31. Finally, high income-inequality countries include Ireland, Switzerland, and the United States, with Ginis of between 33 and 35. Income concept is disposable income; distribution is per equivalent adult using the OECD equivalence scale. According to the empirical evidence presented in Coulter, Cowell, and Jenkins (1992), the use of per capita income (as in table 4.1) will lead to slightly higher estimates of the Gini coefficient than will the use of income per equivalent adult. For a discussion of Coulter, Cowell and Jenkins results, see Banks and Johnson (1994).

Table 4.1. *Changes in Inequality during the Transition*

| Country | Gini coefficient (annual)[a] | | Expenditures per capita |
| | Income per capita | | |
	1987–88	1993–95	1993–95
Balkans and Poland	24	30	
Bulgaria	23[b]	34	
Poland	26	28[e]	31[e]
Romania	23[b]	29[c]	33[c]
Central Europe	21	24	
Czech Republic	19	27[c]	
Hungary	21	23	27
Slovakia	20	19	
Slovenia	22	25	
Baltics	23	34	
Estonia	23	35[d]	31[d]
Latvia	23	31[d]	
Lithuania	23	37	
Slavic republics and Moldova	24	40	
Belarus	23	28[d]	30[d]
Moldova	24	36	
Russia	24	48[d]	50[e]
Ukraine	23	47[c]	44[c]
Central Asia	26	39	
Kazakhstan	26	33	
Kyrgyz Republic	26	55[d]	43[d]
Turkmenistan	26	36	
Uzbekistan	28[b]	33	
All transition	24	33	

Note: For most countries income concept in 1993–95 is disposable income; in 1987–88, gross income. Personal income taxes are small, and so is the difference between disposable and gross income (see the exact definitions in appendix 4). Income includes consumption-in-kind, except for Hungary and Lithuania in transition years. Regional averages are unweighted.

a. Except when stated otherwise.
b. 1989.
c. Monthly.
d. Quarterly.
e. Semiannual.

Source: Calculated from the countries' household budget surveys given in appendix 4. See also the discussion of HBSs and caveats in appendix 1. All expenditure data obtained from the same surveys as income data.

19 and 24, the current range goes from around 20 (Slovakia) all the way to high 40's (Ukraine and Russia), and even mid–50's (the Kyrgyz Republic) (see also figure 4.1).

These results illustrate not only sharply increasing income differentiation among members of a single population, but also growing differences among countries. Central European countries have registered only moderate increases

Figure 4.1. *Dispersal of Gini Coefficients in Transition Economies*

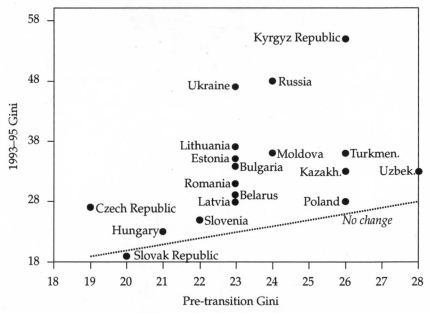

Source: Countries' household budget surveys (see appendix 4).

in inequality: their Gini rose, on average, from 21 to 24. The increase was greater in the Balkans, even greater in the Baltics (where it rose from 23 to 34), and by far the greatest in Moldova and the Slavic republics of the former Soviet Union (where it rose from 24 to 40).

Fourth, Ginis calculated on the basis of 1993–95 expenditures are not, on average, lower than Ginis calculated on the basis of 1993–95 income. In five cases, expenditure Ginis are higher (by 2 to 4 Gini points), and in three cases, they are lower. Higher expenditure than income Ginis suggest that surveys tend to underestimate both income levels (as discussed in chapter 3) and income inequality because we would normally expect to find, particularly during a depression, lower inequality among expenditures than among incomes.

While inequality rose everywhere, the exact shape of this change differed among countries. Figures 4.2, 4.3, and 4.4 show the change between 1987–88 and 1993–94 in income shares received by the five quintiles. [4]

---

4. Income distribution data, as they appear in the original sources, are presented in appendix 4. Decile data (from which the quintiles in figures 4.2–4.4 are calculated) are presented in appendix 2.

Figure 4.2. *Changes in Quintile Shares in Hungary, Slovakia, and Slovenia between 1987–88 and 1993–94: Little Change*

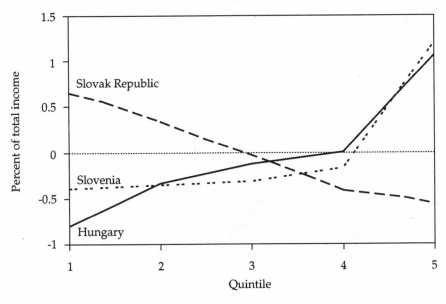

Figure 4.3. *Changes in Quintile Shares in Belarus, the Czech Republic, Latvia, Poland, and Romania between 1987–88 and 1993–94: Moderate Regressive Transfers*

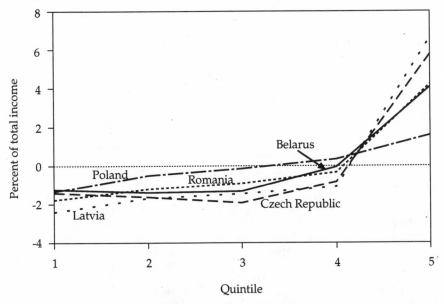

Source: Countries' household budget surveys (see appendices 2 and 4).

Figure 4.4. Changes in Quintile Shares in Bulgaria, Estonia, Lithuania, Moldova, Russia, and Ukraine between 1987–88 and 1993–94: Large Regressive Transfers

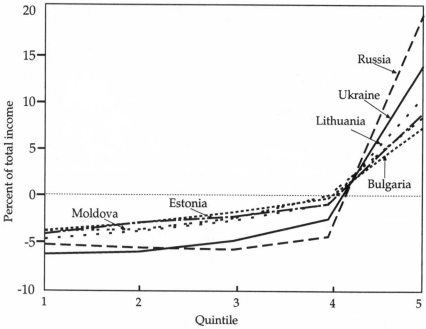

Source: Countries' household budget surveys (see appendices 2 and 4).

We can divide countries into three groups.[5] The first group consists of Hungary, Slovakia, and Slovenia (figure 4.2). Income shares in these countries barely changed at all. No quintile gained or lost more than 1 percentage point of total income.[6]

In the second group, maximum loss ranged between 1 and 2 percentage points of total income, and was sustained by the bottom three quintiles (figure 4.3). The forth quintile either experienced a very small loss or retained its pre-transition share. In all cases, the top quintile alone was the "winner."[7]

---

5. Central Asian republics are not considered here because of the unreliable nature of the data.

6. A similar pattern of change is reported for eastern Germany (see Spéder 1995, table 1). Between 1990 and 1993, the bottom quintile lost 1.2 percentage points of income; the next three quintiles lost between 0.5 and 0.2 points, and the top quintile had gained 2.2 points. The Gini coefficient increased quite moderately from 19.5 in 1990 to 22.4 in 1993 (calculated from data provided by Spéder 1995, table 2).

7. Note that this discussion relates to shares. Because overall income decreased in all countries, even an increased share received by the top quintile did not necessarily guarantee an increase in its real income. The real income decline of the bottom quintiles was that much more severe because both its share of the pie and the size of the pie itself decreased.

However, depending on the amount lost by the bottom three or four quintiles, the gain of the top quintile ranged from less than 2 percentage points in Poland to about 6 points in Latvia and the Czech Republic. On average, the share of the bottom quintile was reduced from 10 to 11 percent of total income to 9 to 10 percent; the share of the top quintile rose from 32 to 35 percent of total income to 35 to 37 percent. By contrast, in 1992 the bottom quintile in the United Kingdom, whose inequality was about average among OECD countries, received about 7 percent of disposable income, while the top quintile received just over 40 percent. Income distribution in this second group of transition countries thus remained more equal than in the United Kingdom.

This was not the case for the countries in the third group (figure 4.4). Their inequality is greater than the OECD average. The extent of income transfer from the bottom 80 percent of the population to the top 20 percent was much larger than among group 2 countries. Income loss by the bottom quintile varied between 4 and 5 percentage points of total income. Only a slightly smaller loss was sustained by the next two quintiles. In Russia and Ukraine, the significant income losses extended to the fourth quintile as well. In these countries, sharp losses by 80 percent of the population translated into large gains for the top quintile. Thus, in Russia, Ukraine, as well as in Lithuania, the top quintile gained 20, 14, and 11 percentage points of total income, respectively. In Russia, the bottom quintile's share was halved, declining from 10 percent of total income to less than 5 percent,[8] while the share of the richest quintile rose from 34 to 54 percent of total income.

These results show that:

- In all cases (except the Slovak Republic), redistribution was regressive.
- As regards poverty, the most unfavorable developments occurred in the countries of the third group (Russia, Estonia, Ukraine, Moldova, Bulgaria and Lithuania), where the poorest suffered greater *absolute* losses than did the middle or top income classes. Because in all these countries, real income decreased by between one-third and one-half, this translated into real income losses of up to two-thirds for the bottom quintile.
- Inequality in Russia, Ukraine, and the Baltics (in that order) seems to be greater than the OECD average. In Eastern Europe, however, inequality remains distinctly less than the OECD average.

Is there a relationship between the type of adjustment identified in chapter 3 ("non-compensators, " "compensators, " and "populists") and increases in the Gini coefficient? The only relationship that could be detected is that be-

---

8. In other words, an average Russian in the bottom quintile had an income equal to half the mean before the transition; now his income is one-quarter of the mean.

Figure 4.5. Relationship between Type of Adjustment and Increase in Gini Coefficient

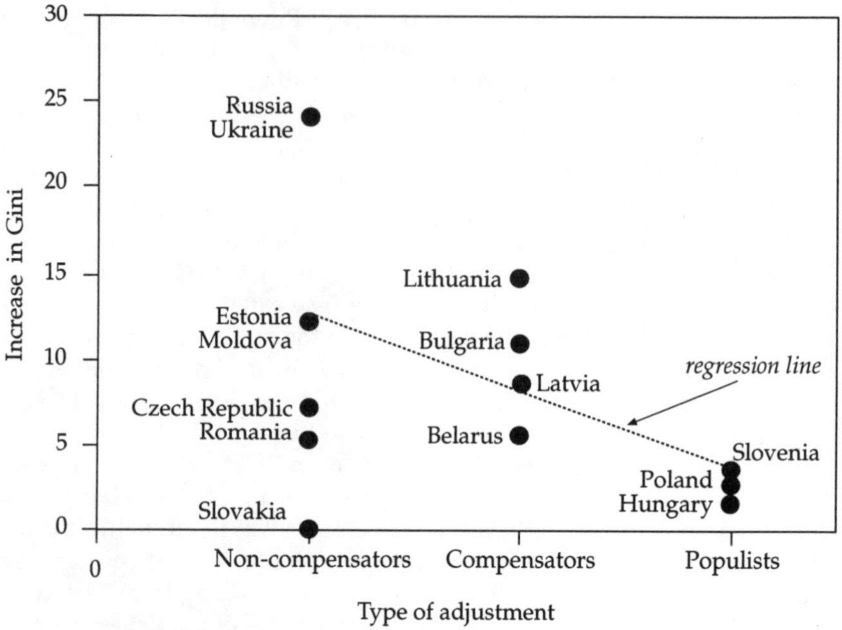

Source: Increases in the Gini coefficient are calculated from table 4.1.

tween the "populist" type of adjustment and low increases in inequality.[9] The average increase in Gini for the three "populist" adjustment countries (Poland, Hungary, Slovenia) was less than 2 Gini points, and except for Slovakia they experienced smaller increases in inequality than any other country. The average increase among "compensators" and "non-compensators" was approximately 10 and 12 Gini points, respectively. Each movement toward "tougher adjustment" (i.e., from "populists" to "non-compensators") was associated, on average, with a Gini increase of about 4 points (see the regression line in figure 4.5). However, if Russia and Ukraine are excluded, the average inequality increase among the "non-compensators" is less than among the "compensators:" the monotonic relationship between "softer" adjustment and lower increase in inequality no longer holds.

9. The partial correlation coefficient between the type of adjustment (where 1 = non-compensators, 2 = compensators, 3 = populist) and the Gini increase is -0.42. On the other hand, there is no statistically significant correlation (r = -0.04) between the type of adjustment and the change in an economic liberalization index (defined for transition economies by de Melo, Denizer, and Gelb 1996) that includes privatization, internal market liberalization, and external market liberalization. Similarly, there is only a weak relationship between the change in the liberalization index and the change in the Gini (-0.11).

Distribution of Income Sources: Wages, Social Transfers, and Private Sector Income

How can the increased income inequality during the transition be accounted for?

Disposable income can be defined as the sum of wages (w), cash social transfers (t), and non-wage private sector income (p). The Gini coefficient of disposable income, (G), is equal to the weighted average of the concentration coefficients of the three income sources (wages, transfers, and non-wage private sector income) C_i where weights are sources' shares (S_i) in total income:[10, 11]

4.1 $$G = \sum\nolimits_{i=1}^{3} S_i C_i = S_w C_w + S_t C_t + S_p C_p.$$

The change in the Gini between two dates (before and after the transition) can be written as:

4.2 $$\Delta G = \sum\nolimits_{i=1}^{3} \Delta S_i C_i + \Delta C_w S_w + \Delta C_t S_t + \Delta C_p S_p + \sum\nolimits_{i=1}^{3} \Delta S_i \Delta C_i.$$

The first term on the right hand side shows the change in Gini due to changing shares of different income sources; the next three terms show the change due to changing concentration coefficients of income sources; and the last term is an interaction term.

Table 4.2 shows the decomposed change in the Gini for selected countries between a pre-transition year and 1993–96. The following conclusions can be made.

First, the change in income composition has had little relation to increased inequality. In the only country where income composition did have a significant impact on inequality (Russia), it contributed to *reduce* inequality; that is, income composition in 1994 was more favorable to equality than it was in 1989. This is chiefly because social transfers, which were the most equally distributed income source in Russia before the transition, increased their share in overall income after the transition. In other countries, only about 1 Gini point was added to or subtracted from total inequality by changes in income composition.

Second, higher concentration coefficients of wages drove the overall Gini up in all countries. It was the most important factor behind increases in in-

---

10. The concentration coefficient captures both the inherent inequality with which a given income source is distributed (source Gini coefficient) and the correlation of that source with overall income. Thus, an inherently unequal source, such as social assistance, with a high Gini coefficient will have a low or negative correlation with overall income (because most social assistance recipients are poor), and its concentration coefficient will be low or negative. For a more detailed definition of concentration coefficient, see footnote 9 in chapter 2.

11. The analysis here is based on HBS data. The three income sources add exactly to disposable income.

Table 4.2. *Decomposition of the Change in the Gini Coefficient between Pre-transition and 1993–96*

| Country (years) | Change in composition of income | Due to: Change in concentration of: | | Out of which: | | | | Overall Gini change |
		Wages	Social transfers	Pensions	Non-pension transfers	Non-wage private sector	Interaction term	
Hungary (1989–93)	-1.3	+5.9	-0.6	+1.4	-0.2	-0.6	-1.3	+2.2
Slovenia (1987–95)	-0.2	+3.6	-0.6	-0.1	-0.4	+0.4	-3.8	+2.6
Poland (1987–95)	-1.7	+3.4	+3.5	+3.2	-0.1	+0.8	+0.9	+7.0
Bulgaria (1989–95)	+1.4	+7.8	+0.9	+0.4	+0.4	-0.4	+0.3	+10.0
Latvia (1989–96)	-1.6	+15.0	-1.5	-2.0	+0.5	+1.4	-3.3	+10.0
Russia (1989–94)	-3.4	+17.8	+5.1	+3.9	+0.4	+3.0	+1.2	+23.6

Note: All data in Gini points. The years in brackets show the dates between which the Gini change is calculated. The data sources and end-years for Bulgaria, Latvia, Poland and Slovenia are not the same as in table 4.1. This explains differences in the overall Gini change.
Source: Calculated from the countries HBSs (see appendix 1).

equality. Increased wage concentration was responsible for between 3.5 and 8 Gini points of increase in Eastern Europe, and for 15 to 18 Gini point increases in Latvia and Russia. In the latter two countries, these huge increases were due not only to a greatly increased concentration coefficient of wages, but also to a high pre-transition share of wages in income. Thus, a very high weight attaches to a more unequal concentration of wages that occurred during the transition. An increase in the concentration of non-wage private sector income was responsible for 3 Gini points of increase in Russia and about 1.5 points in Latvia, while its impact was negligible in Eastern Europe.

Third, the effect of the changed concentration of transfers on inequality was not uniform across countries. In Bulgaria, Hungary, and Slovenia, for example, the concentration of transfers did not change. In Latvia, on the other hand, better targeting of transfers reduced inequality by 1.5 Gini points. In Poland and Russia, transfers contributed to an increase in inequality. This was due to a greater concentration coefficient of pensions. Non-pension transfers, because of their initially small size, did not anywhere have much of an impact on inequality. [12]

Decomposition of the increase in inequality in table 4.2 is based on the change between the two data points (before the transition and 1993–1996). The two end-data points can mask changes in the distribution or shares of various income sources in the intervening years. For the six countries shown in figures 4.6–4.17, annual HBSs are available. They allow us to chart annual developments in the concentration and share of wages, cash social transfers and non-wage private sector.

The developments in Bulgaria illustrated in figures 4.6 and 4.7 are straightforward, and to some extent typical of the transition. The rising concentration of wages (from around 20 to 35) contributed strongly to inequality. The concentration coefficient of non-wage private sector income, which was already high before the transition, remained high while the share of non-wage private sector income increased. This also pushed up overall inequality. Pensions' concentration and share both remained unchanged, thus leaving inequality unchanged. Finally, non-pension transfers were too small (less than 5 percent of total income) to make any difference in the overall Gini.

Polish results illustrate a different story (see figures 4.8–4.9). Although wage concentration increased markedly, the most important development was in the area of pensions: their rising concentration and rising share in overall income. Pensions thus contributed strongly to increase inequality. In 1995, pensions had the same concentration coefficient as wages and non-wage private sector income. The fact that concentration coefficients of the three income sources converge means that income *composition* is almost equal across

---

12. To some extent, this conclusion differs from Cornia's observation that "the relative importance of redistribution [via transfers] has grown... Targeting of these [social] transfers has generally improved or remained sufficiently progressive" (1994, p. 39).

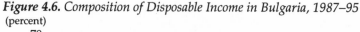

Figure 4.6. *Composition of Disposable Income in Bulgaria, 1987–95*

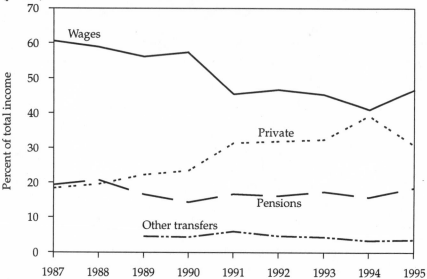

Figure 4.7. *Concentration Coefficients of Wages, Cash Social Transfers, and Non-wage Private Sector Income in Bulgaria, 1989–95*

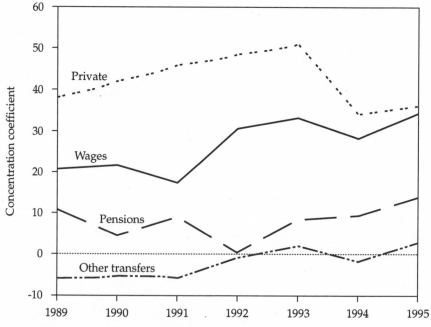

Note: The more unequally distributed the income source, the higher the coefficient of concentration. The concentration coefficient shows how much a given source "pushes" up the overall inequality.

Source: 1989–95 Bulgaria Household Budget Surveys.

Figure 4.8. Composition of Disposable Income in Poland, 1987–95
(percent)

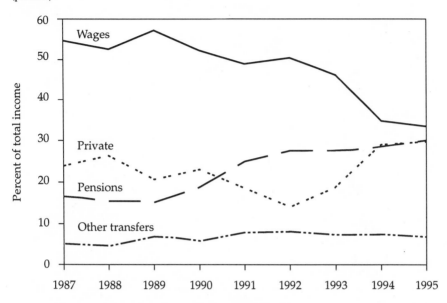

Figure 4.9. Concentration Coefficients of Wages, Cash Social Transfers,
and Non-wage Private Sector Income in Poland, 1987–95

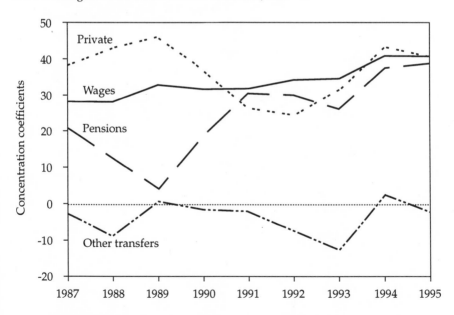

Note: The more unequally distributed the income source, the higher the coefficient of concentration. The concentration coefficient shows how much a given source "pushes" up the overall inequality.

Source: 1987–95 Poland Household Budget Surveys.

Figure 4.10. Composition of Disposable Income in Slovenia, 1987–95
(percent)

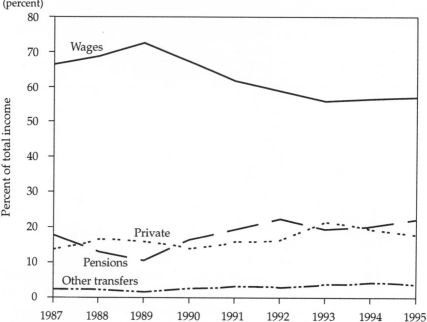

Figure 4.11. Concentration Coefficients of Wages, Cash Social Transfers, and Non-wage Private Sector Income in Slovenia, 1987–95

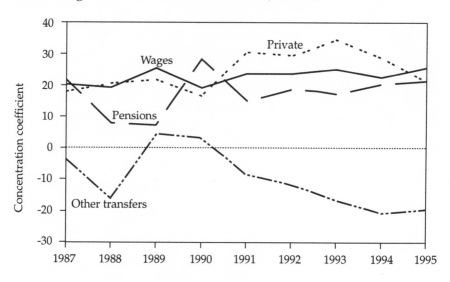

Note: The more unequally distributed the income source, the higher the coefficient of concentration. The concentration coefficient shows how much a given source "pushes" up the overall inequality.

Source: 1987–95 Slovenia Household Budget Surveys.

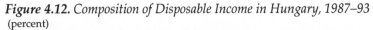

Figure 4.12. *Composition of Disposable Income in Hungary, 1987–93*
(percent)

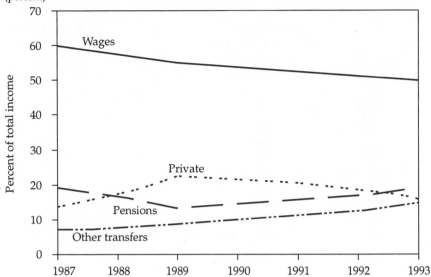

Figure 4.13. *Concentration Coefficients of Wages, Cash Social Transfers, and Non-wage Private Sector Income in Hungary, 1987–93*

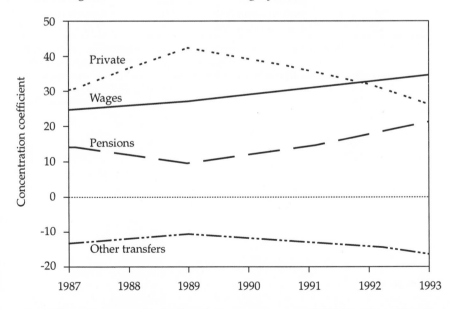

Note: The more unequally distributed the income source, the higher the coefficient of concentration. The concentration coefficient shows how much a given source "pushes" up the overall inequality. "Private income" in 1993 does not include consumption-in-kind.
Source: 1987, 1989, 1993 Hungary Household Budget Surveys.

income brackets: in other words, a poor person will derive the same percent of income from wages, pensions, or non-wage private sector income as a rich person will. This is a rather unexpected outcome.

In Slovenia and Hungary (figures 4.10–4.13) none of the concentration coefficients showed a clear tendency to increase or decrease (the increased concentration of wages in Hungary is the only exception). This explains very small increases in Ginis in both countries.

Russia represents a unique case: *all* income sources' concentration coefficients were higher in 1994 than before the transition and all have pushed overall inequality up (see figures 4.14 and 4.15). The only factor that has moderated the increase in inequality was a shift toward more equally distributed income sources: that is, towards transfers and non-wage private sector income, which prior to the transition had smaller concentration coefficients than did wages.

Transfers and, in particular, pensions either left inequality unchanged (as in Bulgaria, Slovenia, and Hungary) or they contributed to an increase in inequality (as in Poland and Russia). The only exception noted here is Latvia, where an *improved* (that is, more pro-poor) concentration of pensions resulted from the introduction of almost flat pensions in 1992, a development which is reflected in the steep, downward-sloping line for pensions in figure 4.17.[13]

Disparity among Social Groups

Changes in income distribution have also been accompanied by changes in the relative position of social groups. Under previous regime, care was taken to maintain some level of balance (or "parity") between the average income of workers and of farmers.[14] Communist concern with the relative position of various social groups was also reflected in the design of HBSs, where survey representativeness was ensured at the level of the social group, but not necessarily at the level of the population (see appendix 1 for further discussion of HBSs).

Table 4.3 shows what happened to the average per capita income of workers', farmers', and pensioners' households between 1987–88 and 1993–94. [15]

As expected, average real incomes of all social groups have declined. However, it is the *difference* in the decline between the various groups that is of interest here. When the difference in decline between two groups is less than 3 percentage points, it is assumed that no change in the groups' relative

---

13. The concentration coefficient of pensions decreased from 34 in 1989 to -4 in 1995.

14. Okrasa (1988, p. 637) argues that redistribution policies under Communism were mostly designed to insure vertical equality among social groups. In some aspects, however (for example, in access to safe water and sanitation), rural populations, particularly in the less developed republics of the former U.S.S.R., were at a disadvantage.

15. Workers are, in principle, both those employed in the state and private sector. Many private sector workers are self-employed, however, and are thus included in the category "self-employed" or "other" which is not shown here.

Figure 4.14. Composition of Disposable Income in Russia, 1989–94
(percent)

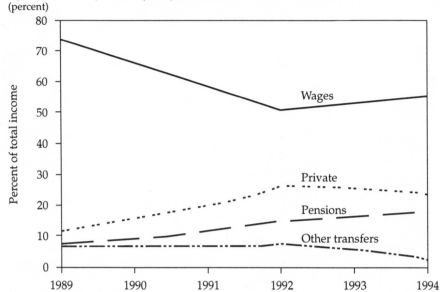

Figure 4.15. Concentration Coefficients of Wages, Cash Social Transfers, and Non-wage Private Sector Income in Russia, 1989–94

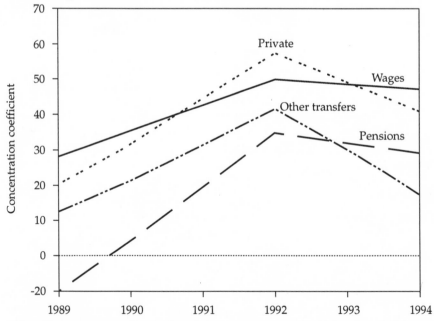

Note: The more unequally distributed the income source, the higher the coefficient of concentration. The concentration coefficient shows how much a given source "pushes" up the overall inequality.

Source: 1989: Family Budget Survey; 1992 and 1994: *Russian Longitudinal Monitoring Survey,* rounds 1 and 4 respectively.

Figure 4.16. Composition of Disposable Income in Latvia, 1989–96

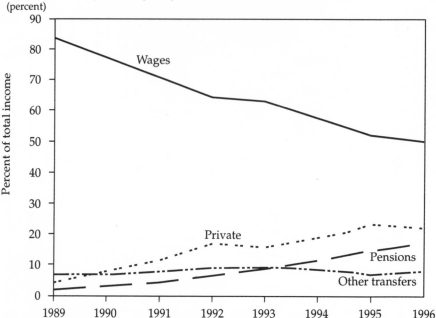

Figure 4.17. Concentration Coefficients of Wages, Cash Social Transfers, and Non-wage Private Sector Income in Latvia, 1989–96

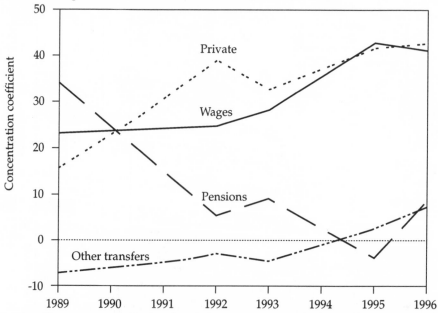

Note: The more unequally distributed the income source, the higher the coefficient of concentration. The concentration coefficient shows how much a given source "pushes" up the overall inequality.

Source: 1989 and 1992–93 Family Budget Survey; 1995–96: New Household Budget Survey.

Table 4.3. *Change in Real and Relative per Capita Income of Worker, Farmer, and Pensioner Households*
(workers' households real per capita income in 1987=100)

Country	1987–88	1993–94	Change in relative position
Belarus			
Workers	102	86	W=F
Farmers	101	85	
Bulgaria			
Workers	102	53	W>F
Farmers	119	64	
Czech Republic			
Workers	102	73	P>W=F
Farmers	93	64	
Pensioners	61	54	
Hungary			
Workers	100	73	P>W
Farmers	90	n.a.	
Pensioners	92	68	
Latvia			
Workers	101	54	P>W>F
Farmers	100	41	
Pensioners	59	34[a]	
Lithuania			
Workers	102	43	P>W>F
Farmers	100	33	
Pensioners	58	46[a]	
Poland			
Workers	107	85	P>W>F
Farmers	121	77	
Pensioners	95	89	
Romania			
Workers	100	76	F>P>W
Farmers	74	59	
Pensioners	88	68	
Russia			
Workers	103	59	W>F
Farmers	88	30	
Slovak Republic			
Workers	102	71	P>W=F
Farmers	95	63	
Pensioners	64	52	
Slovenia			
Workers	94	81	W>F
Farmers	84	66	

a. 1992.

Source: Calculated from the countries' household budget surveys (see appendix 1).

positions has taken place. For instance, if workers' real income lost 15 points and farmers' real income lost 16 points (as in Belarus), their relative positions are considered unchanged. However, if workers lost 49 points and farmers lost 55 points (as in Bulgaria), then workers are considered to have done better than farmers. Remarkably, the following rules apply for all countries here:

- Pensioners' position in relation to workers has improved: $P>W$.
- Workers' position in relation to farmers has either improved (in six countries) or remained the same (in three countries): $W \geq F$. [16]
- Pensioners' position in relation to farmers has improved in all countries: $P>F$.

Farmers' households real incomes have declined the most almost everywhere. This was caused by a variety of factors: decreased agricultural production in all countries; [17] removal of input subsidies (for example, for fertilizer and gasoline) combined with liberalization of food imports (in Poland, Czechoslovakia, Russia, and the Baltic countries); [18] chaos associated with land privatization and uncertainty of ownership (in Albania, Bulgaria, Estonia, Romania, and Russia); and the end of an explicit government policy of ensuring rural-urban income parity (Poland, Czechoslovakia). Workers have done slightly better than farmers, and pensioners have done better than both.

How have the "new" private sector entrepreneurs, and the self-employed done? Anecdotal evidence and common sense suggest that they would be among those who benefited most from the transition. It is important, however, to keep in mind that this group is more heterogeneous than workers or farmers are. The private sector encompasses not only the self-employed professionals (for example, doctors, accountants, engineers, and computer specialists) but also coffee shop owners, shoemakers, hoteliers, and repairmen. It includes also small-scale employers and "capitalists" (that is, owners of larger plants or factories). The difference in income between a self-employed shoemaker and a large-scale capitalist can be so large that it becomes all but meaningless to include them in the same group. From the perspective of the transition, however, both are part of the private sector, because their income comes from private activities.

Poland is the only country for which there is evidence about how the self-employed have done since the transition. The Polish HBS introduced the category of "self-employed" (outside agriculture) as a new social group in 1992. [19] The self-employed represent about 6 percent of the 1993 and 1994 sample. Their

---

16. Except in Romania, where farmers have done better than either pensioners or workers.

17. In 1993–94, agricultural output in Eastern Europe, Russia, and Ukraine was about 20 percent below its 1987–88 level.

18. In addition, wage arrears in the Russian agricultural sector have been particularly severe (see Braithwaite 1997, p. 65).

19. The first HBS results reflecting this new category were published in 1993.

average income and expenditures are the highest of any group: approximately 20 percent above the overall mean in 1993 (World Bank 1995a, p. 10) and 30 percent in 1994 (Polish Central Statistical Office 1995 table 7 and 9). Being self-employed reduces the probability of poverty by 11 percent, when other factors, such as education, type and size of household, location, and so on, are controlled for.[20]

20. This result is obtained using the probit analysis. The coefficients on other explanatory variables are virtually the same whether or not the probit regression is estimated with the self-employment dummy variable.

5

Poverty

What Happens to Poverty When Income Goes Down?

Chapter 3 discussed the dramatic declines in output experienced in transition countries. As incomes decreased, poverty went up. In this chapter, two simple measures of poverty will be used to study poverty: the headcount index and the poverty deficit. The headcount index gives the percentage of people who are poor because their income is below a certain threshold. The poverty deficit is the sum of all income shortfalls (difference between the threshold and one's income). In other words, it gives a weight to each poor individual equal to the amount by which that individual's income falls short of the poverty line. Poorer individuals thus "count" more, according to this measure. The poverty deficit shows the total amount of money needed to bring all those who are poor up to the poverty line. The poverty deficit is often expressed as a percentage of GDP in order to show the effort a country needs to make to "solve" its poverty problem.[1] When the poverty deficit is divided by the total number of the poor, the average income shortfall of the poor (sf) is obtained. This shortfall can then be expressed as a percentage of the poverty line, and will be here denoted by s.

For example, let the poverty line be 4, and let there be three individuals with incomes of 1, 2, and 10. The first two are considered poor. The headcount index is 2 out of 3 (that is, 66.6 percent). The total poverty deficit is equal to (4-1) + (4-2)=5. Five units of income will be needed, then, to bring the poor up to the poverty line. The average income shortfall of the poor in this example is equal to 5 divided by 2, or 2.5. The average shortfall as a percentage of the poverty line is 2.5 divided by 4, or 62.5 percent.

In chapter 4 it was concluded that income distribution has become more unequal. Both the decline in overall income and the more unequal distribution of income will increase the incidence of poverty. The poverty deficit should also then increase: if the poverty line is fixed and everyone's income declines, then the overall amount needed to "solve" the poverty problem must go up. The example provided in box 5.1 may help explain this. We may

---

1. The assumption behind the poverty deficit is that all money used for poverty alleviation is paid only to the poor (with no leakage to the non-poor) and is paid in exact amount needed to bring the poor just up to, but not above, the poverty line (that is, there is no "spillover"). This is the assumption of so-called perfect targeting. In reality, no more than 50 to 60 percent of funds specifically destined for poverty relief are perfectly targeted.

Box 5.1: *How Poverty, According to Certain Measures, Changes as Income Declines*

Suppose there are 100 people with an average income of $10 (so that their total income is $1,000). Let the poverty line be $4 and let there be ten people with an income of less than $4. Let the average income of these ten people be $2. Their average income shortfall is thus $2, and the poverty deficit is $2 times 10 people, or $20. The shortfall represents 2 percent of overall income or GDP. Suppose, then, that income declines uniformly by 20 percent. Total income becomes $800. The ten people who were poor remain poor, and their average income drops to $1.60. The poverty deficit goes up to $2.40 times 10, or $24. In addition, however, let an additional ten people "slide" below the poverty line. Their incomes formerly ranged between $4 and $5 and are now between $3.20 and $4. Let their average income be $3.60. Their poverty deficit will be $(4-3.60) times 10, or $4. The new total poverty deficit will thus be equal to $28, or 3.5 percent of the new GDP.

What does this example show? It shows, first, that a 20 percent uniform decline in income results in a 10 percentage-point increase in the headcount index. This gives an implicit elasticity of 0.5 (10 percentage points divided by 20 percent), which as will be seen later, is realistic. Second, doubling the poverty headcount from 10 to 20 led to a 40 percent increase in the poverty deficit (from 20 to 28). A smaller increase in the poverty deficit than in the headcount is due to the decline in the average income shortfall, which went down from $2 to $1.40. This is also very common as the "new" poor tend to fall slightly below the poverty line. Third, the poverty deficit as a proportion of GDP has risen by 75 percent, both because the poverty deficit has gone up and because the GDP has shrunk. In terms of percentage changes in the poverty measures, the following may be expected to apply:

- The poverty headcount will increase the most.
- The poverty deficit as a share of GDP will increase less.
- The poverty deficit will increase even less.
- The average income shortfall might fall.

also expect that the more income declines and the greater the increase in inequality, the greater the increase in the headcount index and the poverty deficit.

Other aspects of changes in poverty measures in the presence of large income declines can be elucidated through simple algebra. For the sake of simplicity, it is assumed here that income distribution does not change and all incomes decrease by the same proportion. Such changes in income are considered "uniform."

The poverty deficit (PD) is obtained by multiplying the average income shortfall of the poor, s (in percent) by the poverty line (z) and the number of the poor (P). This amount can then be related to the country's GDP written as the product of its GDP per capita ($\bar{y}$) and its population (N). After some simple manipulation, the poverty deficit/GDP ratio becomes:

5.1 $$\frac{PD}{GDP} = \frac{szP}{\bar{y}N} = s\,\frac{z}{\bar{y}}\,\frac{P}{N} = s\frac{z}{\bar{y}}HC$$

where HC is the headcount index.

As income shrinks across the board, the ratio between the (fixed) poverty line and GDP per capita ($z/\bar{y}$) increases by definition, as does the poverty headcount. The average shortfall s may be reduced if the distance between the new poor and the poverty line is small (as per the example in box 5.1).

There is a further change in the poverty deficit that is not directly revealed by equation 5.1, however. To consider this, the poverty deficit is written as:

5.2 $$PD = \int_0^z (z-y)\ f(y)\ dy.$$

The poverty deficit is equal to the sum of all distances between the poverty line and actual income ($z-y$) multiplied by the number of people who have such income, $f(y)$, where $f(y)$ is the density function. An across-the-board slide in income is formally equivalent to a corresponding increase in the poverty line z. Consider what happens to the poverty deficit when the poverty line increases infinitesimally. If equation 5.2 is differentiated with respect to z the following is obtained:

5.3 $$\frac{dPD}{dz} = \int_0^z f(y)\ dy\ +\ (z-z)\ f(z)$$
$$\int_0^z f(y)\ dy\ =\ F(z).$$

Equation 5.3 shows that the change in the poverty deficit following an infinitesimal uniform decline in income is equal to the *area* between 0 and z under the density function $f(y)$ as shown in figure 5.1.[2] The clear implication

---

2. For a more intuitive explanation, see appendix 3.

Figure 5.1. *Income Density Function and the Poverty Line*

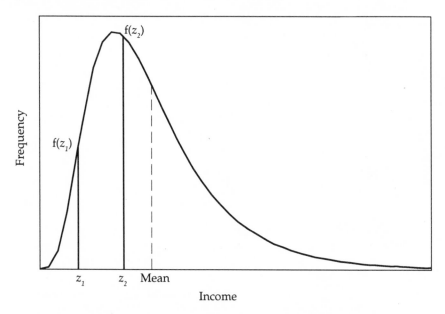

is that the higher the poverty line, the greater the increase in the poverty deficit for a *given* absolute decline in income. If, for example, the poverty line is z_2 then the poverty deficit will increase by more than it would if the poverty line were z_1 (see figure 5.1).

Because in the analysis in this chapter the same real poverty line is used for all countries ($120 per capita per month at international prices; see the section below, *By how much has poverty increased?*), the place of the poverty line within the income distribution curve will differ between the richer and poorer countries. For example, the purchasing power parity (PPP) $120 poverty line amounts to only 38 percent of Hungary's average income (approximately equal to point z_1 in figure 5.1), and 70 percent of Estonia's average income (approximately equal to z_2 in figure 5.1). The area $\int_0^{z_2} f(y)\ dy$ will be greater than the area $\int_0^{z_1} f(y)\ dy$. Thus it can be concluded that:

(A) A *given* absolute decrease in income will raise the poverty deficit more in the case of a poor country (Estonia) than it will in the case of a richer country (Hungary).

In addition, a uniform decline in income (equivalent to an increase in the poverty line) will have a more than a proportional impact on the poverty deficit: if incomes shrink by, say, 10 percent, the poverty deficit will rise by more than 10 percent. This can be seen if equation 5.3 is multiplied by z/PD, thus yielding the elasticity of the poverty deficit with respect to the poverty line (equation 5.4). The elasticity is equal to the reverse of the shortfall, and is always greater than 1. The percentage shortfall would normally increase with z and hence elasticity would decrease with z.[3] This is equivalent to elasticity 5.4 increasing with income.

5.4
$$\frac{dPD}{dz}\ \frac{z}{PD} = \frac{z\ \int_0^z f(y)\ dy}{\int_0^z (z-y)\ f(y)\ dy}$$

$$\frac{z}{z - \overline{y}_p} = \frac{1}{s} > 1$$

where $\overline{y}_p$ = average income of the poor.
In other words,

(B)   If percentage declines in income are the same in poor and rich countries, the poverty deficit will increase, proportionately more, in rich countries.

Finally, with a uniform infinitesimal slide in incomes, the poverty headcount will increase by $f(z)$, that is,

5.5
$$\frac{dHC}{dz} = \frac{dF(z)}{dz} = f(z).$$

(C)   Because the density function is "thicker" (higher) around z_2 than it is around z_1 (see figure 5.1), the poverty headcount will, for a *given* absolute decrease in income, increase more for a poorer than for a richer country.

Another way to express this is to say that the relationship between HC (with a given poverty line) and mean country income (or consumption) is convex: the higher the income, the smaller the effect of a given change in income on the headcount index (see Ravallion 1993, p. 6). The exception to this would be if a country were so poor that the poverty line was situated very much to the right of the mode where the density function is "thin."

By How Much Has Poverty Increased?

One of the central objectives, if not *the* central objective, of a comparative study of poverty is to compare poverty rates and poverty deficits both among

---

3. For example, for an extremely high poverty line equal to the highest income in the country (y_{max}), elasticity becomes $y_{max}/(y_{max} - \overline{y}_p)$ and tends to 1.

countries and within a given country at different points in time. For this sort of comparison, however, a common poverty line is needed.

The same poverty line across countries implicitly treats each individual equally, regardless of where he or she lives. To have the break-down of poor people among countries is important because it helps the development of an international anti-poverty policy. If the objective is to decide where, among a given group of countries, available resources should best be directed in order to help the poor, cross-country comparability is indispensable. It is reasonable to assume that international effort should be directed toward countries in which, according to international standards, (1) many poor people live, or (2) poverty rates are high even if the absolute number of poor is small (because the country's population is small). For the first, it is necessary to use the same poverty yardstick in order to determine the distribution of the poor by country, and for the second, it is necessary to use the same yardstick to compare headcount indexes in different countries. Once the poverty line is fixed in time and among countries, a full comparison is possible. For example, we can compare Hungary's poverty headcount in 1993 not only with Hungary in 1989, but also with Russia in 1989.

The first step in calculating such a poverty line is to establish a single benchmark expressed in the same "currency" for all countries. Four international dollars per capita per day will be used here.[4] These dollars have the same purchasing power over *consumption* goods in all countries. Then it is necessary to find the purchasing power parity PPP exchange rate for each country: how many units of local currency are needed to buy $1 worth of consumption goods at international prices? These data are obtained from the multilateral International Comparison Project (ICP), whose most recent round is for 1993.[5] The PPP exchange rate for each country is then multiplied by $120 per month to obtain the monthly poverty line expressed in domestic currency. Of course, a poverty line that implies the same purchasing power over goods and services across countries requires different amounts of actual dollars in each country: the lower the country's price level compared with that of the world, the fewer actual dollars are needed to buy the same amount of goods. For example, in 1993, $51 per month was needed to reach the $PPP 120 poverty line in Poland; $57 in Hungary; $30 in Bulgaria; and only $21 in Ukraine. By contrast, it would require $165 per month to reach the same poverty line in Switzerland, $125 in Finland, and $59 in Turkey.

Once the 1993 benchmark poverty line in domestic currency is established, poverty lines for other years can be obtained, if needed, simply by inflating

---

4. This is calculated at 1990 international prices.

5. Data supplied to the author by European Comparison Project. Hungary, Poland, and the former Yugoslavia have been included in the ICP since 1985. In 1990, Romania and the U.S.S.R. were added. In the 1993 ICP exercise, all transition economies participated. Data for Central Asian countries were not published, however. For these countries the base price level used is the 1990 ICP result for the Soviet Union as published in United Nations Economic Commission for Europe (1994).

the 1993 poverty line by the cost-of-living index. Full comparability of different points in time for a given country, as well as of different countries is thus possible. It is, however, worth pointing out again that the actual dollar amounts needed to reach the poverty line in each country, and in *each year*, will differ. In Poland, the poverty line in 1987 amounted to $27 per capita per month (at the official exchange rate); in 1993, because of the rapid real appreciation of the zloty, it was, as mentioned before, $51. On the other hand, in Moldova the poverty line in 1988 (as in the rest of the Soviet Union) was $25 per capita per month;[6] but in 1994, one needed only $13 to reach the poverty line.

More formally, the formula for calculating the poverty line can be written as follows:

$$PL_{i,t} = PL_{\$,93} \; ER^*_{i,93} \; COL_{i,(t,93)}$$

where $PL_{i,t}$ = the poverty line in domestic currency for country i and year t; $PL_{\$,93}$ = the common poverty line in international dollars at 1993 prices; $ER^*_{i,93}$ = the consumption purchasing power exchange rate of i country's currency in 1993; and $COL_{i,(t,93)}$ = the change in the cost-of-living index between year t and 1993 for country i.

The amount of $PPP 4 per capita per day is a relatively high poverty line. It is four times higher than the World Bank line of absolute poverty. But the level of income of East European and former Soviet countries, and the compression of their income distributions make $PPP 4 per day per capita a reasonable poverty line.[7]

This line is below the "accounting" social minimum lines for most East European countries, that is, the lines which are not used to define eligibility for social assistance but represent same vague "desirable" minimum. However, they are widely published and often used to calculate the number of the poor. The "accounting" social minimum lines in Eastern Europe range from $PPP 170 to $PPP 300 per capita per month (see Milanovic 1996). For example, the Polish social minimum in 1987 was zloty 14,222 per capita per month, while the $PPP 120 poverty line for the same year is zloty 7,265. The gap is even greater in 1993. The Polish social minimum for June 1993 was zloty 2.1 million per capita per month; the poverty line as calculated here is zloty 880,000. The situation is somewhat different in republics of the former Soviet Union. At the beginning of the transition, like in Poland, social minimum lines[8] were higher than the poverty line used here. The Soviet social

---

6. The 1988 ruble exchange rate is calculated according to a two-to-one "blend" between the official rate (Rs. 0.6) and the parallel market rate (Rs. 4.2).

7. In a recent World Bank study of income distribution and poverty in Latin America and the Caribbean, the poverty line used was $PPP 2 per day per capita (see Psacharopoulos and others 1992).

8. Actually, there was a single U.S.S.R.-wide line until 1991.

minimum in 1987–88 was Rs. 78,[9] while the poverty line used here is only Rs. 54. With time, however, the social minimum in all these republics was scaled down in real terms, and by 1993–94, the new social minimums were very close to the $PPP 120 poverty line. For example, in 1992 Russia officially adopted a new subsistence minimum that was about two-thirds of the old social minimum.[10] In July 1993 (the date of the Russian survey used here), the official minimum was 21,206 rubles per month per capita, almost the same as the poverty line proposed here of Rs. 21,496.[11] Because both lines are indexed by the cost-of-living index, their amounts continue to converge.

The results: universal increase in poverty

Table 5.1 shows the estimated poverty rates for the eighteen countries. For all countries, poverty rates are calculated from "uncorrected" HBS data from the two end-periods: 1987–88 and 1993–95. These "uncorrected" estimates are here referred to as *INCOME1* estimates. The average per capita $PPP incomes range from $PPP 75 per capita per month in the Kyrgyz Republic to $PPP 480 in Slovenia (see also figure 5.2). (For further discussion of data sources, biases, and main problems, see appendix 1.)

The total estimated number of the poor in the eighteen countries has risen twelvefold from nearly 14 million before the transition or about 4 percent of the population, to 168 million in 1993–95, or approximately 45 percent of the population.

Poverty increased in all eighteen countries. The headcount increase, however, was very uneven. In the richer countries of Central Europe (the Czech Republic, Hungary, the Slovak Republic, and Slovenia) the percentage of the poor rose, on average, modestly from less than 1 percent to 2 percent. In Poland, it rose from 6 percent to 20 percent. It is more difficult to interpret results for the former Soviet republics because inadequate coverage of surveys before the transition tended to underestimate poverty, while during the transition, dramatic changes in the economy (such as, the expansion of the informal sector) were not reflected in household surveys, thus biasing current poverty estimates upwards. The two biases reinforce each other when the overall *change* in poverty is being considered. Despite these and other

---

9. Or Rs. 84 if goods were valued at free market prices (see Braithwaite, 1994, p.4).

10. The Russian subsistence minimum defined in 1992 is based on the cost of a bundle of goods, where the share of food is 68 percent. The bundle was devised by the Russian Institute of Nutrition of the Academy of Sciences and by WHO. It became the official standard for poverty measurement in Russia in March 1992. For details, see Gontmakher and others (1995, pp. 43–52) and World Bank (1995e, p. 15).

11. The official poverty line was used in a detailed study of poverty in Russia (World Bank 1995g) and in Klugman (1997). However, in both cases, this "central" per capita poverty line was scaled to take into account economies of size and the lower expenditure requirements of children. This explains why the headcount for Russia found in Foley (1997) is about 40 percent, that is, about 10 percentage points lower than the one presented below in table 5.1.

Table 5.1. Estimated Poverty Headcount and Poverty Deficit in 1987–88 and 1993–95 Using HBS Income

Country	Poverty headcount (%) 1987–88	1993–95	Total number of the poor (millions) 1987–88	1993–95	1993–95 data Shortfall as % of poverty line	Total poverty deficit as % of GDP	Elasticity[a]	Average income per capita ($PPP pm)	Type and year of data
Balkans and Poland	5	32	3.6	22.4	28	2.2	0.5	193	
Bulgaria	2[b]	15	0.1	1.3	26	1.1	0.3	282	A:93
Poland	6	20	2.1	7.6	27	1.4	0.4	213	SA:I/93
Romania	6[b]	59	1.3	13.5	32	5.4	0.7	123	M:3/94
Central Europe	<1	2	0.1	0.4	25	0.1	0.1	348	
Czech Republic	0	<1	0	0.1	23	0.01	0.01	411	M:1/93
Hungary[c]	1	4	0.1	0.4	25	0.2	0.2	266	A:93
Slovakia	0	<1	0	0.0	20	0.01	0.01	332	A:93
Slovenia	0	<1	0	0.0	31	0.02	0.01	481	A:93
Baltics	1	29	0.1	2.3	33	3.1	0.6	204	
Estonia	1	37	0.02	0.6	37	4.2	0.7	172	Q3:95
Latvia	1	22	0.03	0.6	28	2.3	0.5	213	Q4:95
Lithuania[c]	1	30	0.04	1.1	34	2.9	0.5	212	A:94
Slavic republics	2	52	3.5	112.1	39	4.8	0.5	170	
Belarus	1	22	0.1	2.3	26	1.2	0.5	197	Q1:95
Moldova	4	66	0.2	2.9	43	7.0	0.6	115	A:93
Russia	2	50	2.2	74.2	40	4.2	0.6	181	Q3:93
Ukraine	2	63	1.0	32.7	47	6.9	0.5	136	M:6/95
Total without Central Asia	3	43	7.2	137.2	31	3.1		230	

68

	Poverty headcount (%)		Total number of the poor (millions)		1993–95 data				
Country	1987–88	1993–95	1987–88	1993–95	Shortfall as % of poverty line	Total poverty deficit as % of GDP	Elasticity[a]	Average income per capita ($PPP pm)	Type and year of data
Central Asia	15	66	6.5	30.7	47	9.8	0.5	113	
Kazakhstan	5	65	0.8	11.0	39	9.2	0.7	115	A:93
Kyrgyz Republic	12	88	0.5	4.0	68	64.4	0.2	75	Q3:93
Turkmenistan	12	61	0.4	2.4	40	7.7	0.6	124	A:93
Uzbekistan	24	63	4.8	13.3	39	12.4	0.6	118	A:93
Total transition	4	45	13.6	168.0	35	3.5		215	
Comparators									
Brazil	33		48.3		44	4.4	0.3	466	A:89
Colombia		35		11.6	40	5.4	0.3	360	A:92
Ecuador		35		3.9	31	4.4	0.5	219	A:94
Paraguay		44		2.1	51	8.1	0.3	266	A:95
Malaysia	31	18	5.1	3.6	29	0.8	0.3	403	A:87,95
Turkey	31		16.7		33	3.8	0.5	255	A:87
United Kingdom	1	<1	0.6	0.5				900[d]	A:88,92

Note: "Slavic republics" includes Moldova. Poverty line = 120 international dollars per capita per month. A = annual data; SA = semiannual data; M = monthly data; Q = quarterly data. 10/93 means that the data refer to October 1993. I/93 means that the data refer to the first half of 1993.

Poverty rates were calculated using World Bank software POVCAL. For poverty headcount, the number of the poor, poverty deficit as percentage of GDP, and income per capita the regional means are weighted averages; for elasticity and average shortfall, the regional means are unweighted averages.

a. Elasticity is percentage *point* change in poverty headcount divided by percentage change in income (around the poverty line).

b. 1989 data. c. Income does not include consumption-in-kind in 1993–95. d. Estimate based on the ratio between equivalent adult units and per capita measures.

Source: Transition economies: calculated from household budget surveys presented in appendix 4. For caveats and data biases, see appendix 1. For other details regarding calculations, see appendix 5. For comparator countries, the sources are as follows: for the United Kingdom, Family Expenditure Survey data as reported in United Kingdom Central Statistical Office (1991, appendix 1) and United Kingdom Central Statistical Office (1994, appendix 1); for Turkey, *Turkey Statistical Yearbook 1990*, pp. 206–207; for Malaysia, Ahuja (1997, Annex 2); for Brazil, Psacharopoulos et al. (1992); for Colombia, World Bank (1994b, vol. 1, p. 1 and vol. 2, Annex 1); for Ecuador, World Bank (1995d, vol. 2, p. 4); for Paraguay, *Encuesta de Hogares 1995*.

Figure 5.2. *Average Monthly per Capita $PPP Incomes, 1993–95*

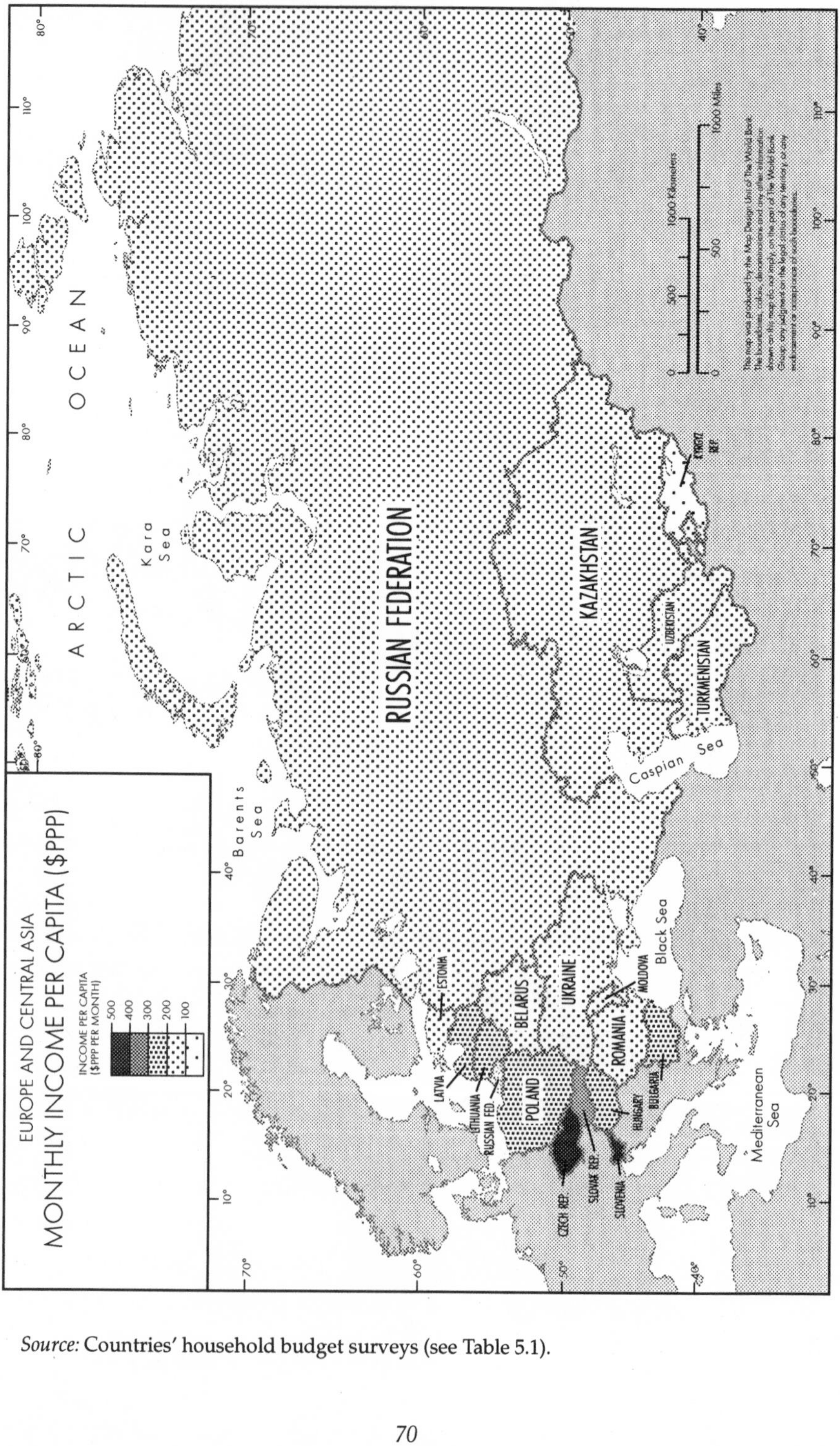
EUROPE AND CENTRAL ASIA
MONTHLY INCOME PER CAPITA ($PPP)
INCOME PER CAPITA ($PPP PER MONTH)
500
400
300
200
100
ARCTIC OCEAN
Kara Sea
Barents Sea
RUSSIAN FEDERATION
KAZAKHSTAN
UZBEKISTAN
TURKMENISTAN
KYRGYZ REP.
Caspian Sea
Black Sea
Mediterranean Sea
ESTONIA
LATVIA
LITHUANIA
RUSSIAN FED.
BELARUS
UKRAINE
MOLDOVA
ROMANIA
BULGARIA
HUNGARY
POLAND
CZECH REP.
SLOVAK REP.
SLOVENIA
1000 Kilometers
1000 Miles

Source: Countries' household budget surveys (see Table 5.1).

caveats (see appendix 1), it is safe to conclude that poverty increased greatly in these countries. The Baltic countries started the transition with low poverty rates, close to those of Central European countries. Their poverty rates recorded very sharp increases reaching almost 30 percent of the population in 1994–95. In Ukraine and Russia, poverty rates increased even more. Russia's poverty headcount is estimated to have risen from 2 percent to 50 percent of the population. Finally, the Central Asian countries began the transition with relatively high poverty headcounts (in double digits for every country except Kazakhstan). Data from 1993 show poverty rates over 60 percent for all countries, including what is probably a too-high 88 percent for the Kyrgyz Republic.

The composition of poverty has also changed. There are now many more poor in the states of the former Soviet Union, as compared with Eastern Europe, than there were at the beginning of the transition. In 1987–88, about as many poor people lived in Eastern Europe as in the European part of the U.S.S.R. In 1993–95, however, for each poor person in Eastern Europe there were five living in the European part of the former Soviet Union. If the Central Asian countries are included, the preponderance of poverty in the former Soviet Union compared with Eastern Europe becomes even greater (six-to-one).

Elasticity of poverty with respect to income

Differences in how much poverty has increased do not depend only on how much real income has declined and how much income inequality has risen, but also on the absolute level of a country's income. This is because we use the same absolute yardstick to measure poverty. Richer countries will have lower poverty headcount than poor countries, even if their incomes declined by the same percentage. The Czech Republic, Hungary, the Slovak Republic, and Slovenia had relatively high average incomes both before the transition and in 1993–95. With the poverty line of $PPP 120 per capita per month, there were very small increases in poverty because almost no one's income was below that level, either in 1987 or in 1993–95. The situation is different in poorer countries, where the same percentage decline in income led to massive increases in poverty as many fell below the poverty line. In these countries, the poverty line lies in the region of "dense" income distribution, as can be seen by comparing Moldovan income distributions to that in the Slovak Republic (see figure 5.3).

The equation 5.6 shows that the elasticity of the poverty headcount with respect to a given uniform percentage decline in income (that is, a decline without a change in the income distribution curve) will vary among countries. Elasticity (as defined here: it is in effect *semi*-elasticity),

5.6 $$\frac{dF(z)}{dz/z} = \frac{dF(z)\ z}{dz} = f(z)\ z$$

Figure 5.3. Income Distributions in Moldova and Slovakia, 1992

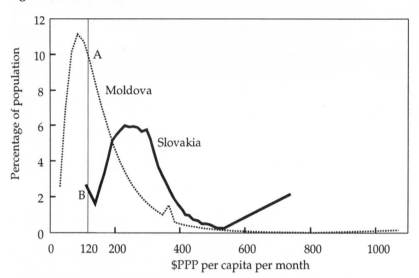

Source: Countries' household budget surveys.

is equal to the product of the density function around the poverty line, and the poverty line. The poverty line is the same for all countries. The value of the density function at *z*, however, will be higher for poorer countries (compare points A and B in figure 5.3 for *z*=$PPP120), and elasticity will tend to be higher for them. (Note that the rule C above refers to the change in headcount for a given *absolute* decrease in income in rich and poor countries.)

Indeed, elasticities in Balkans, Poland, and the former Soviet republics are invariably around 0.5 to 0.6, meaning that an across-the-board decline in income of 10 percent raises the poverty headcount by 5 to 6 percentage points. For example, in Russia every 10 percent decline in income will make an additional 5 percent of the population, or about 7 million people, poor. In richer countries, elasticities are much smaller, around 0.1.

How do these values compare with those in other countries? Are socialist countries likely to have higher elasticities because of a more compressed income distribution? Squire (cited in World Bank 1993, p. 41) estimates the elasticity of poverty headcount with respect to expenditures to be 0.24 after controlling for the initial headcount. His equation is ΔHC = -0.24 growth in mean expenditure - 0.01 HC_0 (where HC_0 = initial headcount). Because initial pre-transition headcounts were small in the countries studied here (0.04 on average), the second term in Squire's equation would be close to zero. Squire's equation would then yield elasticities of around 0.24, which is lower than that observed here for all countries except Central Europe. In a study of approximately twenty countries, Ravallion (1993, p. 7) finds that the elasticity of poverty rates to income (when income alone is included in the equation, that is, assuming that distribution does not change) is about 2.4. When his equation is re-expressed in terms of headcount semi-elasticity as here, its value is around 0.1, which is again much lower than what is found in transition economies.

Another important question is what will happen to elasticity as the economy recovers. Is there likely to be a symmetrical movement that, accordion-like, after having first pushed people below the poverty line, then raises them above it? Whether this occurs depends on the shape of future growth. If income growth occurs first at the top and the middle levels of income distribution, then inequality will continue to rise and poverty will remain stable. This seems to have been the case in Poland, the only transition economy in which real GDP has grown for four consecutive years (1992–95). While GDP grew by 5 percent between 1992 and 1994 (and real personal incomes grew by 4 percent), the poverty rate in 1994 was still slightly higher than in 1992, as inequality seems to have risen. But when growth "trickles down," sharp declines in poverty could result, as relatively large segments of the population now hovering around the poverty line are pulled above it. Several elements suggest that such an optimistic scenario is likely. Most of the poor in transition economies do not represent a distinct "underclass" as they do in Latin America (see the section below, *Who Are the Poor?*): their educational achievements are not much lower than those of the rest of the population; their access to social services; their ownership of consumer durables and apartments is also close to that of non-poor segments of the population.[12] The declines in their incomes are recent and are not yet reflected in a marked deterioration of their asset ownership. If it takes a long time for income growth to "trickle down," however, these relatively favorable elements will be lost.

Alternative poverty calculations

Another implication of the poverty rate's high elasticity with respect to income is that mistakes in income reporting are likely to have a substantial impact on calculated poverty rates. Underreporting of income seems to be widespread in transition economies. Thus, both inadequate income reporting and "bunching" of the population around the poverty line lead to a great variability in calculated poverty rates. The rates "move around" a lot: they

---

12. Trying to "guess" who is poor in transition economies based on asset ownership or access to social services fails (see Dupre 1994 on Russia). A Polish survey of recipients of social assistance shows that almost 20 percent own cars and 60 percent own color televisions (see Polish Central Statistical Office 1993, p. 21). Aside from automobiles and videocassette recorders, a recent World Bank study found, "no strong correlation [in Ukraine] between housing conditions or ownership of most consumer durables and the frequency of poverty" (World Bank, 1996b).

are not robust. For example, if the elasticity around the poverty line is 0.5 to 0.6, then a 20 percent underestimation of income, which is quite likely, will lead to an overestimation of the poverty rate by between 10 and 12 percentage points. Because of uncertainty regarding the "true" poverty rates for the years 1993-95, they are recalculated here in two additional ways. First, rates were recalculated using macroeconomic incomes rather than data from HBSs whenever macroeconomic data showed higher incomes (see table 3.4); then they were recalculated using expenditures instead of income. Estimates based on macro ("adjusted") income data are referred to as *INCOME2*; estimates based on expenditures are referred to as *EXPEN*.

Table 5.2 shows that, using macroeconomic data instead of HBSs, the overall average poverty headcount drops from 45 (as in table 5.1) to 40 percent. The total number of the poor goes down from 168 million to 147 million. The most important changes occur in Romania and Uzbekistan, where estimated poverty rates decline by between 20 and 24 percentage points. Headcounts in Poland and Russia decline by 6 points. Poland, Romania, Russia, and Uzbekistan account for virtually the entire decline in the number of the poor. This is because income adjustments in Central European countries had little effect on poverty rates, because the poverty rates were low and the elasticities small. In terms of regional poverty rates, the picture changes somewhat. There is a sharper split between the Balkans, Poland, and the Baltic countries (except Romania and Estonia), on the one hand, which have poverty rates of about 20 percent, and the Slavic and Central Asian republics of the former Soviet Union, on the other hand, where about half the population is poor. The increase in the number of poor, compared with the situation before the transition, is tenfold: from about 14 million to 147 million (see figure 5.4).

Table 5.3 shows a different set of poverty estimates, where expenditures per capita are used instead of incomes per capita, for the eight countries for which both HBS income and expenditure data are available for the same years. In seven of these countries, the use of expenditures results in lower poverty headcounts than did the use of HBS income. For Belarus, Poland, Romania, and Russia, reported expenditures are significantly higher (between 19 and 30 percent higher) than reported *INCOME1*, and the headcounts are between 8 and 11 percentage points lower (see the two last columns in table 5.3). For example, Russia's headcount goes from 50 to 39 percent; Romania's goes from 59 to 48 percent, and Poland's goes from 20 to 10 percent. The Kyrgyz Republic and Ukraine are in a class of their own, with reported expenditures in these countries more than twice reported incomes. When expenditures are considered rather than incomes, more than one-third of the population in these countries, ceases to be poor! For the three Slavic republics of the former Soviet Union, where the transition has brought about a huge increase in informal sector incomes, the average poverty headcount goes down dramatically from more than 50 percent, when unadjusted survey data are used, to 34 percent, when expenditure data are used. The latter figure probably offers a more realistic estimate of poverty.

Table 5.2. *Estimated Poverty Headcount and Poverty Deficit in 1993–95 Using a Higher (Macro) Income instead of HBS Income*

Country	Poverty head-count (%)	Shortfall as % of poverty line	Total number of the poor (millions)	Total poverty deficit as % of GDP	Income adjustment (%)
Balkans and Poland	22	27	15.6	1.2	
Bulgaria	15	26	1.3	1.1	0
Poland	14	27	5.3	0.9	+15
Romania	39	28	8.9	2.4	+26
Central Europe	1	28	0.2	<0.1	
Czech Republic	<1	26	0.0	0.0	+5
Hungary	2	33	0.2	0.1	+27
Slovak Republic	<1	20	0.0	0.0	0
Slovenia	<1	33	0.0	0.0	+12
Baltics	29	33	2.3	3.1	
Estonia	37	37	0.6	4.2	0
Latvia	22	28	0.6	2.3	0
Lithuania	30	34	1.1	2.9	0
Slavic republics and Moldova	48	38	104.0	4.1	
Belarus	22	26	2.3	1.2	0
Moldova	66	43	2.9	7.0	0
Russia	44	38	66.1	3.3	+10
Ukraine	63	47	32.7	6.9	0
Total without Central Asia	38	31	122.1	2.5	
Central Asia	53	44	25.0	7.5	
Kazakhstan	62	38	10.6	8.2	+4
Kyrgyz Republic	86	67	3.9	57.7	+8
Turkmenistan	57	39	2.2	6.7	+6
Uzbekistan	39	32	8.3	4.4	+44
Total transition	40	35	147.1	2.8	

Note: Poverty line = 120 international dollars per capita per month. HBS incomes are raised across the board (thus leaving inequality unchanged) by the macroeconomic income *minus* HBS percentage difference from table 3.4 (if macroeconomic incomes have declined more than HBS, adjustment = 0).

Source: Calculated from the data presented in appendix 4. For caveats and data biases, see appendix 1.

Figure 5.4. Estimated Number of Poor Before the Transition and in 1993–95
(millions)

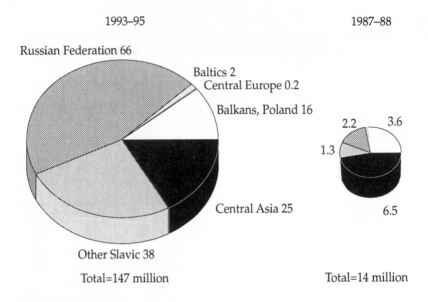

Note: 1993–95 information is based on "adjusted" HBS data (*INCOME2* set). "Other Slavic" includes Moldova.

How Much Is Needed to Cover the Poverty Deficit?

A relatively shallow poverty

Tables 5.1–5.3 indicate that poverty in transition economies, while widespread, is relatively "shallow." This means that the average income of the poor is not substantially below the poverty line. Poverty shortfall (that is, the percentage by which the average income of the poor falls below the poverty line) in the Balkans, Poland, the Baltic countries, and Central Europe is around 30 percent. This means that the average income of the poor person is about $PPP 2.8 per day. Poverty is deeper in the Slavic republics of the former Soviet Union and in Central Asia, where the average shortfall is about 40 percent, and the average income of the poor is thus $PPP 2.4. Broadly speaking, poverty shortfalls increase with higher poverty headcounts. This means that as poverty widens it also becomes deeper which, of course, puts a double pressure on the poverty deficit.[13]

13. In general, there is no reason why this should be the case. The average shortfall in any given country tends to decrease as the poverty headcount goes up (see box 5.1). If the headcount is small, only the very bottom of income distribution (the "down and

Table 5.3. Estimated Poverty Headcount and Poverty Deficit in 1993–95 Using HBS Expenditures

Country	Poverty head-count (%)	Shortfall as % of poverty line	Total poverty deficit as % of GDP	Elasticity[a]	EXPEN compared to INCOME1	
					Head-count	Mean[b]
Poland	10	20	0.5	0.4	-10	+30
Romania	48	34	4.9	0.7	-11	+19
Hungary	7	20	0.3	0.3	+3	0
Estonia	34	28	2.9	0.7	-3	+2
Slavic republics	34	34	3.3	0.4	-17	
Belarus	14	23	0.7	0.4	-8	+21
Russia	39	44	3.7	0.4	-11	+23
Ukraine	26	37	2.3	0.4	-37	+110
Kyrgyz Republic	55	46	27.2	0.5	-33	+132

Note: Poverty line = 120 international dollars per capita per month.

a. Elasticity is percentage *point* change in poverty headcount divided by percentage change in income (across-the-board).

b. The difference between *EXPEN* and *INCOME1* from table 3.3.

Source: Calculated from household budget surveys presented in appendix 4. For caveats and data biases, see appendix 1.

The situation in transition economies may be contrasted with that in Latin American countries. In Latin American countries, using a lower poverty line of $PPP 60 per capita per month, average income shortfalls are approximately 40 percent.[14] The average income of a poor person in Latin America is therefore only $PPP 1.2 per day, or half the average income of a poor person in the Commonwealth of Independent States[15] and even less compared with a poor person in Eastern Europe.

Widespread but shallow poverty has several policy implications. About 2.8 percent of GDP (using the *INCOME2* data set)[16] would be needed to eliminate poverty, assuming perfect targeting, that is, assuming that transfers are received only by the poor and in the exact amounts needed to bring them up to the level of the poverty line.

Poverty deficits as a percentage of GDP vary widely among the countries. The deficits are only 0.1 percent of GDP in Central European countries. In

out") are included, and they are likely to be very poor. As the headcount increases, the poor are the "ordinary folk" whose income is often relatively close to the poverty line.

14. See Psacharopoulos and others (1992).

15. The Commonwealth of Independent States (CIS) comprises all but Baltic republics of the former Soviet Union.

16. Poverty deficits as a share of GDP are calculated in relation to countries' actual GDPs in corresponding years.

Figure 5.5. *Estimated Annual Costs of Poverty Elimination Assuming Perfect Targeting, 1993–95*

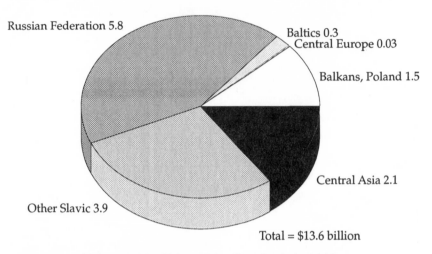

Russian Federation 5.8

Baltics 0.3
Central Europe 0.03

Balkans, Poland 1.5

Central Asia 2.1

Other Slavic 3.9

Total = $13.6 billion

Note: Current $ billion; *INCOME2* data. "Other Slavic" includes Moldova.

Figure 5.6. *Estimated Monthly Spending Required to Lift an Average Poor Person out of Poverty, 1993–95*

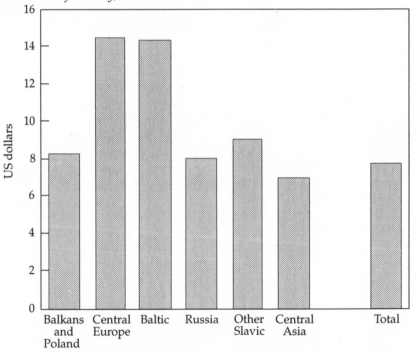

Note: Current dollars using *INCOME2* estimates. The poverty line is $PPP 120 per person per month. "Other Slavic" includes Moldova.

Belarus, Bulgaria, Lithuania, and Poland, the poverty deficit is approximately 1 percent of GDP. In Latvia and Romania, it is about 2 percent of GDP. In Russia, the deficit is 3.3 percent of GDP.[17] In the Central Asian republics, Moldova, and Ukraine, the deficits are even higher.[18] These figures may be contrasted with the poverty deficits of 3.8 percent of GDP in Turkey, 4.4 percent in Brazil, and 5.4 in Colombia, figures which were obtained using the same poverty line of $PPP 120 (see table 5.1). Eliminating poverty in Russia would cost about what it would in Turkey, relative to GDP.

Relatively small poverty deficits (under 3 percent of GDP) in most transition economies appear to carry a favorable message for anti-poverty policies. It seems, at first glance, that elimination or substantial alleviation of poverty is feasible. However, before estimates can be made of actual resources needed to eliminate poverty these numbers must be multiplied by a factor of about 3 to account for realistic estimates of "leakage."[19] Then, even in countries where estimated deficits are about 3 percent of GDP, the welfare spending required becomes an "impossible" 9 percent of GDP.

How much would be needed in *current* dollars, assuming perfect targeting, to eliminate poverty in all eighteen transition economies? The annual total for all countries is estimated at between $13.6 and $17.3 billion, depending on the income assumptions used (the former with *INCOME2* data; the latter with *INCOME1* data). Figure 5.5 shows the regional breakdown assuming higher income and thus lower poverty deficit. As much as 70 percent of the total $13.6 billion needed, would be spent in the Slavic republics of the former Soviet Union and Moldova, with Russia alone accounting for $5.8 billion per year. The Balkans and Poland would need $1.5 billion per year, and the Central Asian republics would need $2.1 billion per year. The requirements of the other two regions, the Baltics and Central Europe, are small: the Baltics would require an estimated $300 annually, while the Central European countries would require only $30 million per year. In the case of the Baltic countries, this is because the population is small, even if the headcount ratios are high (the total population of the Baltic countries is less than that of Bulgaria). Central Europe's needs are very modest because poverty rates there are low.

The *dollar* costs of poverty elimination per one poor person (figure 5.6) are relatively small in Central Asia (about $7 per month), slightly higher in the Slavic republics of the former Soviet Union and the Balkans (about $8 per

---

17. If expenditures are used, almost the same poverty deficit is obtained for Russia (3.7 percent of GDP).

18. If expenditures rather than income are used to calculate the poverty deficit in Ukraine, however, the deficit drops from 6.9 percent of GDP to only 2.3 percent.

19. See the subsection *"Leakage" and actual cost of poverty alleviation* below.

month), and high in the Baltics and Central Europe ($14 per month). This is chiefly because most currencies in the Commonwealth of Independent States are more undervalued with respect to purchasing-power levels, than are those in Eastern Europe and the Baltics. (This is rapidly changing, however, as witnessed by the brisk real appreciation of the ruble in 1992-95.) While the total number of the poor in Russia alone is almost four times as high as in Eastern Europe and the Baltics combined, the estimated dollar costs of poverty elimination are only three times as high. This is not because the poor are less poor in Russia—on the contrary, Russian poor's average shortfall below the poverty line is greater—but rather because the Russian poverty line in *current* dollar terms is relatively low.[20]

How should a given amount of international funds be distributed?

If the objective is to minimize the number of poor in the combined transition economies with a given amount of international funds, in US dollars, then the best approach would be to help those who are nearest to the poverty line. And yet, the situation is not so simple. Those nearest to the poverty line are not necessarily those with the lowest *$PPP* shortfall, but those with the lowest *actual dollar* shortfall. For example, the average poverty shortfall from the $PPP 120 poverty line is 33 percent in Hungary and 67 percent in the Kyrgyz Republic (see table 5.2). Is it less expensive, then, for the international community to help a poor person in Hungary? No—because the Hungarian 33 percent $PPP shortfall translates into $19 per month, while to fill up the 67 percent shortfall in the Kyrgyz Republic requires only $10 per month. The reason for this is simple: although in PPP dollars the gap is greater in the Kyrgyz Republic, in current dollar terms it is much smaller. This is because a dollar is worth much more in the Kyrgyz Republic than it is in Hungary.

If countries are ranked by how inexpensive it is to help the *average* poor person to reach the poverty line, then Uzbekistan, Belarus, and Moldova top the list with less than $6 per person per month.[21] They are followed by Slovakia, Bulgaria, Romania, and Lithuania, which require less than $8 per

---

20. In 1993, the same poverty line ($PPP 120) amounted to $21 in Russia compared with $51 in Poland, $57 in Hungary, and $60 in Estonia.

21. These rankings are only approximate because they disregard differences in income distribution among countries. Although the average dollar shortfall from the poverty line in one country may be less than in another, it does not follow that it would be cheaper to help *all* the poor from the first country. There may be some poor from the second country who are very close to the poverty line and who would be very inexpensive to help. Ideally, all the poor from all the countries would be ranked by the size of the shortfall expressed in current dollars.

person per month. Russia comes next with exactly $8. The most expensive countries are Estonia ($22) and Slovenia ($24). Assuming that the international community has a given amount of funds *F* and that it is concerned with a representative poor in each country, whose distance from the poverty line is equal to the average shortfall, the optimal strategy would be to help first the poor in "less expensive" countries and then, gradually, to move to more "expensive" countries until funds are exhausted. Under this scenario, it is unlikely that "expensive" countries would be helped at all.

A different objective could be envisaged. If what matters is to reduce the level of deprivation among the poor, and deprivation is assumed to be an increasing function of the shortfall, then reducing the poverty of a very poor person by *x* dollars matters more (that is, it yields greater utility) than reducing the poverty of a less poor person by the same amount. Put another way, the marginal utility of money is a decreasing function of income. If deprivation is a quadratic function of the distance from the poverty line, then the objective function, guiding the allocation of funds, becomes:

5.7
$$\min_{d_{ij}} \sum_{i=1}^{k} \sum_{j=1}^{P_i} (z - y_{ij} - d_{ij}E_i)^2$$

where z = the poverty line in $PPP (same across the countries), k = number of countries, P_i = number of poor people in country i, y_{ij} = income of j-th individual in country i in PPP terms, d_{ij} = international transfer to that individual, E_i = purchasing power of a dollar in i-th country (that is, the reverse of the country's price level relative to the world).[22] The objective is to minimize overall deprivation. Equation 5.7 must be minimized under conditions of a given international amount of dollar funds (F), and only for poor people. This means that those whose income is above z are not included in the minimization of 5.7. These two conditions are written:

$$\sum_{i=1}^{k} \sum_{j=1}^{P_i} d_{ij} = F \quad (\textit{fund exhaustion})$$

$$(z - y_{ij} - d_{ij}E_i) \geq 0 \quad (\textit{irrelevance of the non-poor}).$$

The second condition ensures perfect targeting because the income of a poor person after the transfer cannot exceed the level of the poverty line.

Assuming, for the sake of simplicity, that only the representative poor in each country is addressed (that is, disregarding differences in countries' in-

---

22. The minimization of equation 5.7 is equivalent to the minimization of Foster-Green-Thornbeck's function P_2 for all transition economies combined.

come distributions among the poor), the objective function simplifies, and we can write the Lagrangean:[23]

5.8 $$\min_{d_i} L = \sum_{i=1}^{k} (z - y_i - d_i E_i)^2 + \lambda \left(\sum_{i=1}^{k} d_i - F \right)$$

where y_i = average poor person's income in PPP terms. z, E_i's and F are given.

The first-order condition is:[24]

$$\frac{\delta L}{\delta d_i} = -2E_i (z - y_i - d_i E_i) + \lambda = 0$$

and the solution is:

5.9 $$d_i = \frac{1}{E_i} (z - y_i - \frac{\lambda}{2E_i}).$$

In order that all d_i's be positive, λ must be less than or equal to the minimum value of $2(z-y_i)E_i$ (condition A). Let the country with the minimum value of $2(z-y_i)E_i$ be called "the binding country" (because it binds the value of λ from the above). The "binding country" may be denoted by b. λ, the marginal change in deprivation if the amount of available funds, F, changes infinitesimally, reflects how binding the funds constraint is. A high value of λ means that the constraint is fairly binding (that is, the marginal utility of an additional dollar is high).

From equation 5.9, it can be observed that d_i's are not necessarily positively related to E_i: countries with more depreciated currencies (high E) will not necessarily receive more funds per person. This is because the depth of poverty also influences d_i. If poverty of a representative poor $(z- y_i)$ is deep, then gains from reduced hardship may be significant (since the objective function is squared) even if the "bang for the buck" (E_i) is small. The condition for d_i and E_i to move in the same direction is that λ be greater than the country's $(z-y_i)E_i$ (condition B).[25] This condition may or may not be satisfied.

---

23. Note that in the case where $E_i=1$, the problem reduces to:

$$\min_{d_i} L = \sum_{i=1}^{k} (z - y_i - d_i)^2 + \lambda \left(\sum_{i=1}^{k} d_i - F \right)$$

which is minimized when

$$(z - y_i - d_i) = \frac{\lambda}{2}$$

that is, when the poverty deficit after transfers for each country is the same. This is equivalent to the condition derived by Kanbur (1987) namely that to minimize P_2 across several categories (countries, social groups, and so on) one needs to equalize P_1's.

24. The second order condition is satisfied: $2E_i^2>0$.

Figure 5.7. *Optimal Allocation of Funds by Countries if the Objective Is to Minimize Deprivation of the Poor*

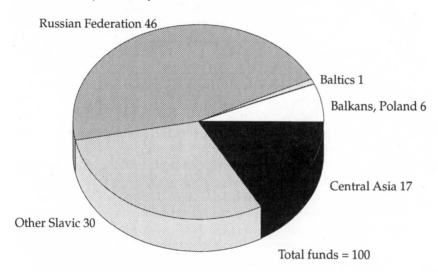

Total funds = 100

Note: "Other Slavic" includes Moldova. Based on *INCOME2* data.

Now, using the actual values for eighteen transition economies, the optimal d_i's are calculated. Optimal d_i's, or transfers per representative poor person, are then multiplied by the number of poor in each country to obtain the optimal allocation of international funds. The optimal distribution of funds, assuming the objective function 5.8, will be such that 46 percent of the funds would be allocated to Russia, 28 percent to Ukraine, 8 percent to Kazakhstan, and 4 percent each to Romania (the highest in Eastern Europe) and the Kyrgyz Republic (figure 5.7). The remaining thirteen countries would share 10 percent of the funds. The optimal allocation of money would thus be very heavily concentrated on five countries. Appendix 6 shows the exact distribution by countries.[26]

The lesson here is threefold:

- In general, it is less expensive for the international community to help the poor in countries where the exchange rate is low in comparison with its purchasing parity.
- It is probably less expensive to help the poor rapidly because the real exchange rates in the CIS countries still seem to be below their long-

---

25. For d_i and E_i to be positively related we must have:

$$\frac{\delta d_i}{\delta E_i} = \frac{-1}{E_i^2} \ (z - y_i - \frac{\lambda}{E_i}) > 0.$$

From the last relation, it directly follows that λ must be greater than $(z-y_i)E_i$.

26. The binding country is Slovenia. The countries for which condition B is satisfied are: Poland, Bulgaria, Hungary, Czech Republic, Slovakia, Slovenia, Latvia, and Estonia.

term equilibrium—that is, they are still rising. It is easy to imagine a situation where real incomes in domestic currency and nominal dollars rise, the poverty rates decline, but the overall cost of poverty alleviation from an international perspective does not fall or even rises, as the effect of currency appreciation offsets the effect of the decreasing number of the poor.

• Since funds are limited, it is useful to try to explicitly model what the objective function is because different objectives lead to different results. If the objective is to reduce the number of the poor, then the distribution of the poor (that is, how many are near the poverty line) will matter a great deal. Countries with much shallow poverty will be helped first. If a representative poor is targeted (for example, because data on the distribution of the poor are not available) and our objective is to minimize the number of the poor or the poverty deficit, then countries with low domestic price levels will benefit, because the cost of "vaulting" an average poor above the poverty line is relatively low. If the objective is minimization of hardship, then the depth of poverty plays a more important role, and the amount of transfers is determined through the interaction between the (squared) depth of poverty and the "bang for the buck" that can be obtained.

"Leakage" and actual cost of poverty alleviation

All these calculations assume perfect targeting. Relaxing the assumption of perfect targeting increases estimated outlays needed to "solve" poverty by a factor greater than 2–2.5, which are the numbers derived from the Western experience.[27] This can be shown as follows. Data on the distribution of social assistance reported here (see table 5.9 below) show that the bottom quintile receives 28 percent of total social assistance in transition economies, and 42 percent in market economies. Assuming that the bottom quintile is targeted in both cases, it follows that to arrive at an estimate of the actual cost of poverty elimination, the poverty deficit needs to be multiplied by a factor of 2.4 in market economies (100 divided by 42) and by 3.6 in transition economies (100 divided by 28).

An implication of the shallowness of poverty in transition economies is that the poor are not a distinct underclass. A lack of distinct poverty features implies that the costs of identifying the poor and the amount of "leakage" can be high.[28] If people who are poor cannot be identified easily through

---

27. See, for example, data quoted in Atkinson (1995, pp. 29–30) or Sawhill (1988, p. 1101).

28. This, in addition to relative inexperience of social assistance offices in transition countries in administering such programs, probably explains their lower targeting efficiency as compared with market economies. This is indirectly confirmed by the fact that there is no difference between the two sets of countries in the targeting efficiency of unemployment benefits, where eligibility criteria are clearer (see table 5.9).

certain categorical criteria (for example, place of residence, age, ethnic group, occupation, family size), and if their income cannot be gauged accurately (because it is barely below or above the poverty line and because it includes much in-kind income and income from the informal sector), then the costs of anti-poverty policies rise. The ratio between overall spending and the amount of cash actually "delivered" to the poor rises. The choice between (i) relying on growth as the primary anti-poverty instrument, or (ii) relying on welfare, then, moves in favor of the former. In conclusion, *shallowness of poverty by itself represents an argument in favor of growth-based (as against redistributive) policies as the tools for poverty reduction.*

Formally, the expected cost of poverty alleviation can be represented as the product of the "real" poverty deficit (PD) and a factor (greater than 1) that represents "leakage" (or payments to the non-poor), "spillover" (or payments to the poor in excess of what they need to reach the poverty line), and administrative costs. Empirical results in Poland show that both "leakage" and "spillover" increase when (a) the percentage of the poor increases, and (b) the poor are less distinct from the rest of the population. An increase in the percentage of potential claimants—if the distinctness of the poor from the rest of the population is assumed to be fixed—means that the probability of errors of targeting goes up.[29] The proportion of mistakes will be greater if, for example, half the population is poor than if only 5 percent is poor. The probability of such errors further increases if income differences between the poor and the non-poor are small, that is, if the poor are not distinct. As shown in equation 5.10, the "effective" poverty deficit as a percent of GDP (PD*/GDP) is equal to the "calculated" PD/GDP "grossed up" by a factor L, which is a positive function of the headcount index and the "shallowness" of poverty ($1/s$). Both a high headcount index and shallow poverty are characteristics of transition economies and increase the cost of poverty alleviation.

$$5.10 \qquad \frac{PD^*}{GDP} = \frac{PD}{GDP}\left(1 + L(HC, \tfrac{1}{s})\right).$$

How to Explain Increases in Poverty?

Letting both income and distribution change

The descent into poverty is the product of two forces: lower income and greater income inequality. This is illustrated in figures 5.8 and 5.9 with the example of the Czech Republic. Individuals are ranked according to their per capita monthly disposable income, and the height of the ordinate indicates the income level for each decile at constant prices. In 1993, real income for all but the top decile was less than it was in 1988. The percentage decline in income was greater for the poor: the lowest income decile lost 24 percent in real terms, while the ninth decile lost only 12 percent. Meanwhile, the top decile gained 20 percent. The Gini coefficient rose from about 19.4 to 26.6.

---

29. See Milanovic (1995a, pp. 43-45).

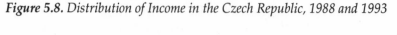

Figure 5.8. *Distribution of Income in the Czech Republic, 1988 and 1993*

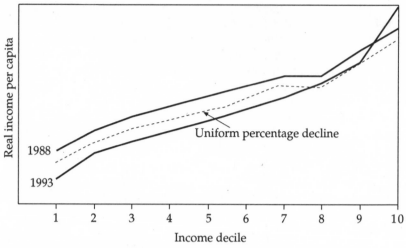

Note: In 1988 crowns. Vertical axis in logarithms.
Source: For 1988, *Microcensus*; for 1993, *Survey of Economic Expectations and Attitudes*. Both
reported in Večernik et al. (1994).

If 900 crowns per capita per month is taken to be the poverty line for 1988,
an amount equal to the poverty line actually used in Czechoslovakia during
that year[30] then approximately 6 percent of the population was poor in 1988
(see point A in figure 5.9 which "zooms" on the bottom quintile from figure 5.8). If income declines across the board by 12 percent, which indeed
was the actual average decrease in real income between 1988 and 1993,
then the percentage of the poor rises to about 10 percent (point B). In addition, however, the income distribution curve itself changed. The actual 1993
distribution is given by the line *Actual 93*. The headcount ratio now jumps
to 17 percent (point C). Thus, both the overall decline in income and the
change in distribution combine during the transition to raise the number
of poor.

When income distribution becomes more unequal, as it did during the
transition, the real income of the poor has to rise dramatically—in this case
it would have to more than double; see the ratio between AF and FG in
figure 5.9) just to maintain the poverty rate constant. Such an increase in

---

30. Czechoslovakia differed from other East European countries in that its poverty
line was not a mere "accounting" poverty line but was used in social policy (see also
section *Should OECD-like Social Assistance Be Introduced in Transition Economies?* in chapter 6). In 1988, the Czechoslovak per capita poverty line (for a family of four) was 875
crowns per month, or the equivalent of 210 international dollars.

Figure 5.9. *Decomposing the Change in the Poverty Rate: Parts Due to Change in Income and Change in Distribution*

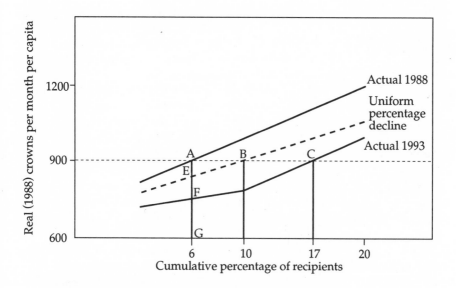

Note: AB=due to decline in income, BC=due to distributional change.
Source: For 1988, *Microcensus;* for 1993, *Survey of Economic Expectations and Attitudes.* Both reported in Večernik et al. (1994).

the income of the poor cannot, of course, take place while overall income declines (that is, it cannot occur at the same time as income distribution "worsens"). A notable feature of all transition economies however is a simultaneous decline in income and an increase in inequality; both effects contributed to rising poverty in these countries. In contrast, in the 1980s in Latin America, when poverty also increased, these two negative changes occurred simultaneously in only two countries: Brazil and Peru (Morley 1994).

Decomposition into growth and distribution effects

The increase in poverty can be broken down into a portion due to declining income and a portion due to more unequal distribution.[31] The typical pattern

---

31. The decomposition procedure used is the one described by Kakwani and Subbarao (1990), and Kakwani (1995, pp. 38–39). The formula for the change in poverty between period 0 and period 1 due to income is

$$Y = \frac{1}{2} \ (P_{10} - P_{00} + P_{11} - P_{01})$$

(Continued on the next page)

in transition economies seems to include first a period of quick decline in output with relatively small changes in the distribution of income, and then a second period in which inequality increases, the GDP bottoms out and, eventually, rises again. Poverty should be driven up by declining incomes during the first period and by increased inequality in the second (at least for as long as growth is not sufficient to offset the impact of more unequal distribution).[32] This pattern is illustrated for Poland and Russia during the period 1990–94 (figures 5.10 and 5.11). In Poland during 1990–93 almost all the increase in the poverty headcount (right-hand side axis) was due to the decline in real income (solid area in figure 5.10). However, beginning in 1992, the increase in the Gini coefficient and the associated change in the distribution also begin to add to poverty (the shaded area). By 1994, rising incomes began to pull poverty down while poverty due to a widening income distribution increased.

In Russia, the income decline was, of course, more severe: in 1994, real income was less than half what it was in 1988. The increase in the poverty headcount was also much sharper. Here again, however, widening income inequality becomes gradually more important in driving poverty up (see the shaded area in figure 5.11). In 1993 and 1994, the growth and distribution effects each explain about the same proportion of the overall increase in poverty. Interestingly, even a slight decrease in the Gini coefficient in 1994 (compared with 1993) did not stop the growing role of income distribution in explaining poverty. This suggests that while Gini might have decreased because of some reduction in the share of the rich, the distributional change continued to be unfavorable to those close to the poverty line and pushed some down into the ranks of the poor.

(Continued from the previous page)

where P_{ij} is the poverty rate with the income level from period i and the distribution from period j. The change in poverty due to change in distribution is:

$$D = \frac{1}{2} \; (P_{01} - P_{00} + P_{11} - P_{10}).$$

It can easily be seen that $P_{11} - P_{00} = Y + D$.

Downscaling all incomes is equivalent to raising the poverty line. To calculate P_{10} the poverty line is shifted upward (because income between 0 and 1 has declined) using the formula:

$$PL_0^* = \frac{PL_0}{1 + r}$$

where PL_0^* is the new poverty line, PL_0 the original poverty line and r = rate of income decline (negative). Similarly, to calculate P_{01} we redefine PL_1 as:

$$PL_1^* = PL_1 \; (1 + r).$$

32. The same pattern is observed by Cornia (1994, p. 39) and UNICEF (1995, Table I.2, p. 11).

Figure 5.10. *Breakdown of the Increase in Poverty Headcount between Growth and Distribution Effects in Poland, 1990–94*

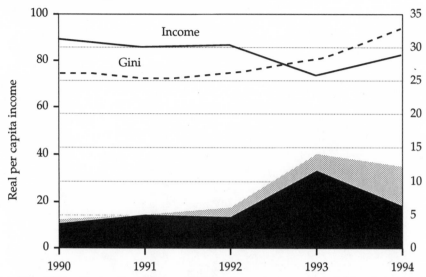

Note: 1987 real per capita income = 100. Real per capita income = solid line (left axis). Gini coefficient = broken line (right axis). Headcount increase compared to 1987 (right axis). Growth effect: solid area; distribution effect: shaded area.

Figure 5.11. *Breakdown of the Increase in Poverty Headcount between Growth and Distribution Effects in Russia, 1990–94*

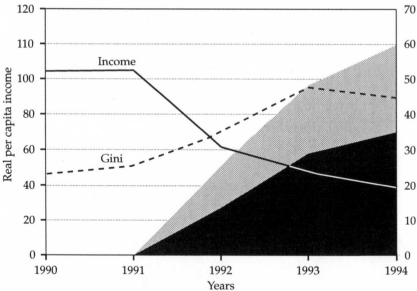

Note: 1988 real per capita income = 100. Real per capita income = solid line (left axis). Gini coefficient = broken line (right axis). Headcount increase compared to 1988 (right axis). Growth effect: solid area; distribution effect: shaded area.

Table 5.4. *Explaining the Increase in Poverty Headcount between 1987–88 and 1993–94*

Equation	Constant (t-value)	ΔINCOME (t-value)	ΔGINI (t-value)	PPP INCOME (1988)	ΔLIB	$\bar{R}^2$ (F)	SE
A	24.0 (1.5)	-0.63 (3.1)[a]	0.50 (0.8)	-0.0041 (1.3)		0.70 (11.8)	14.2
B	1.7 (0.4)	-0.28 (1.6)	1.33 (2.6)[b]			0.44 (6.5)	12.9
C	22.6 (2.1)	-0.75 (4.5)[a]	0.28 (0.5)		-30 (2.0)	0.74 (14.4)	13.2
D	25.2 (3.1)[b]	-0.47 (3.2)[a]	0.94 (2.4)[b]		-41 (3.2)[a]	0.68 (11.0)	9.7

Note: ΔHC (change in poverty headcount) is the dependent variable. It is the difference between the 1987–88 poverty headcount from table 5.1 (column 2) and the 1993–94 poverty headcount calculated using the macroeconomic *INCOME2* data (table 5.2).

ΔINCOME is the change in population real (macroeconomic) income from table 3.4, column 3.

ΔGINI is the difference between the 1987–88 and 1993–94 Ginis from table 4.1.

PPP INCOME is annual per capita household income in 1988 obtained from HBSs and expressed in international 1990 dollars.

ΔLIB is the change in the liberalization index between 1989 and 1994 (maximum value of the index = 1, minimum value = 0).

t-values are in parentheses.

a. Significant at 1 percent.

b. Significant at 5 percent.

Cross-country analysis: economic policy and increase in poverty

The previous analysis of poverty shows that the increase in poverty was driven by two strong forces: a decline in population incomes and an increase in inequality. This can be studied more formally by estimating the first-difference equation 5.11 across all transition economies:

5.11 ΔHC = fct ($\Delta INCOME$, $\Delta GINI$, *PPP INCOME*)

where ΔHC = change in poverty headcount between 1987–88 and 1993–94, $\Delta INCOME$ = percentage change in real income over the same period, $\Delta GINI$ = = change in Gini points over the same period, and *PPP INCOME* = \$PPP income per person (from household surveys) in 1988. *PPP INCOME* is used to control for the fact that poverty headcounts for different countries are calculated using the same real poverty line of \$PPP 4 per day per person. Given the same percentage decrease in income and the same increase in the Gini coefficient, the richer country's headcount will change less because fewer people will fall below the given (real) poverty threshold. In other words, a 10 percent decline in income will push fewer people below the \$PPP 4 line in a relatively rich country such as the Czech Republic, and many more people in the poorer Kazakhstan (see also equation 5.6).

Equation A in table 5.4 shows the results of running equation 5.11 over fifteen transition economies.[33] All coefficients have the predicted signs: lower income and higher Gini increase poverty; higher initial (1988) income level reduces the increase in the headcount. However, only the coefficient of $\Delta INCOME$ is statistically significant; $\Delta GINI$ and *PPP INCOME* are not.[34] Each percent decrease in real population income is associated with an increase of the poverty headcount by 0.63 points. This is virtually the same (semi-) elasticity as found in the section, *Elasticity of poverty with respect to income.*

Equation B takes into account the fact that estimates of poverty increase are not equally accurate. Here, observations are weighted using an explicit indicator of survey quality.[35] Now the $\Delta GINI$ coefficient becomes statistically significant while the importance of $\Delta INCOME$ diminishes.

Is there a relationship between the increase in poverty and the speed of reform, that is, independent from, and *in addition* to, the effect that the speed

---

33. Macroeconomic income data are not available for Bulgaria, Estonia, and Latvia (see table 3.4).

34. Multicollinearity reduces the significance of the coefficients: the partial correlation between $\Delta INCOME$ and $\Delta GINI$ is 0.6 and between $\Delta INCOME$ and *PPP INCOME* it is -0.5. This means that income loss has been accompanied by increased inequality and has been greater in poorer countries.

35. The indicator ranges from 4 = perfect survey to 1 = unreliable survey. Values are obtained as 4 *minus* the estimated bias for 1993–94 surveys given in table A1.4. Thus, the value for Poland is 3.5, for Bulgaria 2, and so on.

of reforms may have on real income and the Gini coefficient (which are already included in the regression).[36] In equation C, an estimate is added for the speed of reforms (*LIB*), expressed as the change in the liberalization index, which ranges from 0 (no reform) to 1 (full-scope reform).[37] In this equation, which is identical in formulation to equation A, the direct effect of reforms on the change in poverty is not significant. However, if a weighted *OLS* formulation is used to account for the quality of observations (equation D), ΔLIB shows that faster reforms reduce poverty. Moreover, with this equation, all coefficients become statistically significant: 1 percent of decrease in real income is associated with an increase in the headcount of 0.47 percentage points; 1 Gini point increase in inequality is associated with a little less than 1 percentage point increase in headcount, and each 0.1 point "increase" in reform reduces the poverty headcount by 4 points.[38] Adjusted R^2 is almost 0.7.

Who Are the Poor?

Poverty by social class

The section in chapter 4, *Disparity among social groups*, demonstrated that the approximate order of gain by socioeconomic group during the transition was as follows: pensioners > workers[39] ≥ farmers. Given this, it would be reasonable to expect the reverse ordering in terms of poverty rates. This is illustrated in figure 5.12, which shows *relative* poverty rates for the main socioeconomic groups. Relative poverty rates are obtained by taking the actual poverty rate for one group—for example, workers—and dividing it by the average rate for all social groups (that is, by the country average). Values smaller than 1 indicate that a given socioeconomic group has a smaller proportion of the poor than the country average. This approach is used here because the data in figures 5.12 and 5.18–5.25 come from a variety of sources that use different poverty lines. Expressing poverty rates in relative terms makes comparisons possible.[40]

Workers' households have, in all countries, lower poverty rates than the average. Poverty incidence among pensioners is also lower than the average, except in Bulgaria and Estonia. In Belarus and the Slovak Republic, the inci-

---

36. That is, speedy reforms might lead to an increase in inequality which, of course, would already be reflected in the Gini coefficient. However, that effect seems negligible as indicated by low correlation coefficients between ΔLIB and $\Delta GINI$ (-0.15), and ΔLIB and $\Delta INCOME$ (-0.13). This also suggests orthogonality of the right-hand side variables.

37. The index is calculated by de Melo, Denizer, and Gelb (1996).

38. The effect is independent of countries' income level. If countries' PPP income level in 1988 is included in regression D as a control, the same results hold.

39. Unless otherwise specified, workers include both white-collar and blue-collar workers who are employed in the public, private, or mixed sectors (but not the self-employed and not those employed in the small-scale private sector).

Figure 5.12. Social Group and Relative Poverty Rates, 1992–95

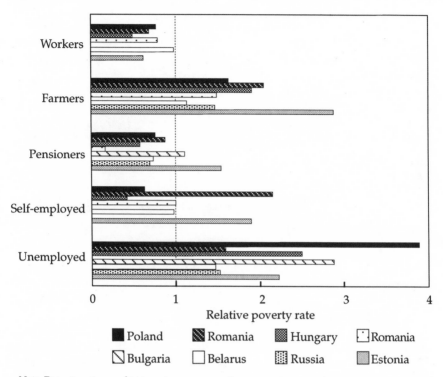

Relative poverty rate

■ Poland   ▨ Romania   ▨ Hungary   ⬚ Romania

◩ Bulgaria   ☐ Belarus   ▦ Russia   ▨ Estonia

Note: Poverty rate equal to country average = 1.
Source: Calculated from: Poland 1993: World Bank (1995, Table 2.5). Romania 1994: World Bank (1995a, Table 3.1, p. 17). Hungary 1992-93: Tóth and Förster (1994, Table 5, p. 34). Slovakia 1992: calculated from *Microcensus* 1992, p. 30. Bulgaria 1992: calculated from HBS 1992, p. 109. Russia 1993: World Bank (1994a), Klugman (1995). Belarus 1995: World Bank (1995c, p. 36). Estonia 1995: World Bank (1996, p. 13).

dence of poverty among pensioners is even less than among workers' households. In all countries, farmers' poverty rates are between $1\frac{1}{2}$ and 2 times the average (three times the average in Estonia). The self-employed, often thought to be among the "winners" in the transition, have lower poverty rates than the average in Hungary and Poland, about average in Belarus and the Slovak Republic, but, interestingly, higher than the average in Esto-

---

40. The resulting comparability, while satisfactory, is not full. This is because the level of the poverty line used will also influence the relative incidence of poverty. To take an extreme example, suppose that the poverty line used is so high that virtually all households in a country are poor. Then all socioeconomic groups will have the same poverty incidence and the *relative* poverty rates will be unity for all. Fortunately, the sources used here all employ broadly comparable poverty lines ranging between $PPP 100 and $PPP 200 per capita per month.

Figure 5.13. *Poverty Headcount by Socioeconomic Group in Poland, 1987–94*

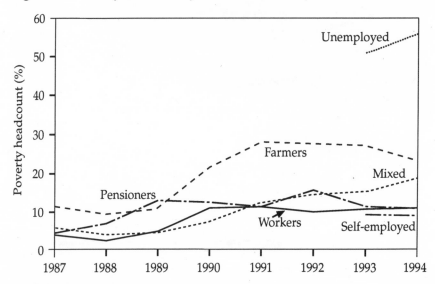

Note: Poverty line = 1993 minimum pension (= official poverty line) indexed by the cost-of-living.
Source: Calculated from Polish HBSs (various years).

nia and Romania. This probably reflects issues of classification (what household are classified as "self-employed") as well as the lack of homogeneity noted above among the self-employed, a group that includes both small-scale subsistence farmers and rich private entrepreneurs. Finally, households with at least one unemployed person have poverty rates of between $1\frac{1}{2}$ (Belarus, Romania, and Russia) and four times (Poland) greater than the average.

From this information the following conclusions can be drawn: the unemployed and farmers are, in all countries, more likely to be poor than the average person; pensioners' likelihood to be poor is about average; and workers' households are slightly less likely. No regularity emerges regarding the position of the self-employed.

In addition to a comparison between countries, historical single country data can be used. Historical data are preferable because they allow for the tracking of changes in poverty, but they are also more difficult to find. For Poland, however, detailed and relatively consistent data are available on the incidence of poverty by social group going back to the late 1970s. In figure 5.13 they are shown dating back to 1987. The incidence of poverty among farmers' and mixed (worker-farmer) households has increased by more than it has among workers and pensioners. Farmers, who traditionally have had high poverty rates, still have the highest incidence of poverty (except for the unemployed), but they are now closely followed by mixed households.[41]

41. During the stagnation of the 1980s, however, mixed households fared better than others (Milanovic, 1992).

Table 5.5. Relative Poverty Rates for Different Types of Unemployed Households

Country	With one un-employed at least	With long-term un-employed	With more than one unem-ployed	Household head un-employed
Estonia 1995	2.2		3.3	
Hungary 1993	1.0	3.3	4.9	3.7[a]
Poland 1993	1.7	2.6	3.2	4.0
Russia 1992	1.5			2.5

Note: Long-term unemployed is unemployed for more than a year.
a. Becomes 9 if head of household is long-term unemployed.
Source: Calculations for Estonia from World Bank (1996); Hungary from World Bank (1995b); Poland from World Bank (1995); and Russia from World Bank (1995a, p. 17).

The self-employed and the unemployed are two socioeconomic groups that have become more important during the transition, and are, for the first time, included in Polish HBSs. These two groups have the lowest and highest incidence of poverty, respectively. The absence of data for the years prior to 1993 does not allow a comparison of the position of these two groups before and after the transition. Anecdotal evidence suggests, however, that the incidence of poverty among the self-employed has always been low. On the other hand, the current unemployed once belonged to either workers' or mixed households[42] and their poverty incidence was probably not too dissimilar from the average of these groups. Thus, during the transition their position must have deteriorated markedly.

Unemployment and poverty

The link between unemployment and poverty is clear. The higher the rates of unemployment and, particularly, the higher the share of the long-term unemployed (that is, those who are unemployed for more than a year), the greater the poverty. The long-term unemployed either lose their entitlement to unemployment benefits or receive only a fraction of earlier benefits. A low rate of unemployment and a virtual absence of long-term unemployed make the correlation between unemployment and poverty weak in the Czech Republic.[43] But the situation is different in countries where unemployment rates are greater and the share of the long-term unemployed is high. As shown in table 5.5, in Poland and Hungary in 1993, households with a long-term unemployed member had poverty incidences that were 2.6 and 3.3 times higher

---

42. Only very few current unemployed would have been farmers. Polish agriculture was private, and it is unlikely that a farmer would abandon agriculture to register as an unemployed without right to benefits.

43. A point made by Professor Jiří Večerník at the Third Central European Forum held at the Institute for Human Sciences, Vienna, 21–23 January 1994.

than the average, respectively; households with two or more unemployed members were 3.2 and 4.9 times more likely, respectively, to be poor than the average; and households headed by an unemployed person were about 4 times more likely to be poor than the average.

In Poland and Bulgaria, 30 percent of poverty could be attributed to unemployment. In Hungary, the share is even 60 percent (see table 6.1 below). In Russia, where the unemployment rate is much lower, this is true for only 11 percent of the poor.[44] Even if unemployment does not continue to rise in transition economies, the share of the long-term unemployed will probably still increase, and the link between unemployment and poverty will become stronger.

How the working population became poor

The working poor represent a sizable proportion of those who were pulled below the poverty line during the transition. A study of poverty in Poland finds that in 1993 60 percent of the poor were working poor (World Bank 1994a, vol. 1, p. iv); similar results are obtained for Russia, where 66 percent of the poor are working poor (World Bank 1994a, p. 15). Those whose relative wage position appears to have deteriorated during the transition were primarily manual workers (in declining industries) and low-skilled clerical staff who often had only a vocational education or less. The latter were probably the most overstaffed professional category in socialist countries. The streamlining of production, together with a reduced need for various reporting functions related to the bureaucratic management of the economy, reduced demand for this category of worker. In Poland, for example, the position of people with only a vocational education has deteriorated more than that of any other educational group (World Bank 1995, p. 81).

Two examples illustrate how working people have slid below the poverty line. The first is that of Ukraine, and to some extent Russia, where even the minimum conditions necessary for working people to stay ahead of poverty are no longer satisfied. The second is that of a richer country, Poland, where the minimum conditions are satisfied even if many working people are still poor.

The situation in Ukraine and Russia is depicted in figures 5.14 and 5.15. The average wage and average pension are expressed in terms of a constant real per capita poverty line, which is taken to be the 1993 official Russian poverty line (also virtually equal to the poverty line discussed above of $PPP 120). At minimum, the average wage should be twice the (per capita) poverty line. This means that the "typical" dual-income working couple that is, a couple that has two children and is earning the average wage, should not be poor. Not all such dual-income, four-member families would remain above the poverty line, however, because approximately 60 percent of workers nor-

---

44. The same figure for Canada in 1990 was 28 percent (calculated from Statistics Canada, 1991, pp. 154–64).

Figure 5.14. *Average Wage, Pension, and per Capita Income as a Ratio of the Poverty Line in Russia, 1987–96*

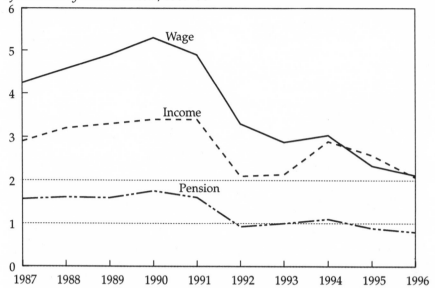

Note: The poverty line is the official Russian Ministry of Labor minimum subsistence line for 1993. In 1993, the average subsistence minimum per person was Rs. 20,562, or $22 per month, or $PPP 120. This line is indexed using consumer price index. Average income comes from macroeconomic income data. All amounts are monthly averages.

Figure 5.15. *Average Wage, Pension, and per Capita Income as a Ratio of the Poverty Line in Ukraine, 1987–95*

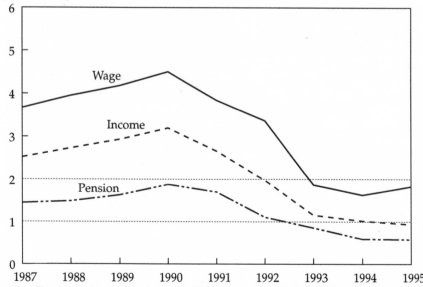

Note: The poverty line for Ukraine is the official Russian Ministry of Labor minimum subsistence line for 1993 (average value). This line is indexed using Soviet and Ukrainian (as appropriate) CPI index. Average income comes from macroeconomic income data. All amounts are monthly averages.

Figure 5.16. *Cumulative Wage Distribution in Ukraine (1992) and Poland (1993)*

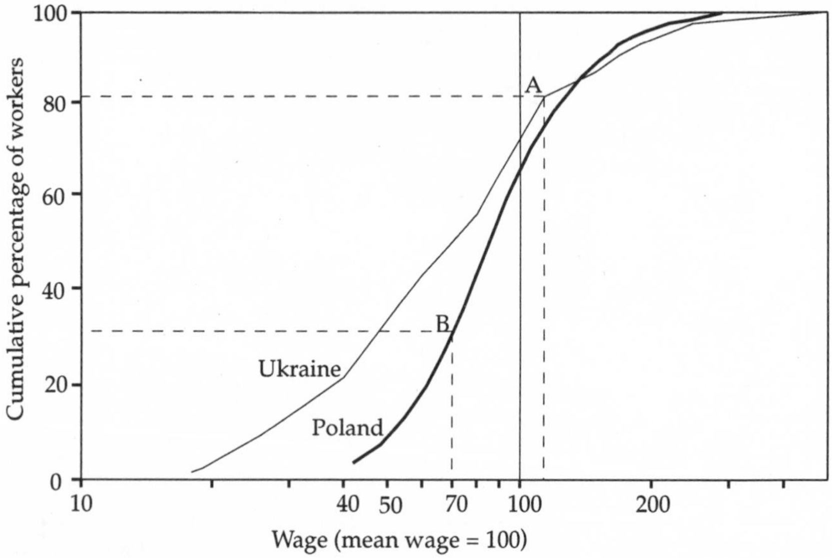

Note: Horizontal axis in logarithms.

mally earn less than the average wage. But because there are offsetting elements such as women who are systematically low earners marrying men
who are high earners, family allowances, income-in-kind,[45] and so on, the
average wage-to-poverty-line ratio of 2 to 1 seems a satisfactory approximation. In Russia and Ukraine, the ratio declined from about 4 (and even 5 in
Russia, due mostly to high wages paid to workers in Siberia) before the transition, to about 2 in 1995 and 1996. (In Ukraine, the ratio has been slightly
below 2 since 1993.) Thus, a dual-income couple earning the average wage
cannot be sure of staying above the poverty line in Ukraine, and barely man-
ages to do so in Russia. Because the average wage-to-poverty-line ratio in
Ukraine in 1995 is only 1.8, only those earning approximately 10 percent above
the average wage should be able to stay out of poverty. As figure 5.16 shows,
fewer than 20 percent of the employed fulfill this condition (point A).

Similar conclusions emerge if the relationship between the average pension and the poverty line is considered. The average pension should, at a
minimum, be equal to the poverty line: one-person or two-person pensioners' households with no dependents and no other sources of income should
be able to avoid poverty. With that objective in mind, governments often link
the minimum pension to the official poverty line, as in the Czech Republic,
Hungary, Poland, Russia, and Slovakia. The "average" pensioner should, then,

_____

45. Workers' families receive about 20 percent of total income from non-wage payments.

be able to avoid poverty. This, however, is not always the case. The minimum pension that is linked to the poverty line may be the minimum full-entitlement pension. Disability, social, family, or early-retirement pensions may be below the minimum pension. The vagaries of slow indexation, or delays in pension payments, may further push some pensioners (at least temporarily) below the poverty threshold, and the overall average pension may barely stay at the subsistence level. In Russia, this has been the case since 1992 (see figure 5.14). In 1995 and 1996, because of huge pension arrears, the paid-out average pension was 10 to 20 percent *below* the official poverty line.[46] In Ukraine, the average pension has been less than the poverty line since 1993, and in 1994–95 it was approximately 40 percent below the poverty line. Thus even the minimum pension requirement identified above is no longer satisfied in Russia and Ukraine.

The average per capita income in Ukraine, as estimated using macroeconomic sources (see figure 5.15), is equal to the poverty line since 1993. Putting aside for the moment possible underestimations of macroeconomic income, this fact alone (combined with a log-normal income distribution) ensures that approximately 60 percent of the population lives below the poverty line.[47]

In Poland, the wage requirement is satisfied, as the average wage in 1996 was about $2\frac{3}{4}$ times greater than the Polish official poverty line (see figure 5.17).

Who are the working poor in Poland? The Polish per capita poverty line was 35 percent of the average wage in 1995 and 1996. This means that if only one member of a "typical" family of four is employed earning the average wage, the family will fall short of the poverty threshold (because the family income needed to stay above the poverty line is 35 percent times 4, or 140 percent of the average wage). Even if economies of scale in consumption, lower needs of children, and additional sources of income are accounted for, such a family is clearly hovering near the poverty line. If the spouse is outside the labor force, or his/her unemployment benefit has expired, or even if she is receiving an unemployment benefit[48] but the earning of the working spouse is less than the average wage, the family is in a precarious situation. Translated into practical terms, this means that to stay ahead of poverty, a typical Polish family has to have two wage earners. While this was typical under Communism, it no longer is, as participation rates have declined and many have become unemployed. Consequently, many families in Poland with only one employed member will probably be poor or near poverty.

But this is not all. If both husband and wife are employed and each earns approximately 70 percent of the average wage or less, they too will be poor.

---

46. The average pension includes all supplementary pension payments.

47. The mean of the log-normal distribution is at approximately the 60–65th percentile.

48. The unemployment benefit was a flat 35 percent of the average wage.

Figure 5.17. *Average Wage, Pension, and per Capita Income as a Ratio of the Poverty Line in Poland, 1987–96*

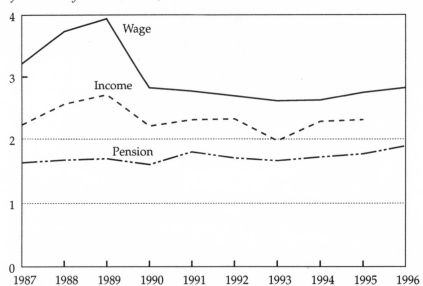

Note: The poverty line is the 1993 minimum pension equal to $68 per month or almost $PPP 170. It is indexed using the cost-of-living index. Average income comes from macroeconomic income data. All amounts are monthly averages.

Figure 5.16 shows that about 30 percent of the employed in Poland fall into this category (point B).

The working person's situation in Poland can be contrasted with that of his counterpart in the United Kingdom or the United States. The *minimum wage* in the latter two countries is a little more than $30 per day.[49] This is three (in the United States), and four times (United Kingdom), greater than the per capita poverty line for a four-member household.[50] This means that, for a typical family, only one member of the household need work at the minimum wage for the whole family to be near the poverty line.[51] Virtually all "typical" families with one or more employed members earning more

---

49. This assumes an eight-hour work day and twenty-two work-days per month.

50. The U.S. federal poverty line for a four-member household is about $10 per person per day. The U.K. Income Support is about $5 per person per day plus about $3 for the housing allowance.

51. The U.S. federal poverty line is among the highest (in PPP terms) in the world. It differs from European poverty lines, however, because it does not represent a "guaranteed minimum income." It defines which individuals and households are eligible for federal assistance (for example, housing benefits, Medicaid, food stamps). The states define their own—lower or higher—effective poverty lines for the allocation of state-financed benefits.

Figure 5.18. *Household Size and Relative Poverty Rates, 1993–95*

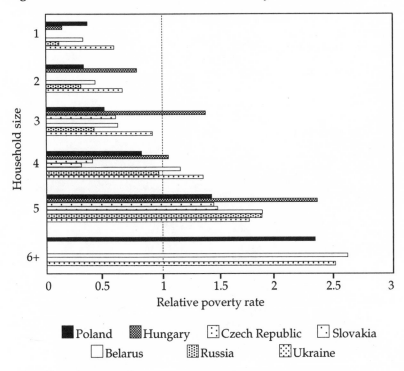

Note: Poverty rate equal to country average = 1.
Source: Calculated from: Poland 1993: World Bank (1995). Hungary 1992-93: Tóth and Förster (1994, Table 4). Czech Republic and Slovakia 1993: Večernik et al. (1994). Belarus 1993: Roberti (1994, Table 3). Russia 1993: Center for Economic Conjuncture (1994). Ukraine 1995: *Family budget surveys* 1995 reported in Ukrainian Committee for Statistics (1996).

than the minimum wage will be above the poverty threshold. *The position of minimum-wage workers in the United States and the United Kingdom vis-à-vis their countries' poverty lines therefore, is similar to that of an average-wage worker in Poland vis-à-vis the Polish poverty line.*[52] In both cases, if only one member of the household is employed at that wage (the minimum in the United States and United Kingdom, and the average wage in Poland), the household is in a precarious position.

Poverty by size and type of household

Poverty also varies as a function of size and type of household (see figure 5.18). In general, larger households tend to be poorer both in per capita terms

---

52. Note that, in addition, the poverty line is approximately $PPP 10 per person per day in the United States, $PPP 8 in the United Kingdom, and $PPP 6 in Poland.

Figure 5.19. *Relative Poverty Rates for Single-parent Households, 1993–95*

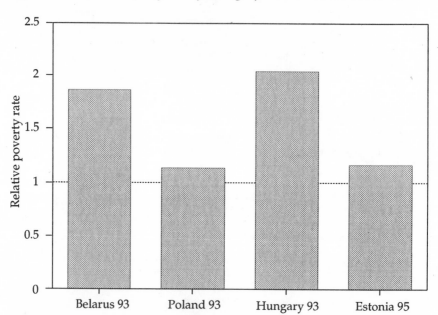

Note: Poverty rate equal to the country average = 1.
Source: Calculated from: Belarus: Roberti (1994, Table 3). Poland: World Bank (1995, Table 2.17). Hungary: World Bank (1995b, p. 22). Estonia: World Bank (1996).

(meaning that total household income rises more slowly than the number of household members) and in equivalent terms (when economies of scale and lower consumption needs of children are taken into account). The position of larger households is the same in transition economies. Poverty rates for five-member households are everywhere between 1.5 and 2.5 times higher than the average. On the other hand, for one- and two-person households, poverty rates are less than one-half the average almost everywhere. Exceptions include declines in poverty rates in the Czech Republic and Hungary from three-person to four-person households.

Not surprisingly, single-parent households also have a higher-than-average incidence of poverty (see figure 5.19).

Poverty by age

The high correlation between household size and poverty implies that children will be one of the most poverty-stricken groups. This is shown in figure 5.20. Children under the age of fourteen are between 20 and 70 percent more likely to be poor than the average person. In all eight countries shown here, there is a remarkable similarity in the way in which poverty rates decline with age. Poverty rates for people of retirement age (55 for women, 60 for men) are only about one-half the country average in Hungary and Poland,

Figure 5.20. *Age and Relative Poverty Rates, 1992–95*

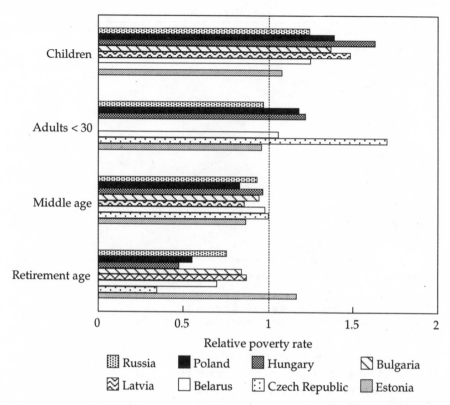

Note: Poverty rate equal to the country average = 1.

Source: Calculated from: Russia Q2/1993: McAuley (1994, p. 37). Poland 1993: World Bank (1995, figure B, p. iii). Hungary 1992-93: Andorka and Spéder (1994, table 2). Bulgaria 1992: HBS 1992, calculated from table 4, p. 111. Latvia 1992: HBS 1992, calculated from p. 23 and p. 26. Belarus 1995: World Bank (1995c, p. 36). Czech Republic 1993: Večernik and others (1994, tables IV/3a and IV/3b, pp. 21-22). Estonia 1995: World Bank (1996, p. 17).

and even less in the Czech Republic and Slovakia,[53] a finding consistent with findings above regarding the relatively favorable position of pensioners in Eastern Europe. Among the countries shown here, only in Estonia do the elderly have higher-than-average poverty rates. This is due to low and flat (i.e. almost equal for all) pensions in existence in Estonia since 1992.

The most dramatic reversal in relative poverty rates between the old and the young probably occurred in eastern Germany in the wake of the 1990 Unification. In the German Democratic Republic, the aged had relatively high poverty rates because the pension-wage ratio, as in the Soviet Union, was

---

53. Slovakia is not shown in figure 5.20 due to lack of space.

Figure 5.21. *Age and Relative Poverty Rates in Eastern Germany, 1990 and 1992*

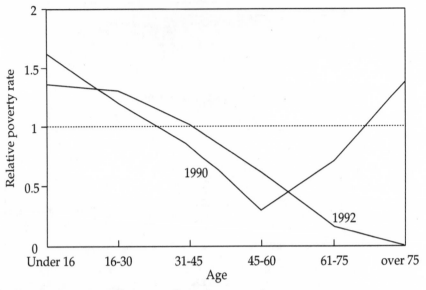

Note: Poverty rate equal to eastern German average = 1.
Source: Calculated from Krause (1992, reported in Heimerl [1993]).

low (about 35 percent). Pensioners in the former German Democratic Republic "gained" from the Unification, however, because their pensions were first converted from Ostmarks into DMs at a favorable one-to-one rate, and then the pensioners were absorbed into the more generous West German pension system.[54] As shown in figure 5.21, almost no eastern German pensioners in 1992 were among the poor. By contrast, the relative poverty rate among children in 1992 was about the same as prior to Unification. The figure 5.21 also shows that in 1992, poverty rates were steadily decreasing with age, as they were in other transition economies. Before Unification, however, poverty rates peaked for the very young and the very old.

---

54. For example, at the time of the Unification the average income of a pensioner household in West Germany was 90 percent of the country-wide average while in East Germany, it was 76 percent (Heimerl, 1993, p. 77).

55. Večernik (1994a) finds that in the Czech Republic the rate of return to one additional year of education has increased from 3.5 percent before the transition to 6.2 percent after the transition. Similarly, in comparing Czech and Slovak earnings distributions for 1984 and 1993, Chase (1995) finds the rate of return to education to have risen by between 2 and 3 percent. World Bank (1995) and Rutkowski (1996) find that in Poland this rate went up from 6.4 percent in 1989 to 7.5 percent in 1992. Rutkowski (1995, p. 29) also finds increasing returns to education in Bulgaria.

Figure 5.22. *Education of Household Head and Relative Poverty Rates, 1993–95*

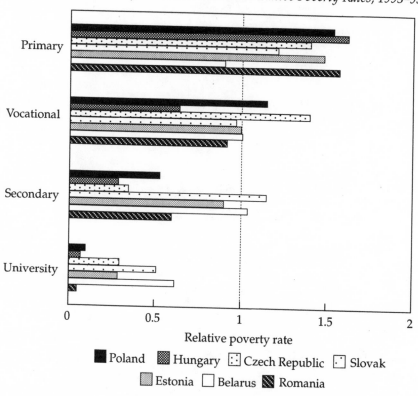

Relative poverty rate

■ Poland ▨ Hungary ⸬ Czech Republic ⸫ Slovak

▨ Estonia ☐ Belarus ◆ Romania

Note: Poverty rate equal to the country average = 1.
Source: Calculated from: Poland 1993: World Bank (1995, Table 2.8). Hungary 1993: World Bank (1995b, p. 24). Czech Republic and Slovak Republic 1993: Večernik and others (1994, Tables IV/3a and IV/3b, pp. 21-22). Estonia 1995: World Bank (1996, p. 14). Belarus 1995: World Bank (1996a, pp. 6-7). Romania 1994: World Bank (1995a, Table 3.1, p. 17).

Education and poverty

The educated, not surprisingly, are less likely to be poor. In addition, increasing returns to education have probably further strengthened the link between high levels of education and low levels of poverty.[55] As can be seen from figure 5.22, university education virtually guarantees in every country but the Slovak Republic and Belarus that a household will not be poor.[56] Households whose head has only an elementary education are between 20 and 60 percent more likely than the average household to be poor. Vocational education yields an average probability of being poor. Secondary education reduces the probability to about half the average.

---

56. In these two countries, the probability is half the country average.

Figure 5.23. *Size of Locality and Relative Poverty Rates, 1993–95*

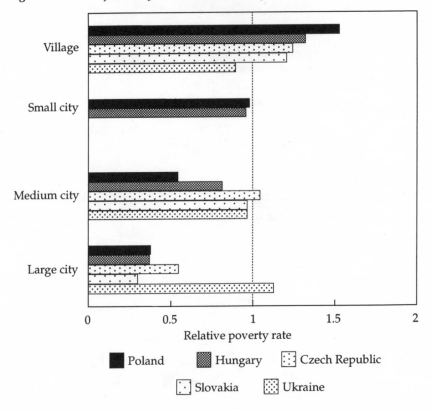

Note: Poverty rate equal to the country average = 1.

Source: Calculated from: Poland 1993: World Bank (1995, Table 2.16). Hungary 1992–93: Tóth and others (1994, Table A 1.2). Czech Republic and Slovak Republic 1993: Večernik and others (1994, Tables IV/3a and IV/3b, pp. 21-22). Ukraine 1995: World Bank (1996b, p. 22).

Hungary displays the sharpest decline of poverty with education level. In Belarus and Slovakia there is an increase in the incidence of poverty as one moves from household heads with vocational education to household heads who are secondary school graduates. This might suggest a slower restructuring as typically demand for workers with vocational education declines during the transition.

Regional aspect of poverty

Poverty rates decline with increase in the size of the locality. Low rates of unemployment and the concentration of highly skilled people in capital cities, increasing returns to education, and the finding above that farmers experience higher levels of poverty than other groups, suggest that larger cities would be richer. Figure 5.23 confirms it for four East European countries.

Unfortunately, reliable data do not exist for the rest of Eastern Europe and countries of the former Soviet Union, except for Ukraine, where, on the contrary, urban poverty is more prevalent. The importance of home-consumption in total population income in Ukraine, and particularly in rural areas, is the key reason for lower poverty in Ukrainian villages. Whether this feature may be shared by other countries of the former Soviet Union is likely but impossible to confirm because of lack of data.

Poverty and gender

Figure 5.24 exhibits poverty rates by age and sex. Data from Bulgaria and Russia (the only two countries for which data is available) show that poverty rates for men decrease as they retire, while for women they remain unchanged. Figure 5.25 contrasts age profiles of poverty in female-headed and male-headed households in Poland. Female-headed households have a higher incidence of poverty than male-headed households, regardless of age. The differential rises with age, however. As in Bulgaria and Russia, the poverty rate for people over 70 years old continues to decrease for male-headed households, and rises for female-headed households. This finding may be due to the fact that women receive lower pensions. It explains, in part, why overall poverty rates tend to be higher for women than for men. It would also seem that most of the overall reduction of poverty with age (such as noted in figure 5.20) may be due to lower poverty among males.

Figure 5.24. *Sex, Age, and Relative Poverty Rates in Bulgaria and Russia, 1992–93*

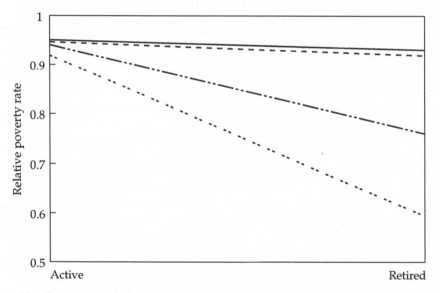

Note: Poverty rate equal to the country average = 1.
Source: Calculated from: Russia Q2/1993: McAuley (1994, p. 37). Bulgaria 1992: HBS 92, table 4, p. 111.

Figure 5.25. Poverty Rates for Male- and Female-headed Households in Poland, 1993

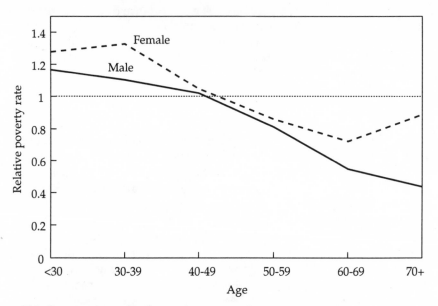

Note: Poverty rate equal to the country average = 1.
Source: Poland 1993: World Bank (1995, Annex Table 5.11).

The Incidence of Cash Social Transfers

In this section, the extent to which cash social transfers are focused on the lowest income groups is analyzed. The analysis will not address pensions except for income-tested state pensions because, strictly speaking, pensions are not an anti-poverty transfer. They are a deferred labor income. Although in all pension schemes there is some redistribution in favor of poorer people (in the sense that pensions do not exactly mirror contributions made during a person's active life), pensions are nonetheless "earned" incomes in the same sense as wages. Their main function is income-smoothing over a person's lifetime.

The second reason not to discuss pensions here is somewhat more complicated. Pensions account for between 70 and 80 percent of total cash social transfers. They also represent most of the income received by pensioners: on average, more than 80 percent. The result is that, if the average level of pensions in a country is relatively low, pensioners will tend to be poor. The poorer the pensioners, the better targeted pension spending will appear simply because most pensions will be received by the poor. Thus, the "good" poverty-focus of pensions in countries where pensions are low, as in Russia, will be misleading. Other more extreme and erroneous conclusions regarding targeting may be drawn if a comparison is made between the number of pen-

Table 5.6. *Concentration Coefficients of Family Benefits
before the Transition (1988–89) and in 1993–95*

Country	1988–89	1993–95	Change in targeting
Eastern Europe	-20	-17	
Bulgaria	-17	+5	Worse
Hungary	-20	-18	Same
Poland	-28	-22	Worse
Romania	-9	-19	Better
Slovakia	-28	-30	Same
Baltics		-12	
Estonia		-12	
Latvia	-4	-12	Better
Slavic republics		-2	
Russia	+15	-2	Better
Ukraine		-1	

Note: Family-related benefits include monthly and regular family allowances, one-time child allowances (given at birth), maternity allowances and other family-related transfers. Individuals are ranked by their household's disposable per capita income. The regional averages are unweighted.

Source: Bulgaria is calculated from 1989 HBS and 1995 *Gallup* survey; Estonia, Hungary, Latvia, Poland, and Slovakia from countries' HBSs presented in appendix 4; Romania from data given in World Bank (1995a, Table 2.3, p. 8); and Russia from *Russian Longitudinal Monitoring Survey*, Round 4 October 1993–February 1994; Ukraine from World Bank (1996b, Table A9).

sion recipients who are poor before and after receiving the pension. For an important transfer like pension, most recipients would obviously be poor without it. Pensions would then appear to be extremely well-targeted as they would lift a large proportion of their recipients out of poverty. The same could be, however, said about wages, because without wages almost all workers would be poor. It therefore makes sense only to look at the targeting of transfers (1) whose implicit or explicit function is poverty alleviation (for example, only income-tested pensions should be included). If it is not entirely clear that (1) is satisfied—as, for example, in the case of a universal family allowance—then the following condition must hold: (2) the size of transfer must be such that it cannot decisively influence the position of the recipient household. This condition is needed to avoid including transfers such as pensions which will always lift many recipients out of (pre-pension) poverty. Family benefits satisfy condition (2). For almost no family are they likely to be a major source of income so that they determine the family's position in the income distribution curve. Then if it is established that family benefits are paid mostly to the poor, one can infer that they are well targeted.

Table 5.6 compares the targeting of family benefits before the transition and in 1993–95. Targeting is approximated by the concentration coefficient:[57]

---

57. For definition see footnote 9, chapter 2.

the lower its value, the better the targeting (with negative values indicating a negative correlation between the absolute amount of a transfer and the rank of a household according to disposable income).

Family-related benefits have negative concentration coefficients every-where, except for Bulgaria in 1995 and Russia before the transition. These benefits appear not to have become more pro-poor during the transition. This is rather surprising because children and larger families have become poorer (relative to the rest of the population). Benefits that are, by definition, tied to children should show more focus on the poor simply because their recipients have slid down the income distribution ladder. The fact that this has not happened, and that the reverse seems to have happened in Bulgaria and Po-land, is probably due to the changes in the eligibility rules, for example, in-troduction of income testing that has led to some poor families being refused the benefit or to the declines in take-up rates among the poor.

Table 5.7 shows the targeting of a new transfer (the unemployment ben-efit) that did not exist before the transition, and an "old" transfer (social as-sistance) that has gained in importance since the onset of the transition. Un-employment benefits are well targeted—with concentration coefficients, in Eastern Europe and the Baltics, all exceeding -15 in absolute amounts (Rus-sia and Ukraine, where unemployment benefits, even if low, are received by better-off households rather than the poor, represent exceptions.) This is a good, although not a surprising, result because the unemployed are often among the poor, and payment of unemployment benefits is governed by clear rules, so there are relatively few classification errors (for example, a poor

Table 5.7. Concentration Coefficients of Unemployment Benefits and Social Assistance, 1993–95

Country	Unemployment benefits	Social assistance
Eastern Europe	-26	-17
Bulgaria	-36	-3
Hungary	-28	-25
Poland	-18	-13
Romania	-17	+9
Slovakia	-29	-53
Baltics	-31[a]	-5
Estonia	-37	-16
Latvia	-25	+10
Lithuania		-10
Slavic republics	+27	+13
Russia	+33	+25
Ukraine	+21	+2

Note: Data for Slovakia are from 1992. Individuals are ranked by household's per capita disposable income. The regional averages are unweighted.

a. Does not include Lithuania.

Source: As given in table 5.6, *plus* Lithuania as reported in Cornelius and Weder (1996).

unemployed person who is denied a benefit). These results show that unemployment benefits do have an important anti-poverty role to play, and that their progressivity is similar in most transition countries reflecting in turn similarities among countries in the position of the unemployed and the size of the benefit.

How well the system of poverty alleviation performs is best assessed by looking at social assistance. Social assistance (or welfare) is a discretionary benefit the targeting of which reflects both the rules that govern it and the ability of social assistance offices to implement these rules, that is, to income- or means-test potential claimants. Social assistance benefits should be more focused on the poor than any other kind of transfer because they are the only transfer whose function is specifically poverty alleviation. Good targeting may be difficult to achieve, however, because social workers lack the relatively clear rules that govern the payment of categorical benefits, such as family or unemployment allowances. Also, social assistance as defined in statistics and household surveys is often a "mixed bag" that includes not only discretionary cash or in-kind payments, but also many heterogeneous benefits such as expenditures on nursery homes for the aged, mental institutions, benefits paid by enterprises to their poor workers, and enterprise-provided free meals. Both the extent of these "other" social assistance benefits and their statistical coverage vary from country to country, which makes results regarding social assistance transfers particularly difficult to compare. These elements explain, at least in part, why social assistance in virtually all countries seems less well targeted than unemployment benefits. The Slovak Republic, however, stands out for its good performance, while Latvia, Romania, and Russia stand out for their poor performance.

Did transfers become better targeted during the transition as GDPs declined and both poverty and inequality increased? Unfortunately, it does not seem that there was any systematic improvement in targeting since the transition. Pre-transition data are not available for most countries of the former Soviet Union, but in Eastern Europe, all non-pension transfers combined appear to have become only slightly more pro-poor: the overall concentration coefficient moved from an average of -13 before the transition to -18 in 1993-95 (see table 5.8). This improvement is due primarily to the introduction of relatively well-targeted unemployment benefits. Distribution of non-pension benefits in the three Baltic countries is close to a flat per capita amount given across income distribution. In Russia and Ukraine, the incidence of non-pension transfers is, paradoxically, pro-rich: only family benefits are "neutral" (almost equal per capita); other cash transfers are pro-rich.

The absence of significant improvements in targeting shows that social transfers have not contributed much toward mitigating increases in poverty since the onset of the transition. This is in contrast to Chile—a country that also experienced a sharp decline in income—where since the mid-1970s very focused transfers have played an important role in checking the spread of poverty (see Graham 1994, chapter 2). Similarly, better targeting of transfers

Table 5.8. *Concentration Coefficients of Non-pension Cash Social Transfers before the Transition (1988-89) and in 1993-95*

Country	1988–89	1993–95	Change in targeting
Eastern Europe	-13	-18	
Bulgaria	-6	+2	Worse
Hungary	-13	-16	Better
Poland	-17	-22	Better
Romania	-10	-36	Better
Slovakia	-14	-21	Better
Slovenia	-16	-17	Same
Baltics		-2	
Estonia		-6	
Latvia	-7	+3	Worse
Lithuania		-4	
Slavic republics		+16	
Russia	+13	+14	Same
Ukraine		+23	

Note: Non-pension transfers include family-related benefits, unemployment benefits, social assistance, sickness benefits, scholarships, and miscellaneous cash and in-kind transfers.

Source: Bulgaria is calculated from 1989 HBS and 1995 *Gallup* survey; Estonia, Hungary, Latvia, Poland, Slovenia, and Slovakia from countries' HBSs presented in appendix 4; Lithuania from data in *Lithuanian Statistical Yearbook 1994–95*; Romania from data given in World Bank (1995a, Table 2.3, p. 8); Russia from *Russian Longitudinal Monitoring Survey*, Round 4, October 1993–February 1994; Ukraine from World Bank (1996b, Table A9).

played a role in the United Kingdom by offsetting the impact of declining overall cash social transfers and increased inequality. Between 1979 and 1989, the share of social transfers in the income of the British population went down from 17 to 13 percent; meanwhile, the concentration coefficient of transfers improved from -20 to -30 (Milanovic 1994, table 2, p. 181 and figure 5, p. 190).

Table 5.9 contrasts results for transition economies with those for advanced market economies (Targeting is approximated by the percentage of transfer that reaches the bottom quintile of income distribution.) It must be noted that market economies are not a homogeneous category. There is much variance among them in the focus of non-pension transfer payments. Some, such as Australia and Chile, have extremely narrowly targeted social assistance, unemployment benefits. Others, such as the United Kingdom and the United States, have very focused social assistance but not unemployment benefits. Finally, in the Northern European countries (the Netherlands, Norway, and Sweden), all three types of transfers are unfocused. Table 5.9 shows, first, that social assistance is much better targeted in market economies: in six of twelve market economies, the bottom quintile receives at least 40 percent of social assistance. Only one transition economy (out of eight) meets this level. Second, there is virtually no difference between market and transition countries in the targeting of unemployment benefits. Third, all non-pension trans-

Table 5.9. *Percentage of Social Assistance, Unemployment Benefits, and Non-pension Cash Social Transfers Received by the Bottom Quintile of Population*

Country (year)	Social assistance	Unemployment benefits	All non-pension cash social transfers
Transition economies	28 (16)	29 (19)	22 (8)
Slovakia (1992)	52	37	31
Estonia (1995)	36	56	26
Bulgaria (1995)	36	46	19
Hungary (1993)	35	33	29
Poland (1993)	29	26	25
Romania (1992)	23[a]	25	25
Russia (1994)	6	8	12
Ukraine (1995)	6	0	8
Market economies	42 (17)	27 (15)	23 (6)
Australia (1989)	78	50	30
United States (1991)	70	15	19
United Kingdom (1991)	55	29	33
Chile (1990)	51	57	31
Finland (1991)	43	20	26
West Germany (1984)	40	26	14
Belgium (1992)	35	38	23
Ireland (1987)	35	34	28
Netherlands (1987)	31	11	18
Norway (1986)	27	13	21
Switzerland (1982)	25	20	16
Sweden (1987)	21	10	9

n.a = not available.

Note: Shares for transition and market economies are unweighted averages. Standard deviations are shown between brackets. Countries are ranked according to the share of social assistance accruing to the lowest quintile. Individuals are ranked by their household's disposable per capita income.

a. Also includes other unspecified allowances.

Source: Market economies: calculated from individual household data from LIS (Luxembourg Income Study) using unemployment compensation (variable V21), means-tested social transfers (variables V25 and V26), and all government cash transfers except pensions (sum of variables V16 through V26 minus V19). Chile was calculated from Schkolnik and Aguero (1993, p. 245). All non-pension cash social transfers for Chile include income-tested state pensions. Transition economies: sources are as given in table 5.6, except for Romania: HBS 1992.

fers are about equally focused in the two types of economies. In both cases, the poorest quintile receives only slightly more than its population share. Even the within-group variability in targeting seems to be about the same as shown by the very similar standard deviations.

The only area where transition economies clearly seem to lag, in terms of targeting, is therefore social assistance. If, for the sake of simplicity, the poor— that is, those whom policymakers want to reach—are assumed to occupy exactly the bottom quintile, and only the bottom quintile, then little over one-fourth of expended social assistance in transition economies can be said to reach them. The poverty deficit—calculated on the assumption of perfect targeting—would then have to be multiplied by a "gross-up" factor of 3.6 (that is, 100 divided by 28) to get an estimate of the actual amount of money needed to eliminate the poverty deficit (see equation 5.10 above). By contrast, the gross-up factor in market economies is less than 2.4.

Unlike social assistance, targeting of unemployment benefits cannot be much improved. Unemployment benefits are relatively "passive" instruments: they are paid after certain requirements are satisfied—for example, if someone has been dismissed, or is without a job and looking for one, or has contribution record. These requirements do not generally include a low income. In addition, the gap between transition and market economies in progressivity of unemployment benefits is almost non-existent. Of course, unemployment benefits could be income-tested, as they are in Chile,[58] but this does not seem a politically acceptable option in Eastern Europe and in countries of the former Soviet Union.

How much could better targeting of non-pension transfers contribute to reducing poverty? There the illustrative analysis must proceed by several steps. First, non-pension cash and in-kind transfers normally account for only 5 percent of household disposable income in transition economies. From equation 4.2 it is clear that with a concentration coefficient of -18 (equal to the average value for Eastern Europe in 1993-95, as per table 5.8) and a share of 5 percent, non-pension transfers reduce the overall Gini coefficient by slightly less than 1 point (-18 times 0.05 = 0.9). If targeting were improved so that it reached the OECD level of social assistance targeting (that is, a concentration coefficient of -30),[59] the overall Gini would be reduced by 1.5 points. The gain from better targeting would be 0.6 Gini points. Second, how would a Gini reduction of 0.6 translate in terms of poverty reduction? According to table 5.4 (equation D), each one-point decline in the Gini is associated with about a 1 percentage point reduction in poverty. Achieving the OECD level of targeting could therefore be expected to reduce the poverty headcount by approximately 0.6 points. Third, because the estimated poverty headcount in transition economies is about 40 percent (see table 5.2), approximately one in sixty-six poor people (0.6 divided by 40), would cease to be poor thanks to better targeting of social transfers. In terms of actual people, it would mean that about 2.2 million people in transition countries would escape poverty.

---

58. Which explains a very high share received by the bottom quintile.
59. The average concentration coefficient of means-tested social assistance for market economies included in table 5.9 is -31.

6

Selected Issues in Social Policy

Should OECD-like Social Assistance Be Introduced in Transition Economies?

Probably the key issue that faces policymakers designing safety net programs in transition economies is choosing between the following two concepts of social assistance.

The first is the OECD or, more narrowly, the northwest European concept. Its key features are (1) there is an official poverty line;[1] (2) income below the poverty line and assets below a certain minimum are a sufficient condition for welfare eligibility; and (3) social assistance offices try, in principle, to cover the entire gap between the poverty line and income, and that gap is filled with cash. Such a concept can be termed the minimum income guarantee (MIG) system.[2] The overall cost of means-tested benefits in OECD countries is typically between 0.75 and 1.5 percent of GDP and benefits account for about 2 percent of household disposable income.[3] No transition economy has such a system.[4]

The second concept of social assistance is what exists in transition economies—shorn of the enterprise-based welfare where still present. The system differs from MIG in the following respects. First, although income testing is

---

1. Examples include the French *revenu minimum d'insertion*, the minimum pension in Finland and Norway, and the survey-based (that is, calculated from actual expenditures of the bottom decile or quintile of the population) poverty lines in Belgium, the Federal Republic of Germany, and Sweden (see Veit-Wilson 1996, pp. 45–47). Differently, there may be a *de facto*, even if not *de jure*, official poverty line. For example, the British government is, for political reasons, adamant that the Income Support Line is not an official poverty line, even if it functions as such.

2. In reality, not all the gap will be identified (that is, the take-up rate is less than 100 percent) or filled (because of mistakes in assessment). The MIG system can be implemented in different ways: through direct payments that bring recipients up to the poverty line, a universal negative income tax (that is, the same amount is paid to everybody and then is subject to taxation), or a specific negative income tax to the poor (like the earned-income tax credit in the United States).

3. OECD countries included here are the "old" OECD countries: Western Europe, Northern America, and Japan. More recently, Hungary, the Czech Republic, Poland, South Korea, and Mexico have joined OECD, but their welfare systems differ from those of other OECD countries.

4. Social assistance in the former Czechoslovakia and in today's Czech Republic and Slovakia comes closest to it (see Večernik 1991, p. 2 quoted by Sipos 1992, p. 38).

an integral component of the system, having an income less than the poverty line is a necessary but not sufficient condition for receiving social aid. Additional criteria must also be fulfilled. These criteria are related to households' low earning capacity (almost zero elasticity of labor supply): single-parent status, presence in the household of handicapped or elderly members; or "dysfunctionality": alcoholism in the family, drug abuse, mental incapacity. For example, Poland's 1990 law on social assistance lists eleven such additional criteria, at least one of which must be present, in addition to low income, before a household can be eligible for social assistance (Fijalkowski 1992, pp. 63–85); Latvian 1994 law lists four additional criteria (Latvia, 1994, articles 53 and 81). The Czech Republic's 1991 social assistance law also stipulates that beneficiaries must be unable to "increase their income due to their age or health situation" (Večernik 1994, p. 7) the wording which is identical to the one used in the Ukrainian law on social help to the "underprovisioned" families (Ukraine Council of Ministers, 1995, pp. 44–45).

Second, social assistance in transition economies is viewed as a temporary relief and is often provided in-kind—for example, through hot meals or food vouchers, drugs, child care assistance, payment for kindergartens, payment of utilities and rent, provision of wood and coal, and so on.

Third, categorical social assistance in transition economies plays a more important role than under MIG—for example, through state pensions for the aged, family allowances, additional allowances for large families, milk and food for school children, and special assistance for regions with a high concentration of poor. Although most OECD countries have categorical programs in addition to MIG, the scope and financial importance of these programs are smaller, particularly when compared to countries of the former Soviet Union, where practically all social assistance is (still) based on indicator (categorical) targeting.[5]

Fourth, social assistance in transition economies does not aim to cover the entire difference between the poverty line and actual income. The amount covered depends on the judgment of local social assistance workers. Such systems may be called income testing as screening (ITS) systems to indicate that income is tested in order to screen applicants, but that there is no minimum income guarantee. MIG and ITS systems are similar respectively to the "Type A" system, which seeks to eliminate poverty, and the "Type B" system, which only seeks to alleviate it, as defined by Sipos (1994).

ITS systems exist in virtually all countries in Eastern Europe and the former Soviet Union. Officially, the Czech Republic, Estonia, Hungary, Poland, and

---

5. For example, in Lithuania in 1994 there were no less than ten types of family allowance (childbirth grant, child care benefit, adoption and foster parents' allowance, single-mother benefit, preschool child benefit, military-family child benefit, alimony benefit, and so on; see Cornelius 1995). A World Bank study of Ukraine (1996b, p. 49) lists twelve types of family benefits and ten types of social assistance (for example, social pensions, housing subsidies, cash allowances for Chernobyl victims, food subsidies for Chernobyl victims, funeral aid, and transportation subsidies). In Hungary, in 1995, there were 35 kinds of family and social assistance benefits (Sipos, 1995, Annex 1).

Table 6.1. The Composition of the Poor, 1993–95

	Hungary 1993	Bulgaria 1994	Estonia 1995	Poland 1993	Russia 1993–4	Belarus 1995
Total "categorical" poor	77	76	73	62	56	44
Unemployed[a]	60	30	24	30	11	5
Pensioners[a]	3	35	9	6	26	21
People in single- parent families	3	2	32	1	3	3
Children[b]	12	9	8	25	16	15
Other poor	23	24	27	38	44	56

Note: All poor = 100. Poverty line is $PPP120 per capita per month except in Belarus (about $PPP100).

a. All individuals living in poor households whose head is a pensioner or where there are unemployed are included in these two groups, respectively.

b. All children living in poor families where the head is not a pensioner, unemployed, or a single parent.

Source: Hungary: HBS 1993; Bulgaria: HBS 1994; Estonia: HBS July–September 1995; Poland: HBS 1993; Russia: RLMS (*Russian Longitudinal Monitoring Survey*) Round 4 (October 1993 to February 1994); Belarus: New Household Budget Survey 1995.

Slovakia have ITS systems, where low income *plus* family dysfunctionality or zero elasticity of labor supply are the requirements for social assistance. In Russia and Ukraine, a "weaker" form of ITS system is applied. Although social workers are supposed to observe official poverty lines (which in a country as vast as Russia vary by region), much is left to the workers' discretion; moreover, implementation depends on local availability of funds (see Foley and Klugman 1997).[6]

To guide a policymaker choice between these two social assistance concepts (MIG and ITS), four criteria are proposed.

First, it is necessary to ascertain the correlation between poverty and characteristics that are both observable and difficult to hide or alter. The stronger the correlation, the stronger the case for ITS, which relies more heavily on categorical benefits. Thus, in countries where family size and age are good predictors of poverty, categorically based benefits (such as family allowance and minimum pension) can be efficient instruments for combating poverty. As shown in table 6.1, in Bulgaria, Hungary, and Estonia unemployment benefits, the minimum pension, and family allowances may be expected to reach more than three quarters of all poor. In Belarus and Russia, where the working poor are more numerous, categorical benefits are not likely to be as efficient.

The same, of course, applies to the correlation between poverty and other characteristics, such as age and region. For example, in countries such as

---

6. A regionally diverse system does not exist only in large countries such as Russia and Ukraine. Latvia, too, has a regionally based social assistance system, with the result that the poor in different parts of the country are treated differently.

Bolivia and Chile (see Grosh 1994; Graham 1994; World Bank 1995f, chapter 1), where poverty is strongly regionalized and the distances between the poor and rich areas are relatively great, governments subsidize staple foods that are sold only in poor areas. A regional approach may be relevant for large countries with low population densities and a heavy regional concentration of inefficient industries. Russia would be an obvious candidate.

Second, income-testing must be feasible for MIG to be chosen. If the correlation between poverty and easily observable household characteristics is weak, thus favoring adoption of MIG, one needs to check if it is possible to determine incomes with sufficient precision. During the transition, personal incomes have become difficult to monitor. Many people are engaging in unreported economic activities; the "gray economy" is blossoming. The relationship between reported and actual income becomes weak. If many in the private sector operate on the margins of legality, then certifications produced by their employers (for example, vouching that workers' wages are sufficiently low so that they can qualify for various benefits) may be worthless for determining actual incomes.[7] The lower the correlation between reported and actual income, the weaker the case for MIG because both effectiveness (the number of poor reached by programs) and efficiency (the proportion of money disbursed to the poor) will be low. In the section, *Decline in real population income*, in chapter 3, it was noted that income underreporting seems to be particularly great in the Slavic, Central Asian, and Caucasian republics of the former Soviet Union. The case against using MIG will be strong in these countries.

The third criterion relates to financial feasibility. In all transition economies, a new transfer has already emerged: unemployment benefits. Is there room for yet another transfer: MIG-based social assistance? This is an empirical question. If other types of transfers (pensions, family allowances, and so on) are scaled down, then universal welfare may be introduced. But how costly will universal welfare be? The answer to this question hinges on how high the guaranteed minimum income is pitched, how many people are likely to fall below that line and by how much, and what are the expected take-up rates, and the "leakage." As discussed in the section, *How Much Is Needed to Cover the Poverty Deficit?*, in chapter 5 the "true" poverty deficit in transition countries amounts, on average, to 9 to 10 percent of GDP. Clearly these costs cannot be financed. Only in some Central European countries where the pov-

---

7. For example, private firms in some transition economies pretend to employ people who then "work" for six months until they qualify for unemployment benefits and are then promptly "fired." The employer's only cost would be, say, 45 percent payroll tax for six months. If the wage replacement rate is 60 percent and the duration of unemployment benefits is a year, then both the employer and employee can make a profit.

8. Note that this discussion does not address the issue of whether "leakage" is more or less under MIG than it is under ITS. The point is simpler: if "leakage" is assumed to be the same under both systems, then MIG programs will be more expensive because they aim to eliminate the entire poverty deficit, whereas ITS attempts only to alleviate poverty.

erty deficit-to-GDP ratio is relatively low can the guaranteed income be a financially feasible option. It is almost certainly not financially feasible in the Soviet successor states.[8]

The fourth criterion is the ability of local administrations to implement centrally mandated schemes. Even if MIG is feasible on the basis of the three previous criteria, it may be impossible to implement because of administrative weakness. Or it may be impossible to implement in some less developed parts of a country. Then a case could be made for simpler local schemes.

Based on the above discussion, two types of conclusions can be made: conclusions regarding elements that favor the selection of either system and conclusions regarding information needed to make an informed choice.

When is a MIG-like system to be preferred? (1) If the correlation between household characteristics and poverty is weak, (2) if determination of household incomes is reliable, (3) if the poverty gap is not large, and (4) if local administration is reasonably capable. In market economies, for example, the last three criteria are satisfied, and the correlation between household characteristics and poverty is probably the same as in Eastern Europe.[9] In Central Asian countries, on the other hand, none of the last three criteria is likely to be satisfied.

Because the choice between MIG and ITS is an empirical question, the information needed to make an informed choice becomes relatively easy to define. To address the first criterion—the correlation between household characteristics and poverty—household surveys and poverty profiles are needed. Using this information, it is possible to learn whether poverty is strongly related to some household characteristics or not (as has been done for example in the section, *Who Are the Poor?*, in chapter 5).

To address the second criterion—can household incomes be ascertained?—information regarding the functioning of personal income taxation, the estimated size of the unrecorded economy, the relationship between incomes and expenditures (based on household surveys), is needed.

To address the third criterion—is universal welfare financially affordable?—a calculation of poverty deficits for a set of "reasonable" $PPP poverty lines is required.[10]

To address the fourth criterion—is local administrative capability satisfactory?—information is needed from those with first-hand experience in deliv-

---

9. The unemployed and pensioners accounted for 47 percent of all poor in Canada in 1990 (calculated from Statistics Canada 1991, pp. 154–64), a percentage almost the same as in Poland (see table 6.1).

10. It is not necessary to spend too much time calculating sophisticated social minima. These are long and costly exercises, subject to much controversy, and may be irrelevant. If the poverty deficit is too big (more than 2 percent of GDP) for almost any "reasonable" range of poverty lines (say, between $PPP 60 and $PPP 120 per capita per month) then it does not make sense to investigate what the "best" poverty line might be. Complicated poverty line exercises should be postponed until a case can be made that the poverty line lies within the financially feasible range.

ering social assistance. This is an important task. Even if it is established that MIG does not make sense in a given country, there are still at least two reasons to look at the local administration: to learn whether local administrations would be able to administer even simple local schemes and to help the central administration define such local schemes.

Transfer Payments to Different Groups of Recipients

A key problem encountered when designing social transfers is to balance the needs of individuals with disincentive effects (mostly on the supply of labor) that can arise due to "over-generous" social payments.

The disincentive effects of transfers on different types of recipients can be considered using the following example. Let there be three categories of people. *A* are people with a zero elasticity of labor supply (*Ls*) such as invalids, the handicapped, and social pensioners. Group *B* are poor (unemployed) people with a positive *Ls* who are net recipients of government transfers and who, at the margin, have to decide between receiving government transfers and working. Group *C* are working people, net tax payers, whose labor supply is a function of net wage (equal to gross wage *minus* tax to finance social transfers to *A* and *B*). Let there also be the restriction that the disposable (post-transfer and post-tax) income of *A* and *B* must be lower than the disposable income of *C*s.

Labor decisions of *A*s are unaffected by transfers. Their supply of labor is inelastic.[11] The supply of labor by *C*s will be reduced, however (the labor supply curve will shift from Ls_0 to Ls_1, figure 6.1) because they have to pay taxes to finance transfers to *A*s. The output loss is $X(L^*) - X(L)$, where X = output, L^* = the equilibrium labor supply of *A*s in the absence of taxation, and L = equilibrium labor supply with taxes, where, implicitly, the price of output = 1 and output depends on L alone. The deadweight loss represented by the cross-hatched area in figure 6.1 is the cost of the scheme. The gain is the utility gain of *A*s. If the utility gain is greater than the deadweight loss, then the move (that is, the progressive transfer from the richer *C*s to the poorer *A*s) is acceptable.

*C*s have to pay additional taxes to finance transfers to *B*s, however. The analysis for *C*s is the same as before. *B*s' work effort will decrease because they receive transfers and the elasticity of their labor supply is positive (figure 6.2). Their labor supply schedule shifts to the left because *B*s receive some income—unemployment benefits—without working (that is, their consumption of leisure increases with higher income). The amount of output loss will depend on the elasticity of labor demand (*Ld*) for *B*s. If *Ld is* fixed, then *B*'s work effort and, thus, output will stay the same. If *Ld* is perfectly elastic and

---

11. If the elasticity of the labor supply is zero, the welfarist perspective (where utility of leisure is taken into account) and the non-welfarist perspective (where leisure is ignored or does not matter) coincide (see Kanbur, Keen, and Tuomala 1995).

Figure 6.1. *The Effect of Taxes on Supply of Labor of the Working Population*

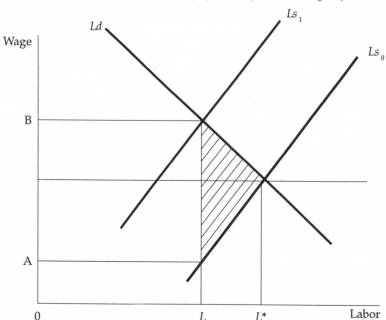

Note: OB = gross wage = OA (net wage) + AB (taxes).

the wage rate for Bs is given, then there will be maximum output loss (see movement from Q to P in figure 6.2).

Consequently, when the demand for Bs' labor is fixed, there is no difference in the analysis of C-financed transfers to As and Bs because in both cases, output produced by the latter two groups is not affected. For all intents and purposes, then, As and Bs can be treated as the same group. If the demand for Bs' labor is elastic, however, transfers will lead to a decrease in Bs' work effort and output. The argument could then be made that to minimize output loss, transfers to Bs should be reduced to below the level paid to As, or should even be eliminated altogether.

In practical terms, much will depend on who the poor (the Bs) are. The greater the labor demand and supply elasticities of Bs, the greater the output loss and the stronger the argument for giving low transfers to Bs. If, for example, labor demand for skilled and unskilled unemployed is the same, and labor supply of the skilled less elastic, then the argument can be made that skilled Bs should receive higher transfers than unskilled Bs, for example, through past earning-related unemployment allowances.

This point illustrates the importance of assessing the elasticities of labor demand and supply when designing social transfers for various types of recipients. A strong case can be made for transfers to As, or to those Bs who have obsolete skills and for whom labor demand is inelastic. The case is not so strong for Bs whose labor supply and demand are elastic.

Figure 6.2. Labor Supply of the Poor (with and without Transfers)

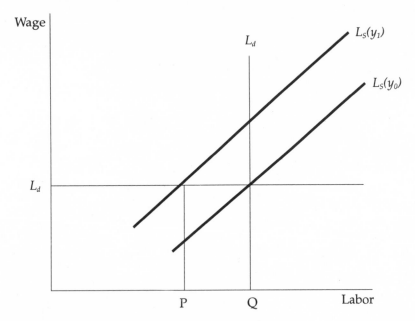

Note: y_0 = income without transfers. y_1 = income with transfers.

Guaranteed Minimum Income and the Supply of Labor

When people are paid the exact difference between their income and the social minimum (i.e., guaranteed minimum income is in place), their disposable income does not change if they work because the additional earnings are "taxed away" through lower social transfers. A typical situation is illustrated in figures 6.3 and 6.4. Up to point A, which is equal to the guaranteed minimum income, all earned income is taxed at the rate of 100 percent; between points A and B (where B is the income level at which social assistance is entirely phased out), the marginal tax rate is less than 100 percent but still in excess of the statutory tax rate. Only if gross income is greater than B does the effective tax rate become equal to the statutory rate. A typical marginal tax schedule then looks as in figure 6.4: lowest incomes are the most heavily taxed. Labor supply of those with lowest income is likely to be reduced, particularly up to point B because the marginal tax rates are high. The reduction in labor supply represents an additional "cost" of guaranteed minimum income.

All things being equal, the cost increases if the guaranteed social minimum and the minimum wage are very close (and if the country is poor, the two cannot be very different). Thus, for example, if a person's maximum

Figure 6.3. *Gross and Net Income if There Is a Minimum Income Guarantee*

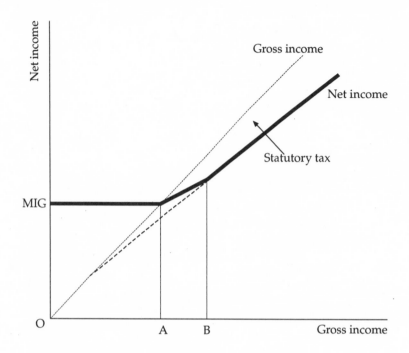

Note: The net income schedule is shown by a bold line.
OA = minimum income guarantee (=MIG). B = social assistance phased out.

attainable earned gross income is barely in excess of MIG, he will be subject to an almost 100 percent marginal taxation throughout. Gains to working are minimal. Browning (1993, pp. 9–10) argues that the costs, i.e., foregone output due to lower labor supply, are substantial and that they increase when income distribution is compressed. In a poor country, the costs in terms of GDP increase for two reasons. First, direct costs increase because more people fall below the poverty line than would in a richer country with the same poverty line. The expenditures needed to close the poverty gap are greater. Second, because the guaranteed social minimum is not much less than the minimum wage, people have weak incentives to work, and foregone output is greater.

The relationship between the poverty line and minimum wage is illustrated for six transition economies (arranged from left to right in ascending order according to their average dollar manufacturing wage) in table 6.2. If the poverty lines that are currently used to *screen* social assistance applicants

Figure 6.4. Marginal Tax Rate in the Presence of a Minimum Income Guarantee

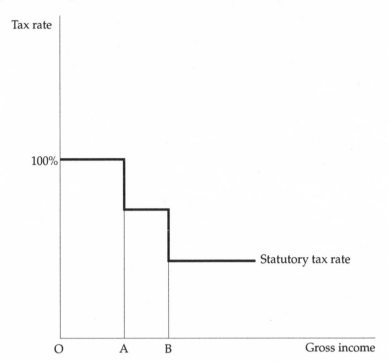

Note: OA = guaranteed minimum income. B = social assistance phased out.

(see line 3) were used as the guaranteed minimum income (gapfill lines), then returns to working at the minimum wage, compared to receiving welfare, would be substantially negative in Russia, only 5 percent in Estonia, 35 percent in Poland, and from 50 to 60 percent in Bulgaria and Hungary. For a "typical" family (of two adults and two children) the returns to both adults working would be even less. Only in Hungary, where wages are relatively high (almost 4.5 times higher in dollar terms than in the former Soviet Union), and thus the wedge between the minimum wage for both adults and the poverty line for the entire family is relatively wide (50 percent), would it be worthwhile to work. In other countries, even if MIG system were financially feasible, disincentive effects would be strong. These results may be compared with results for market economies, where returns to working are between 120 and 190 percent in Portugal, France, and the United Kingdom. The last two have a MIG-type system. The data also show why, using the current federal poverty line, a MIG-type system would be difficult to implement in the United States: the returns to work would be about the same as in Hungary.

Table 6.2. *Relationship between Poverty Lines and Wages, 1992–94*
(in current dollars at current exchange rates, per month)

	Estonia early 1994	Russia April 1994	Bulgaria June 1993	Poland end-1993	Hungary Q2/93	Portugal 1993	France 1992	U.K. mid-1993	U.S. 1993
Poverty line for 1 adult (PL$_1$)	22	45	29	68	72	90	383	285	614
Poverty line for 2-adult, 2-children household (PL$_4$)[a]	59	121	78	184	194	243	825	750	1,230
Minimum wage	23	15[b]	45	92	115	255	1,000	825[c]	930
Universal family allowance (FA) per child[d,e]	9	7	9	9	32	17	175[f]	60	0
Income-to-poverty line ratio									
Minimum wage to PL$_1$	1.1	0.3	1.6	1.3	1.6	2.8	2.6	2.9	1.5
Both adults at the minimum wage plus 2 FAs to PL$_4$	1.1	0.4	1.4	1.1	1.5	2.2	2.8[h]	2.4[g]	1.5[h]
Average manufacturing wage	92	110	122	240	325	560	1,600	1,750	1,950

Note: Poverty line for one adult: Russia: Ministry of Labor subsistence minimum; Bulgaria, Poland, and Portugal: the minimum pension; Estonia: official subsistence benefit; France, *revenu minimum d'insertion*; United Kingdom: income support and housing benefit; United States: the federal poverty threshold (the effective poverty line is less and varies by state).

a. The poverty line for the standard four-member household is calculated using the OECD equivalence scale, where requirements of a four-member household are equal to 2.7 adult units except for the United States, United Kingdom, and France where the actual four-member family poverty lines are used.

b. The official minimum wage in Russia was less than $10 but few were paid that little (0.2–0.3 percent of workers). The official minimum wage is used mostly as a scalar to calculate various social payments. An estimated effective minimum wage is used here instead.

c. There is no official minimum wage in the United Kingdom. An effective minimum wage is used here.

d. Family allowances vary with the number of children and their ages. An approximate average value was chosen in each case.

e. To compare working and not working, only the universal part of the family allowance is relevant because the income-tested part is lost if working.

f. Spending on universal family allowance is about a half of total family allowance expenditures (see d'Agostino and Trombert, 1992, p. 180). Only a half of total in inputed here.

g. Becomes 2.7 if family credit (allowance received by low income working families) is included.

h. Does not include family tax credit received if working (earned-income tax credit in the United States and France).

Source: Transition economies: World Bank data; France from d'Agostino and Trombert (1992); United Kingdom: United Kingdom Central Statistical Office (1994, pp. 71, 184); United States: US Bureau of the Census, CD-Rom, *Income and Poverty* 1993, Table 1; Portugal, personal communication by Luisa Ferreira. Data on average manufacturing wage from *Institut der deutschen Wirtschaft* reported in *German Brief*, June 5, 1993.

Informal Sector and Pension Reform

Transition economies presently function as two-sector economies. On the one hand, there is a shrinking formal sector on which are assessed all pension contributions and other taxes. On the other hand, there is the informal sector, which, by definition, pays no taxes and whose workers do not accrue any social security (including pension) rights.

The situation in transition economies is not unique. In many developing countries there is also a sharp division between the formal and informal sectors. There are, however, two important differences between transition economies and developing countries. First, transition economies face a much greater current liability in the form of pensions that must be paid. In developing countries, few people—mostly public sector employees—have accrued pension rights: current public sector workers, who may account for less than 10 percent of the labor force, are taxed to pay for pensions of past public sector workers, who are similarly few in numbers. In transition economies, on the other hand, a shrinking labor force in the formal sector must pay for pension rights accrued by almost 90 percent of the former labor force. Second, transition economies have a more unfavorable demographic structure with a higher percentage of older people and a correspondingly smaller percentage of people of working age.

The model

In this section, a model is presented that shows the link between growth of the informal sector and the need for pension reform. The economy consists of two sectors: the formal and informal sectors. Both sectors produce the same good, which they price the same (it is the numeraire); both use the same technology; and both have the same demand for labor and face the same labor supply. They are identical in all respects, except that in the formal sector there is a tax on wages that is used to finance current pensions.

In the formal sector, workers are paid M_f which is take-home cash wage plus αT_f where T_f is the payroll tax and α is the parameter that indicates how much of these taxes current workers expect to get back in the future in the form of pensions. In other words, the actual wage is composed of two components: the current cash wage and the expected value of the future pension. For example, if current taxation is perceived simply as yielding an equivalent net present value in the form of (future) pensions, the tax is in effect a deferred wage and α takes the value of 1. More generally, α shows the expected net present value of future pensions to be obtained from paying a dollar in current taxes. If workers perceive current taxation as likely to yield nothing in terms of future income, then $\alpha = 0$ and T_f is a pure tax.[12]

12. Gramlich (1996, pp. 64–65) shows α ratios for U.S. workers of different age cohorts and household sizes. Many "baby boomers" are likely to receive less than what they paid. This is true for all single workers (with $\alpha=0.8$ for those with low earnings to $\alpha=0.4$ for those with steady high earnings) as well as for most married workers (although their α is higher).

In the informal sector, workers are paid only in cash, a money wage $M_{i'}$ which we assume equal to the sum of M_f and T_f in the formal sector.

Suppose now that for workers in the formal sector $\alpha=1$. They are, at the margin, indifferent between current and deferred wage. The labor supply curves in the formal and informal sector will be the same, as would employment and wages. In order to have the pension system in balance, it is necessary simply to solve for such a T_f which is sufficient to pay for all current pensions. The level of equilibrium T_f, whether high or low, would have no effect on the formal sector labor supply because workers view their current taxes simply as equivalent deferred wage.

Now let α be less than 1. This could happen for a variety of reasons. Current workers could believe that demographic trends are so unfavorable that the state would be unable to impose a tax rate on future workers that is high enough to pay for their pensions (this is the situation in the United States). A variant of this is the belief that because of a future disequilibrium in the social security system, the state would renege on its current promises and would, for example, income test future pensions. Workers can also perceive the state to be fundamentally unstable and untrustworthy. This is the case in many transition economies. Political and social changes in the last several years have been dramatic: not only have the states repudiated their implicit and explicit promises, they have also conducted confiscatory policies—for example, wiping out nominal savings and imposing high inflation taxes on the population. The credibility of these states is low. Additional uncertainty has been created by the political turmoil that gave birth to many new states. A given state may not even exist when it is time for a worker to claim his or her pension rights, an unpleasant experience that many pensioners in the former Soviet Union and Yugoslavia have already had to face.

In general, α may be thought of as a function of the expected future tax rate. If workers expect that the future tax rate, needed to finance their future pensions, will be very high, they are more likely to believe that such a tax would be unsustainable and that it would ultimately lead to the government's reneging on its obligations. The relationship between the current α and the future tax rate t^*_f (future variables are denoted by asterisk) is depicted in figure 6.5. There is a threshold tax rate $t^*_{f,min}$ below which $\alpha = 1$. As the expected future tax rate increases, workers expect to lose some of their contributions, and α declines. At some $t^*=t^*_{f,max}$ the whole current contribution is thought of as a pure tax.

In addition, independent factors (for example, lack of confidence in the state) may also shift the relationship so that α declines more sharply. The curve may shift inward (see the southwesterly movement shown by the arrow in figure 6.5).

When α becomes less than 1, a part of t_f is perceived as a pure tax. There is a wedge between gross and net wages. The labor supply curve in the formal sector shifts leftward from A_1A_1 to A_2A_2 (figure 6.6). The equilibrium formal sector employment declines, and the equilibrium gross wage rises (the new equilibrium moves from O to E in figure 6.6). The relative size of the formal sector (compared to the informal sector) shrinks.

Figure 6.5. *Relationship between the Expected Future Tax Rate on the Formal Sector and Current Value of Contributions*

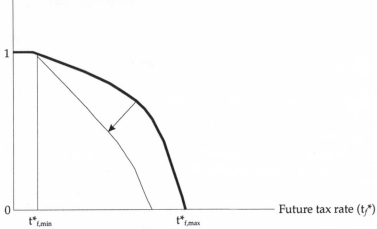

Current value of contributions (α)

Note: Current value of contributions shows the share of current contributions that workers expect to receive through future pensions.

The new formal sector equilibrium will depend on how important the decrease in α is, how elastic labor supply is with respect to both wage and α, and how elastic labor demand is. At any event, it is clear that the equilibrium gross wage in the formal sector, G_f will now be greater than the equilibrium wage in the informal sector, but that the money wage in the formal sector M_f will be less than money wage in the informal sector.[13]

In addition, T_f must be such that current pensions are paid out. This is shown in equation 6.1, where P is the current average pension, N_p is the number of current pensioners, and N_f is the number of current formal sector workers:

6.1 $T_f N_f = P N_p.$

Since N_f and G_f depend on α, and $T_f = t_f G_f$ where t_f is the tax rate on current gross wages in the formal sector, and p = ratio between current pension and gross wage, the following is obtained:

6.2 $t_f G_f(α) N_f(α) = \overline{p} G_f(α) \overline{N}_p.$

Both $\overline{p}$ and $\overline{N}_p$ are fixed in the short run as denoted by the bars in equation 6.2. The first is fixed by law; the second is fixed by demographics and past pension practices and rules.

---

13. Note that the gross (and net) wages in the two sectors were initially the same (when α was 1).

Figure 6.6. *Shift of Formal Sector Labor Supply Curve as a Function of Current Discount of Contributions*

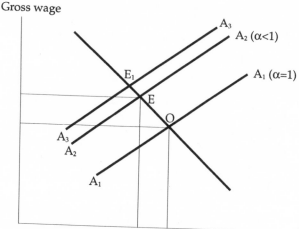

Note: Current discount of contributions is equal to 1-α.

If the ratio between those currently employed in the formal sector and the stock of current pensioners is written as $R = N_f/N_p$, equation 6.2 becomes:

6.3 $\qquad t_f R(\alpha) = \overline{p}.$

Relation 6.3 simply states that if the current pension-to-current wage ratio ($\overline{p}$) is, say, 50 percent and the ratio of current contributors to current pensioners is 2 (a situation common in many transition economies), then the payroll tax needed to pay pensions alone must be 25 percent.

The same identify must hold in the future. If the expected R^* is less than the current R, the future tax rate will have to be higher than the current rate (to maintain $\overline{p}$ at the same level). If this is indeed the case and this future tax rate is $t_f^* > t_f$, then it follows from equation 6.3 that the future equilibrium will depend on the future α. Current workers clearly cannot guess what future workers' expectations will be. So it can be assumed that current workers assume that future workers' α^* will be the same as their current α. To obtain the current equilibrium it is then necessary to solve equations in 6.4 for t_f, t_f^* and α:

6.4 $\qquad \begin{aligned} t_f\, R\,(\alpha) &= \overline{p} & \textit{(present equilibrium)} \\ t_f^*\, R^*(\alpha) &= \overline{p} & \textit{(future equilibrium)} \\ \alpha &= f(t_f^*) & \textit{(determination of } \alpha\textit{)}. \end{aligned}$

Let the solution be t_{f1}, t_{f1}^* ($t_{f1}^* > t_{f1}$ because $R^*<R$) and α_1. The formal sector equilibrium will obtain at point E_1 (see figure 6.6). With still lower employ-

ment and higher wages than before (i.e., than at point E), the share of the formal sector will be further reduced. This illustrates the dynamic nature of the process. A simple exogenous shock, such as decreased confidence in the state, is sufficient to shift the labor supply curve leftward, leading to a reduction in formal sector employment. Suppose that the new tax rate is sufficient to ensure current payment of pensions (so that the current equilibrium condition is satisfied). However, workers begin to notice that the current size of the formal sector compared to the future stock of pensioners has decreased. They realize that to keep the present replacement (pension-to-wage) rules in the future, future taxes need to be even higher. As they realize this and begin to doubt the ability of future governments to impose such high taxes, their discount of future pensions rises, and their labor supply shifts further to the left—upsetting the existing equilibrium. There is thus a vicious circle which leads to the shrinking of the formal sector. Solving the current pension problem is not sufficient for the long-run equilibrium because the way the current problem is solved (by raising taxes) may influence workers' perceptions about the future taxes and thus their current expectation of how much of their present taxes they are likely to recoup.

Heterogeneous workers

Current workers are not all the same: they belong to different age cohorts, and they have different expectations regarding the likelihood that their government will stick to its obligations. Older workers who are closer to retirement age will make the same type of calculation as younger workers, but their expected R^* will be larger simply because the demographic picture is expected to deteriorate less within a few years than over a longer period. Consequently, older workers' expected future tax rate, that is, the tax rate that will finance their pensions, is less and their α is greater than younger workers'. Their formal sector labor supply curve will therefore shift to the left by less than that of younger workers. This is in fact what can be observed in transition economies. The formal sector is "aging." Young people are loath to join the formal sector, among other reasons, because they do not expect that the state will make good its promise to pay future pensions. They prefer, quite rationally, to move to the informal sector where, even if the gross wage is less, the net wage is greater. There is thus an interesting reversal in discounting: discount is high for the young, low for the old. An additional reason why the older workers' discount may be lower is that because of demographics, older workers and pensioners may feel sufficiently numerous to use their political power to ensure payment of pensions.

The problem to which the "aging" of the formal sector leads is twofold:

1. If predominantly older cohorts remain in the formal sector, there may be abrupt declines in formal sector employment as these cohorts retire. The tax rate that then would have to be imposed on remaining formal sector workers would become sharply higher, which in turn

would lead to a withdrawal of their labor supply, and then to an even further increase in the tax rate. The vicious circle would be in full swing.

2. At some point in the future, a large percentage of the population would be without any formal pension rights. However, governments may be politically unable to ignore them, and may be obliged to provide for their old-age support.

The solution

There are several possible solutions to this vicious circle. It is clear that if the trend is to be reversed, the net present value of future payments must be brought closer to the level of current contributions paid. This can be done in two ways.

One possible solution is to introduce private, fully funded pension schemes where current contributions and future payments are automatically linked. In principle, α would increase, but in practice, however, a higher α cannot be taken for granted. Workers must be sure that private pensions are not part of a scam to despoil them of their contributions. Thus rigorous regulation of private pension schemes would be needed to inspire confidence in their future solvency.

If a private pension plan is voluntary, the equilibrium between contributions and future payments is established, by definition. No worker who believes that the net present value of future payments is less than his or her contribution would join. It is doubtful, however, that entirely voluntary private pension plans would be large enough to allow for risk-sharing. This is why avoiding adverse selection requires that contributions be mandatory.

The second possible solution is a sharp reduction in current pensions. The effect of such a reduction would be to reduce the current tax rates paid in the formal sector, to reduce future expected pensions (by less than current taxes), and thus to reduce the wedge between current contributions and expected future returns (pensions). Workers could again begin to expect that the state would honor its obligations because the current and future tax burden (needed to finance pensions) would appear sustainable.

7

A Look Ahead

Under the twin impact of declining incomes and rising inequality, poverty in transition economies has risen dramatically. The increase was driven first by abrupt declines in income and then, as the income decline stabilized and, in most countries, turned to positive growth, by widening income disparities. Of the eighteen countries studied here, only one (the Slovak Republic) shows unchanged inequality, as measured by the Gini coefficient. In terms of inequality, Central European countries are still slightly below average OECD levels, while the Baltic republics, Central Asian republics, and Russia are overtaking high-inequality OECD countries such as Switzerland and the United States and are approaching levels of the more unequal developing countries. These findings are not surprising. Based on a sample of approximately 100 countries and covering almost the entire post–World War II era, Deininger and Squire (1995, p. 25) find that in 70 percent of cases, when the GDP declines, the poor lose relatively more in terms of income—that is, inequality increases.

What will the future bring? Will, for example, the Central Asian republics and Russia exhibit the inequality and poverty characteristics of today's developing countries? Will the turn-around in growth that has already taken place in Eastern Europe and is expected in 1998 in Central Asian countries, Russia, and Ukraine eventually pull most of the current poor out of poverty? Or will those who have become poor during the transition remain poor?

These are difficult questions—almost impossible to answer with any degree of confidence. For the sake of simplicity, they are divided into two questions: (1) assuming that growth picks up, will today's poor be pulled quickly out of poverty, and (2) will income inequality stabilize? With regard to the first question, it is clear that the current poor, according to many household indicators, such as education levels, housing conditions, and ownership of essential consumer durables, are not much worse off than the rest of the population. Furthermore, the average income or expenditure shortfall of the poor (20–30 percent of the poverty line) is relatively small, which explains the high flows in and out of poverty observed in transition economies (for Russia, see Commander, Tolstopiatenko and Yemtsov, 1997). Both facts are grounds for optimism. The economy could, after pushing some people below the poverty line during its decline, bring them back up during a phase of growth. In addition, given the existing poverty shortfall, several years of broadly shared moderate growth (4 to 5 percent per year) *should* be sufficient to help the poor cross the poverty threshold. The experience of Poland, however—the

Figure 7.1. *The Year When the Countries are Expected to Reach Poverty Headcount of 10 Percent*

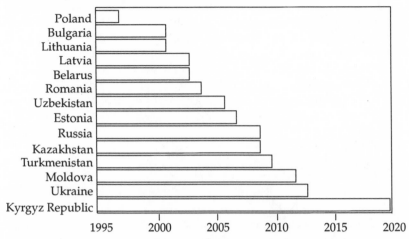

Note: The Czech Republic, Hungary, Slovakia, and Slovenia are not included because their headcounts are less than 10 percent. All other headcounts are calculated on the assumption of unchanged Gini and a constant annual growth rate of 5 percent per capita.

only transition economy that has witnessed five years of consecutive growth—or of Estonia—one of three countries of the former Soviet Union to have grown for two years in a row—is not very encouraging. Economic growth in these countries does not seem to have helped the poor much. The poverty headcount in both countries has stabilized or slightly decreased since 1993–94, but average shortfalls of the poor appear to be increasing as inequality continues to rise. In Latin America, similarly, resumption of growth in the 1990s after a period of GDP decline in the 1980s reduced inequality in only one country—Colombia (see Schwartz and Ter-Minassian 1995, p. 5). Predictions about the ability of growth to pull people out of poverty must therefore be made cautiously. Furthermore, the danger is that if economic growth fails to help the poor quickly, they can become an underclass whose characteristics may gradually diverge more and more from those of the non-poor.

Thus, if growth is to make a substantial dent in poverty relatively quickly, it will be necessary to stabilize income inequality at current—often high—levels. Assuming that inequality remains at current levels, and using the average growth rate of 5 percent per capita per year,[1] the time when current

---

1. Because "current" levels in this context refers to survey results for 1993–95, allowance is made in the calculations presented here for actual growth rates between the time of the survey and 1996. The calculations also assume that the average income shortfall is as it was in 1993–95, and that the income shortfall of the poor is uniformly distributed (that is, the shortfall ranges from 0 percent to twice the average shortfall). For example, if the average poverty shortfall is 25 percent and the poverty headcount is 20 percent, then each 5 percent of annual growth will "vault" 2 percent of the people over the poverty line.

headcounts should drop to 10 percent of the population—probably an acceptable share of the poor, both from political economy and fiscal aspects—can be easily calculated. Leaving aside the countries where poverty rates are already less than 10 percent, only Poland, among the other countries, can expect to reduce poverty to 10 percent before the year 2000 (see figure 7.1). Lithuania, Bulgaria, Latvia, Belarus, and Romania could reach this level between the years 2000 and 2005. All other countries will not reduce poverty headcount to 10 percent of the population until well into the next century—even under the very favorable circumstances assumed here. Poverty appears to be here to stay in transition economies.

Appendix 1

Description of the Surveys Used and Data Problems

The Surveys Used

Because there are considerable differences in the quality and type of data used for East European countries and countries of the former Soviet Union, the sources for these two groups will be discussed separately. Conclusions regarding biases, however, will be made with respect to both groups, although there too, as will become clear, certain differences exist.

Sources for the transition years: Eastern Europe

Type of surveys. For all countries in Table A1.1, except the Czech Republic, data come from official surveys conducted by the countries' statistical offices (CSOs). The Czech source is the "socioeconomic" survey of *Economic Expectations and Attitudes (EEA)* conducted twice per year on a representative (although small) sample.[1] The *EEA* survey was selected in this instance because official survey data, based on large, representative samples, were not available for the transition period studied here (1993–96). Such surveys (called microcensuses) are conducted in the Czech and Slovak Republics every five years; the most recent microcensus was conducted in Czechoslovakia in 1992, and the next was planned for the two republics in 1997.

Representativeness. For all countries, except Slovakia, the surveys are nationally representative. Family budget surveys (FBSs) for 1993 were used for the Slovakia. FBSs include five social groups (blue-collar workers, white-collar workers, the self-employed, farmers, and pensioners) but they do not include pensioner-headed households with economically active members and households headed by the unemployed.[2]

---

1. For example, Hungary's CSO survey covers more than 8,000 households; the *EEA* survey, for a country of about the same population size, includes fewer than 2,000 households.
2. The same FBS survey exists for the Czech Republic, but income-distribution statistics are published only for workers (blue-and white-collar), farmers, and pensioners, and not for the self-employed who represent about 13 percent of the sample (see Czech Statistical Office 1994). It is unclear why full data from this survey were not published.

Table A1.1. Characteristics of the Transition-year Surveys Used for East European Countries

Country	Source of data; survey conducted by:	Data reported in:	Period covered	Representative survey	Access to individual data	Income concept	Income includes consumption-in-kind	Expenditures exclude personal (direct and wage) taxes	Other problems with income or expenditure definitions
Poland	CSO, 1993; HBS.	Individual data available; some results in Polish Central Statistical Office (1994).	First half of 1993	Yes	Yes	Disposable	Yes	Yes	No
Hungary	CSO, 1993; HBS.	Individual data available.	1993	Yes	Yes	Disposable	No	Yes	No
Czech Republic	Czech Academy of Sciences, EEA survey.	Personal communication by Jiří Večerník, Academy of Sciences; some results in Institute of Sociology, *Economic Expectations and Attitudes, I-VII,* Prague.	January 1993	Yes	No	Disposable	Yes	n.a.	No information on expenditures.
Slovakia	CSO, 1993; FBS.	Individual data available. Grouped data reported in Slovak Statistics (1994).	1993	No[a]	Yes	Disposable	Yes	Yes	No distribution of expenditures.[c]

136

Country	Source of data; survey conducted by:	Data reported in:	Period covered	Representative survey	Access to individual data	Income concept	Income includes consumption-in-kind	Expenditures exclude personal (direct and wage) taxes	Other problems with income or expenditure definitions
Slovenia	CSO, 1993; HBS.	Personal communication by Irena Krizman of the Statistical office of Slovenia. Some results published in Slovenian Statistics (1994).	1993	Yes	No	Disposable	Yes	Yes	Income definition incorrect.[b] No distribution of expenditures.[c]
Romania	CSO, Integrated household survey.	Individual data available. Survey discussed in World Bank (1997), vol. 2.	March 1994	Yes	Yes	Gross	Yes	n.a.	
Bulgaria	CSO, 1993; HBS.	Biudzeti na domakinstvata v Republika B'lgariya, National Statistical Institute, Sofia 1994, p. 68.	1993	Yes	No	Gross	Yes	No (taxes included in other expenditures)	Income definition incorrect.[b] No distribution of expenditures.[c]

Note: CSO=country's statistical office. HBS=Household budget survey. FBS=Family budget survey. EEA=*Survey of economic expectations and attitudes*. n.a.=not available.

a. Excludes pensioner-headed households with economically active members and households headed by the unemployed.

b. Disposable income calculated by deducting some revenue items from the income concept used by the CSO (and according to which the individuals and households are ranked).

c. There is only distribution of expenditures by income groups or deciles formed according to income.

Time period. For four countries (Hungary, Slovakia, Slovenia, and Bulgaria), surveys include income or expenditures for all of 1993. For Poland, the survey covers only the first six months of 1993, and for the Czech Republic and Romania the survey covers only one month (January 1993, and March 1994 respectively). The Czech and Romanian data are the least satisfactory as there is reason to believe that a shorter survey time period will lead to overestimation of both inequality and poverty. This is because incomes (and, to a lesser extent, expenditures) do not follow a uniform pattern. Individuals may be sick or unemployed or out of the labor force for a month, and their family's income may be temporarily low, so that the household is classified as poor. In reality, over the period of a year, the household may be relatively well off. The same is true for households with sudden income gains (for example, payment of overdue wages) with the result that both ends of income distribution and the overall inequality are overestimated.

Type of data. Individual income data were available for four countries (Poland, Hungary, Slovakia, and Romania). For the other three (Bulgaria, the Czech Republic, and Slovenia), decile or group data formed according to CSOs' definitions of per capita income were available. However, the definition of income is not satisfactory for Bulgaria or Slovenia, as it includes some revenue items (for example, withdrawal from saving accounts, and money received from sale of assets). These items had to be deducted from CSO-defined income in order to obtain a correct disposable income. When this operation is performed on grouped data (as opposed to individual data) income inequality is underestimated because, strictly speaking, it is not the Gini coefficient of disposable income that is being measured but rather the concentration coefficient of disposable income. The problem is negligible in the case of Bulgaria because the "wrong" items account for less than 1 percent of CSO-defined income, and the rankings of individuals according to one or another definition of income cannot change much. In Slovenia, however, they account for about 8 percent of CSO-defined income.

Income concept. For all countries except Bulgaria, the income concept used here is disposable income. Disposable income equals gross income minus payroll and direct personal income taxes (PIT). For Bulgaria, gross income is used. The difference between gross and disposable income, however, is small because in Bulgaria, gross income already excludes payroll taxes withdrawn at the source, and payroll taxes represent by far the largest share of personal taxes. In all cases except Hungary, consumption-in-kind is included in income.

Data on expenditures. For the Czech Republic, no data on expenditures were available. For Bulgaria, the Slovak Republic, and Slovenia, expenditure data exist, but only for households ranked by their per capita income. Because

---

3. The concentration coefficient of expenditures can be calculated when recipients are ranked by income. But this statistic is likely to be significantly lower than the Gini coefficient of expenditures because of reranking of recipients.

individual data were not available for these countries, individuals could not be reranked by expenditure, so neither expenditure distribution nor Gini coefficients of expenditures could be obtained.[3] Both income and expenditure individual data were available for Poland, Hungary, and Romania.

Definition of income and expenditures. The components of disposable income and expenditures used here are standard. Disposable income is equal to all wage earnings (from primary and secondary jobs, and so on) *plus* cash social transfers *plus* income from property and entrepreneurship *plus* received gifts *plus* the value of consumption-in-kind. It excludes payroll and PIT taxes. Expenditures include expenditures on food, housing, education and culture, health, transportation and communication, clothing, private transfers given, and the value of consumption-in-kind. To make expenditures consistent with disposable income, personal taxes (both those withdrawn at the source and direct PIT) are excluded. The same definitions apply to all countries except Bulgaria where, as mentioned above, PIT could not be separated from other expenditures for either income and expenditure calculations.

Sources for the transition years: countries of the former Soviet Union

The sources for these countries are much more diverse (see table A1.2). Because the quality of pre-transition Soviet official Family Budget Surveys (FBS) was not satisfactory, there was a pressing need to revise the surveys and, often, to undertake entirely new ones.

Basically, countries adopted three approaches to the revision of Soviet surveys. In the Baltic countries and Belarus, new, representative surveys were introduced between 1994 and 1995 to replace the old Soviet-style surveys; it is the results of these new surveys that are used here.[4]

In the Kyrgyz Republic, Russia, and Ukraine, new survey instruments were introduced through the cooperation of international agencies (the World Bank, in particular) and CSOs. Alongside these new and improved surveys, however, the old FBSs continued to exist. The design of the FBSs was somewhat improved (as in Russia), but they were increasingly plagued by high refusal rates and remained unrepresentative. Eventually, it is hoped, the current FBS will be replaced by a better official survey—a process that has begun in Russia. This gives in total seven countries with new surveys.

For Moldova and the Central Asia countries (except Kyrgyz Republic), the old FBSs are being used here, either because the countries had not yet introduced new surveys (by the time of this writing) or because the existing *ad hoc* surveys are not fully representative. Some of these countries, however, are in

---

4. For a detailed description of the new surveys for Belarus, see Martini, Ivanova, and Novosyolova (1996); for Latvia, see Lapins and Vaskis (1996); for Estonia, see Statistical Office of Estonia (1995), pp. 30–36; and for Lithuania, see Zaborskas (1996) and Kazlauskas and Jensen (1993).

Table A1.2. Characteristics of the Transition-year Surveys Used for Countries of the Former Soviet Union

Country	Source of data; survey conducted by:	Data reported in:	Period covered	Representative survey	Access to individual data	Income concept	Income includes consumption-in-kind	Expenditures exclude personal (direct and wage) taxes	Other problems with income or expenditure definitions
Estonia	CSO, 1995; HBS.	Individual data available.	Third quarter of 1995	Yes	Yes	Disposable	Yes	Yes	No
Latvia	CSO, 1995; HBS.	Data provided by the Latvian Committee on Statistics.	Fourth quarter of 1995	Yes	No	Disposable	Yes	n.a.	No information on expenditures.
Lithuania	CSO, 1994; HBS.	Lithuanian HBS reported in *Statistical Yearbook of Lithuania 1994-95*, Vilnius: Lithuanian Dept. of Statistics, p. 188 and Cornelius (1995, table 3).	1994	Yes	No	Gross	No	n.a.	No information on expenditures.
Russia	*Russian Longitudinal Monitoring Survey* Round 3.	Individual data available.	Third quarter 1993	Yes	Yes	Disposable	Yes	Yes	No
Ukraine	*Ukraina 1995 survey*.	Individual data available; some results reported in World Bank (1996b, table A9).	June and first week of July 1995	Yes	Yes	Gross	Yes	No[a]	Large underestimation of incomes.

Country	Source of data; survey conducted by:	Data reported in:	Period covered	Representative survey	Access to individual data	Income concept	Income includes consumption-in-kind	Expenditures exclude personal (direct and wage) taxes	Other problems with income or expenditure definitions
Belarus	CSO, 1995; HBS.	New Household budget survey (data provided by Anna Ivanova).	First quarter 1995	Yes	No	Disposable	Yes	Yes	No
Kyrgyz Republic	Kyrgyzstan Multipurpose Poverty Survey.	Individual data available.	October-November 1993	Yes	Yes	Disposable	Yes	Yes	Large under-estimation of incomes.
Moldova Turkmen. Kazakh. Uzbek.	CSO, 1993; FBS.	Statistical Bulletin CIS, August 1994.	1993	No	No	Gross	Yes	n.a.	No information on expenditures. Income definition incorrect.[b]

Note: CSO=country's statistical office. HBS=Household budget survey. FBS=Family budget survey.
a. Personal income taxes minimal (less than 1 percent of expenditures).
b. Income includes some revenue items (for example, insurance compensations; sale of assets) that could not be deducted.

the process of either overhauling its old official survey, as is the case in Moldova, or conducting a new parallel survey, as is the case in Kazakhstan.

The diversity of the surveys in the former republics of the Soviet Union, mentioned above, is illustrated in table A1.2. All but two of the new surveys are quarterly surveys: the Lithuanian survey is an annual survey, and Ukraine's is virtually a monthly survey. As was the case with the Czech survey, discussed above, the Ukrainian survey is likely to produce an overestimation of inequality and poverty. The Ukrainian and Kyrgyz surveys also yield a major difference between income and expenditure amounts. In other surveys where both expenditure and income data are available, overall expenditures range from being equal to overall income to being approximately 20 percent higher. In Ukraine and the Kyrgyz Republic, however, expenditures are *twice* as great as income. Income underreporting is clearly a large problem with both surveys.

All seven new surveys listed here are representative. For four (Estonia, Russia, Ukraine, and Kyrgyz Republic) individual income and expenditure data were available. For the other three (Latvia, Lithuania, and Belarus), decile data were available.

The income concept used is either disposable or gross income. In Lithuania and Ukraine, where gross income is used, PIT is minimal, so the difference between the two income concepts is negligible.

All surveys except that of Lithuania include consumption-in-kind. Because the importance of consumption-in-kind has increased in transition economies (see chapter 3), and particularly in the countries of the former Soviet Union, Lithuanian survey is likely to underestimate disposable income, thus yielding an overestimation of poverty. In addition, as consumption-in-kind plays an income-equalizing role, calculated inequality in Lithuania will be higher than actual inequality.

Expenditure data were available for five countries: Russia, Ukraine, Belarus, the Kyrgyz Republic, and Estonia.

Comparing pre-transition and transition years

Table A1.3 lists the characteristics of surveys used for the pre-transition period.

The type of survey used for Bulgaria, Hungary, Poland, and Slovenia is the same for pre-transition and transition years. With the exception of Poland's survey, whose representativeness has improved,[5] there was no substantive change in these surveys. For the Central Asian countries and Moldova, pre-transition and transition surveys are also the same: the Soviet-style FBS. Given

---

5. Households whose principal earner was employed in the private sector outside agriculture were not included in pre-transition Polish surveys; army and police personnel were also excluded.

significant shortcomings with FBSs, however, this is more of a problem than an advantage (see the following section). For all other countries, the survey instruments before the transition and the transition differ.

The systemic change—transition from a planned to a market economy—affected the survey's results in three different ways. First, refusal rates have increased, particularly among the rich. Second, coverage of wage and social transfer income has deteriorated from nearly 100 percent before the transition, as reported household earnings are no longer double-checked against enterprise or pension authority records. Third, the omission or inadequate coverage of informal (and illegal) sector income has become an even greater problem as such incomes have increased in both absolute and relative terms. Users of the surveys cannot correct these problems; they must be corrected by the agencies that conduct the surveys. The bottom-line effect of these systemic changes—assuming an unchanged survey design—is that incomes are more underestimated than they were in the past (and that *increases* in poverty will therefore be biased upwards); the effect of these changes on inequality estimates is less clear. In the past, surveys underestimated inequality by not taking into account the many fringe benefits received by the elite and, in the Soviet case, by systematically excluding the poor.[6] Today, they might underestimate inequality by not covering those with high incomes who refuse to participate.

It is up to individual researchers to determine how strong an emphasis they wish to place on such systemic changes—that is, to decide on whether they believe that these changes vitiate comparisons between pre-transition and transition surveys. Here it is assumed that systemic changes in Eastern Europe were not great enough to render comparisons of poverty and inequality before and after the transition unreliable. An argument could be made, however, that comparisons are much less reliable in some republics of the former Soviet Union. Not only was the systemic change there much more profound than it was in Eastern Europe (witness the explosion of the informal sector and rising refusal rates), but pre-transition surveys were fundamentally flawed in that they were basically surveys of employed families to which a quota of pensioners was added.

Comparisons between 1987–89 and 1993 survey results for Bulgaria, Hungary, Poland, and Slovenia are both straightforward and warranted: the survey instruments are the same, and the systemic changes that affected survey results are minimal. The situation is somewhat different in the Czech and Slovak Republics. For these countries, pre-transition data are derived from the 1988 microcensus, whose quality is fairly high. The quality of data for Czechoslovakia in 1988 is better than the quality of 1993 data for the Czech and Slovak Republics for reasons of population coverage (in Slovakia) and shortness of survey time period (in the Czech Republic).

---

6. Subsidies were also not included; yet the effect of subsidies (with the possible exception of housing subsidies) was to reduce inequality.

Table A1.3. Characteristics of Pre-transition Surveys Used for East European Countries and the Soviet Union

Country	Source of data; survey conducted by:	Data reported in:	Period covered	Representative survey	Access to individual data	Income concept	Income includes consumption-in-kind	Other problems with income definitions
Poland	CSO, 1987; HBS.	Budżety gospodarstw domowych w 1987. roku, Central Statistical Office, Warsaw, 1988.	1987	No[a]	No	Gross[c]	Yes	No
Hungary	CSO, 1987; HBS.	Családi Költségvetés 1987, Central Statistical Office, Budapest, 1989, pp.78-9, 102-3, 126-27.	1987	Yes	No	Disposable	Yes	No
Czech Republic, Slovakia	CSO, 1988; Microcensus.	Microcensus, Czechoslovak Statistical Office, Prague; based on the decile calculations reported in Večerník (1994).	1988	Yes	No	Disposable	Yes	Recipients ranked by money income (i.e. exclusive of consumption-in-kind).
Slovenia	Yugoslav SO; 1987 HBS.	Anketa o potrošnji domaćinstava u 1987, Federal Statistical Office, Belgrade, 1988 (all data presented by republics).	1987	Yes	No	Disposable	Yes	Income definition incorrect.[b]
Bulgaria	CSO, 1989; HBS.	Biudzeti na domakinstvata v Republika B'lgariya, National Statistical Institute, Sofia.	1989	Yes	No	Gross[c]	Yes	Income definition incorrect.[b]

Country	Source of data; survey conducted by:	Data reported in:	Period covered	Repre-sentative survey	Access to individual data	Income concept	Income includes consumption-in-kind	Other problems with income definitions
Romania	CSO, 1989; FBS.	Provided by the Statistical office.	1989	No[e]	No	Gross[c]	Yes	No
Soviet Union[d]	CSO, 1988 FBS.	Narodnoe khozyaystvo SSSR 1988, Moscow:Goskomstat SSSR, p. 94.	1988	No[f]	No	Gross[c]	Yes	Income definition incorrect.[b]

Note: CSO=country's statistical office. HBS=Household budget survey. FBS=Family budget survey.
a. Non-agricultural private sector, army and police not included.
b. Disposable or gross income calculated by deducting some revenue items from the CSO income concept and according to which the individuals and households are ranked.
c. Taxes are less than 1 percent of gross income.
d. The only exception is Uzbekistan where the same (FBS) source is used for 1989.
e. Overrepresentation of wage-earners; underrepresentation of pensioners. Households headed by the unemployed are excluded (see Rashid, 1994, pp. 8-9).
f. Based on the "branch of production" sampling. Overrepresentation of workers, and "average" earners and "typical" families; underrepresentation of pensioners. See the discussion in the text below.

What Biases Are Inherent in the Data?

Having reviewed the data sources and their differences, data problems and deficiencies, the next obvious question is: what can be said *a priori* about the bias inherent in each of the surveys?

The fact that these biases are listed here is an indication that not much can be done to remedy them. Yet they are worth mentioning here for two reasons: to encourage caution in interpreting the results, and to delineate areas that most clearly need to be improved in the future.

Survey design

First there is a problem with sampling. The household surveys used here have been justly criticized for containing several biases. The East European surveys were sample surveys. In several countries, however (for example, Poland), they were not designed to be representative of the entire population but rather to be representative of individual socioeconomic groups. This probably reflected a Marxist view of society as composed of social classes and an overriding concern with intergroup equity. The data were thus representative of households where the primary earner worked in the state sector or of pensioners' households, but they could not be combined easily to obtain an accurate picture of the whole population. This was the case for two reasons. First, the sample shares of the groups that were included were not always proportional to their shares in the population (for example, there were too many workers represented and not enough pensioners), and the results were not corrected for systematic differences in refusal rates. Second, some groups were left out of surveys altogether. These groups included both those with high incomes (self-employed entrepreneurs, and army and police personnel) and those with low incomes (the institutionalized population and the unemployed). Income distribution was thus truncated at both ends of the income spectrum.

Soviet data were even more problematic. Surveys were based on quota sampling rather than on random sampling. Households were selected through the so-called branch (of production) approach. Workers and farmers were chosen by their managers and asked to cooperate with statistical authorities. The results, then, were biased: the employed were systematically overrepresented in relation to the non-employed, though to correct some of the bias a quota of pensioners and students was added;[7] workers in large enterprises

---

7. Pensioners' households were simply "added on"—that is, statistical offices were asked to add a quota of pensioners which was often below their true share in the population.

8. If results are to be unbiased, then the probability of selecting a larger household should be proportionately greater than the probability of selecting a smaller household. If the selection criterion is employment, however, and participation rates are high, then households (e.g., one with two adults and three children, and another with two adults only) will have approximately the same probability of being selected, regardless of their size.

and with longer work records were selected more often than those working in small firms and with shorter work records. Because the selection criterion was employment, larger households were undersampled.[8] The survey essentially functioned as a panel—the same households stayed in the sample year after year—but to further complicate matters, the survey was not explicitly designed to be a panel, and household identification numbers were not systematically maintained. The panel nature of the survey further biased the results: because households remained in the sample indefinitely, the share of older working households, which presumably had higher-than-average earnings, was too high.

In conclusion, there were two kinds of biases in many pre-transition surveys. First, there was a bias toward sampling representative of various socioeconomic groups but not of the population as a whole. People who did not "fit" into one of these social groups were likely to be left out, and often these people were at greater risk of poverty than the average citizen. Second, there was a bias in Soviet and Romanian household surveys that followed the so-called branch principle toward the "average" or "typical" household.[9]

Of concern here is the bias against including the poor in surveys (or, more broadly, misrepresenting the distribution curve so that its left-end tail is shown as being "thinner" or "shorter" than it is in reality). Some bias against the coverage of the poor happens in virtually all household surveys. The very poor are difficult to survey: institutionalized population, homeless people, poor ethnic minorities, and illegal foreigners are almost always left out. For example, it has been argued that Hungarian surveys leave out almost all of the poor Gypsy population.[10] The same is the case with other East European countries, such as the Czech Republic, Romania, and the Slovak Republic, where Gypsies represent a sizable minority.

Table A1.4 assesses the reliability of HBS estimation of poverty, both before and during the transition. An ordinal value of -3 means that the survey, in the judgment of the author, strongly underestimates poverty; a value of -0.5 indicates the "usual" bias caused by inadequate coverage of minorities or institutionalized populations; a value of 0 indicates an unbiased HBS, at least from the perspective of poverty estimation.[11] A positive value indicates a likely overestimation of poverty. In all countries of the former Soviet Union, the bias against including the poor is estimated to have been strong before the transition (a value of -3). This seems to have changed in about half of the countries (Baltic and Slavic republics) where underestimation of poverty is now smaller. East European data were already more reliable than the Soviet data before the transition, and since the transition, data from some countries (Poland and Romania) have improved.

---

9. In addition, Romanian results prior to 1989 were doctored to such an extent that they are worthless. Bulgaria also followed "the branch principle" in the 1970s, but abandoned it later.

10. This point was made by Zsuzsa Ferge in a personal communication to the author.

11. The survey could still be biased toward, say, underreporting of top incomes.

Table A1.4. *Estimated Bias against Including Poor People in Household Budget Surveys*

Country	1987-88	1993-94
Eastern Europe	-1	-1
Poland	-1	-0.5
Bulgaria	-2	-2
Romania	-3	-2
Hungary	-0.5	-0.5
Czech	-0.5	-2
Slovak	-0.5	-0.5
Slovenia	-0.5	-0.5
Baltics	-3	-1
Lithuania	-3	-1
Latvia	-3	-1
Estonia	-3	-1
Slavic	-3	-2
Russia	-3	-1
Ukraine	-3	-2
Belarus	-3	-1
Moldova	-3	-3
Central Asia	-3	-3
Kazakhstan	-3	-3
Kyrgyzstan	-3	-3
Turkmenistan	-3	-3
Uzbekistan	-3	-3

Note: The surveys assessed here are the same ones listed in Tables A1.1, A1.2 and A1.3.
-3: very strong bias against including the poor. -0.5: bias similar to that in developed market economies.
Source: Author's estimates.

One implication of table A1.4 is that the bias against including the poor has decreased most significantly in Baltic countries, where surveys have all improved significantly during the transition. Bias has also decreased in Belarus, Russia, and Ukraine. This means that poverty increases between the pre-transition period and 1993–94 are particularly likely to be overestimations for these countries. Bias in Eastern Europe and Central Asia has not changed much. In Easter Europe, surveys were already quite good before the transition, and improvements in Romania and Poland are matched by an apparent deterioration in the Czech Republic. In Central Asia, either new surveys were not undertaken or, if they were (as in the Kyrgyz Republic), their quality was not significantly better than that of the old surveys.

Underreporting of income

The second problem has to do with income. The use of income data rather than expenditure data tends yield underestimations of "true" welfare because people tend to underreport their sources of income.[12] People are less careful, however, when asked to remember their expenditures. An example of this tendency is shown in figure A1.1, which gives income and expenditure data by ventiles (5 percent of recipients) for Poland in 1993. Individuals are ranked on the horizontal axis according to their household per capita income. The lowest ventile reports expenditures equal to twice reported income and equivalent to expenditures reported by the third ventile. This suggests that those in the lowest income ventile may not in fact be very different from those who report significantly higher incomes. Either they have severely underreported their income or permanent income substantially diverges from current income. Whatever the case, in the statistics used here these people would be considered poor.

Poverty rates are thus biased upwards. In general, countries with larger informal sectors ("gray economy") and small-scale private sectors will be more affected. Data in such countries will systematically show lower incomes and higher poverty rates than data from countries in which most income is earned either in the state sector or in the wage-reporting (and thus tax-paying) private sector, or is received in the form of social transfers. Comparisons over time will also be affected. As the share of the informal sector increases during the transition, the problem of income underreporting becomes more serious. On the other hand, surveys have been improved and greater effort is being made to include "gray" sources of income. For example, all countries except those that still use the Soviet-type surveys, now include the self-employed in their HBSs. Hungarian statistical authorities have been imputing tips, "fees" (a polite term for bribes), and "gray" income. Finally, while "gray" income often remains illegal (because people do not pay taxes on it), it is no longer politically necessary to ignore it. In the past, both households and enumerators were aware that such sources of income were not only illegal but also "politically incorrect." Both preferred to look the other way and ignore all non-official sources of income. This source of bias is now gone.

To account for the problem of income underreporting, poverty calculations here use HBS data for *both* income and expenditures. Moreover, to adjust for frequent underreporting in HBS data, as compared with macroeconomic income data, HBS income data here are increased by the percentage difference between the two measures. When HBS data show higher income than macroeconomic data, no adjustment is done, however. These are re-

---

12. Underreporting is also a problem in market economies, particularly with regard to self-employment income and capital income. Atkinson, Rainwater, and Smeeding (1995, table A3) find, using Luxembourg Income Study data, that self-employment income is underestimated in market economies (compared with national accounts data) by between 10 percent (Canada) and 60 percent (West Germany). They also estimate that property income in almost all industrialized countries (United States, United Kingdom, Italy, Germany, Finland, Canada, and Australia) is underestimated by one-half. According to Michel (1991, p. 185), the U.S. Current Population Survey understates so-called non-earned income by about 40 percent.

Figure A1.1. *Income and Expenditures per Capita, Poland, 1993*

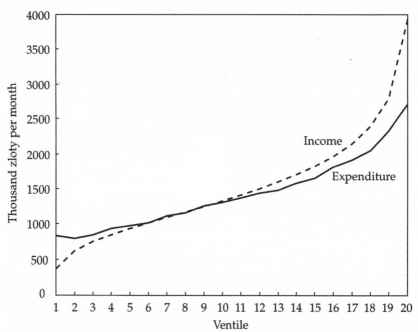

Note: Ventile is 5 percent of the population.
Source: Polish 1993 Household budget survey.

ferred to as "adjusted" or "corrected" income data (*INCOME2* data). The adjustment, however, is a crude one, in the sense that it raises everyone's income by the same percentage. In the absence of data on the pattern of underreporting, however, this is the only available solution.

Per capita versus equivalent units

International comparisons of poverty are complicated, to say the least. The choice of units of analysis (per capita or per equivalent adult) may also lead to differences in results. First, the use of a per capita poverty line, rather than an equivalent-scale derived poverty line, exaggerates poverty. This is because with an equivalence scale the needs of additional family members (often children) do not rise in proportion to number of people as they do when a per capita measure is used. The use of a per capita poverty line exaggerates poverty even more, then, in countries with a larger average family size.[13] For

13. Coulter, Cowell, and Jenkins (1992) show that the poverty headcount charts a *U*-shaped pattern, first decreasing and then rising, as the equivalence scale moves from 0 (full economies of scale, where only total household income matters) to 1 (per capita calculations). The same results are obtained by Michael Förster (1993, p. 21) in an empirical study of thirteen OECD countries.

example, Marnie and Micklewright (1993) compare Ukraine and Uzbekistan using the same Soviet FBSs for 1989. They find that of the 38 percentage point difference in the headcount index between the two republics obtained using a per capita measure, the larger household size in Uzbekistan accounts for 14 percentage points. There are several reasons why the per capita line is used here. First, data from all countries are published in that form. Second, economies of scale in consumption under socialism were typically less than in market economies because the main source of such economies of scale (housing, utilities, and so on) were heavily subsidized; and this is still true, although not to the same extent.[14] Third, the use of per capita poverty comparison allows for an easy transition from per capita comparisons to GDP per capita comparisons.

Quarterly versus yearly data

A final problem concerns the period over which data are collected. Normally, surveys are designed so that households report (that is, keep track of or recall) income and expenditures for one quarter or one month.[15] These data are then "blown up" for the entire year. The same thing is done by another (quarterly or monthly) set of households, until four or twelve such sets are added up to obtain the final annual survey results. Under conditions of high inflation, however, data collected during different months, and even weeks and days, represent wholly different real quantities of goods and services and cannot be summed up without being adjusted for inflation. Statistical agencies, however, sometimes do not make such adjustments, or if they do, they sometimes make them inadequately. Under such conditions, quarterly data on income or expenditure distribution—from which poverty figures are calculated here for several countries of the former Soviet Union—are preferred because they refer to a shorter time period and imply about the same real command over goods and services. The usual drawback of the short-period data—namely, that they overestimate income inequality and poverty (because the shorter the time period, the more people who will report extraordinarily low and high incomes)—is then more than offset by the advantage of using data where the same reported money amounts represent approximately the same real quantities.

---

14. If the price of all goods that provide economies of scale in consumption is zero, then economies of scale no longer matter.

15. To increase the response rate (which was a main source of bias), Polish household surveys began requiring households to track their income and expenditures for one month rather than three months. The response rate increased from 65 to 80 percent (see Kordos 1994).

How Biases Affect Comparability between Pre-transition and Transition Years

Ideally, a household survey would: (a) be representative of the country as a whole; (b) gather information regarding annual income and expenditures; (c) use disposable income or net expenditures as welfare indicators; (d) include consumption-in-kind; and (e) define both income and expenditures "correctly," that is, the way they are defined in economic theory. Note, however, that even the "best" achievable survey could still contain biases. The "best" survey would still probably understate the two tail-ends of income distribution, because the poorest and the richest segments of society are typically undersurveyed, and it would also underestimate some sources of income, such as property (which is routinely underestimated by up to 50 percent in industrial countries) and entrepreneurship.

No transition-year survey used here meets all five criteria (see table A1.5) but several come close. Bulgarian and Slovenian surveys have only a slightly incorrect definition of income; adjustments could not be fully made to account for this as individual data were not available. Hungary's 1993 survey does not include consumption-in-kind in income,[16] and semi-annual rather than annual data were available for Poland.

Among the East European data, the Czech data are the least satisfactory. Both the poverty headcount and inequality are overestimated, because the time period of the survey is so short (see table A1.5).

In Hungary, the absence of consumption-in-kind leads to a slight increase in inequality and poverty, because consumption-in-kind is generally greater in poorer households.

Poland's poverty headcounts may also be slightly overestimated, because the pre-harvest period only—that is, the first six months of the year—was included—and incomes are generally higher among the agricultural population during the second half of the year.

In Bulgaria, the use of gross income reduces the poverty headcount and inequality to the extent that PITs are progressive. PITs are small, however, as most taxes are deducted at the source, so the downward bias is negligible.

Finally, Slovak data exclude pensioner-headed households with economically active members. It is not clear how this exclusion might affect poverty and inequality, because it is not clear if excluded households are richer or poorer than the average, or how they are distributed along the income spectrum.

In conclusion, with the exception of Czech and Slovak data, the quality problems and the conceptual differences between the various East European data sets are not significant.

---

16. It includes consumption-in-kind in expenditures.

Table A1.5. *Survey Defects: Pre-transition and Transition Years*

Country	Pre-transition	Transition
Poland	Incomplete coverage of recipients	Semi-annual data
Hungary	None	No consumption-in-kind
Czech		Monthly data
Slovakia		Not fully representative
Slovenia	Income definition problem	
Bulgaria	Income definition problem; gross income instead of disposable	
Romania	Not fully representative income definition problem	Monthly data
Estonia		Quarterly data
Latvia		Quarterly data
Lithuania		Gross income; no consumption-in-kind
Russia	Quota sample, not fully representative; income definition problem	Quarterly data
Belarus		Quarterly data
Ukraine		Monthly data; large underestimate of income
Kyrgyz		Quarterly data; large underestimate of income
Moldova Kazakhstan Turkmenistan Uzbekistan	Quota sample, not fully representative; income definition problem	

Note: The surveys assessed here are the same ones listed in Tables A1.1, A1.2 and A1.3.
Source: Author's estimates.

For data from countries of the former Soviet Union, the problems are more serious. At most, Soviet surveys satisfied only three of the five criteria listed above: use of annual data, inclusion of consumption-in-kind and use of disposable income.[17] The new, improved surveys suffer from too short an observation period (between one month and one quarter), and in Kyrgyz Republic and Ukraine, there is large-scale income underreporting (see table A1.5).

What can be said, then, regarding non-systemic biases in estimating *changes* in the poverty headcount and in inequality between 1987–89 and 1993–95

---

17. Even if, strictly speaking, income was defined as gross, the difference between gross and net income was negligible.

Table A1.6. Bias in Estimating Change in Poverty and Inequality
During the Transition

Country	Poverty headcount bias	Inequality bias
Poland	Unclear	Overestimates increase
Hungary Czech republic	Overestimates increase	
Slovakia	Unclear	Unclear
Slovenia Bulgaria	None	
Romania Estonia Latvia Lithuania Russia Belarus Ukraine Kyrgyz republic	Overestimates increase	
Moldova Kazakhstan Turkmenistan Uzbekistan	Unclear	

Note: The surveys assessed here are the same ones listed in Tables A1.1, A1.2 and A1.3.
Source: Author's estimates.

(see table A1.6)? For Poland, the exclusion (in 1987) of the non-agricultural private sector and of army and police personnel yielded too-low inequality estimates; the measured increase in inequality during the transition will therefore be overestimated. For Hungary, absence of data on consumption-in-kind in transition years will lead to an overestimation of both income-poverty and income inequality. For the Czech Republic, increases in both poverty and inequality will be overestimated because monthly rather than annual data were used in 1993. For Bulgaria and Slovenia, no biases can be discerned *a priori*. In Romania and the former Soviet Union, pre-transition coverage was biased toward "average" or "typical" households, thus underestimating both inequality and poverty. In the countries where the quality of surveys has improved, then comparisons over time will show increases in poverty and inequality that are greater than actual. Where the quality of surveys has remained unchanged (Moldova and Central Asia, except the Kyrgyz Republic), it is unclear which way the bias will go.

What do these biases imply, in a nutshell, for the estimation of poverty rates? In the past, income data were reliable for those covered in a survey, but the surveys' coverage was biased. They excluded the poorest and overrepresented average, "standard" households. As a result, poverty rates were shown to be lower than they were in reality. Improvements in survey design mean that current data are more representative of the population as a whole. On the other hand, however, households now underreport income more than they did in the past,[18] so that while survey design is now adequate, income reporting is now biased. Unfortunately, rather than offsetting each other, both elements (more representative surveys and income underreporting) tend to show the increase in poverty rates to be greater than actual. The gap between current (high levels of) poverty and pre-transition (low levels of) poverty, while certainly large, then appears even larger.

---

18. In Poland, in the past, wages and pensions reported by survey participants almost perfectly matched the macroeconomic values. Currently, they underestimate macroeconomic values by 10 to 20 percent (see Kordos 1994).

Appendix 2

Decile Shares of Total Income

In tables A2.1—A2.18, decile shares are calculated from the original HBS data given in appendix 4. All the detailed sources are given there.

Note: A = annual data; SA = semi-annual data; M = monthly data; Q = quarterly data. For example, M:10/1993 means that the data refer to October 1993, Q:1/1995 that the data refer to the first quarter of 1995, and SA:I/1993 that the data refer to the first half of 1993.

Table A2.1. Belarus

Decile	A:1988	Q:1/1995
First	4.47	3.38
Second	6.01	5.32
Third	6.99	6.38
Fourth	7.89	7.31
Fifth	8.80	8.30
Sixth	9.76	9.34
Seventh	10.83	10.58
Eighth	12.12	12.03
Ninth	13.92	14.46
Tenth	19.20	22.88

Table A2.2. Bulgaria

Decile	A:1989	A:1993
First	4.49	2.80
Second	6.14	4.31
Third	7.05	5.54
Fourth	7.86	6.65
Fifth	8.67	7.74
Sixth	9.53	8.90
Seventh	10.51	10.25
Eighth	11.75	12.03
Ninth	13.59	14.95
Tenth	20.42	26.84

Table 2.3. Czech Republic

Decile	A:1988	M:1/1993
First	5.41	4.60
Second	6.51	5.90
Third	7.41	6.60
Fourth	8.11	7.30
Fifth	8.91	8.00
Sixth	9.91	8.90
Seventh	11.01	9.90
Eighth	11.11	11.40
Ninth	14.11	13.90
Tenth	17.52	23.50

Table 2.4. Estonia

Decile	A:1988	Q:3/1995
First	4.20	2.06
Second	5.79	4.07
Third	6.88	5.41
Fourth	7.91	6.68
Fifth	8.93	7.83
Sixth	9.99	9.03
Seventh	11.15	10.48
Eighth	12.49	12.50
Ninth	14.24	16.03
Tenth	18.41	25.90

Table 2.5. Hungary

Decile	A:1987	A:1993
First	4.96	4.40
Second	6.46	6.22
Third	7.31	7.22
Fourth	8.08	8.03
Fifth	8.85	8.79
Sixth	9.66	9.60
Seventh	10.58	10.51
Eighth	11.72	11.79
Ninth	13.37	13.65
Tenth	19.00	19.79

Table 2.6. *Kazakhstan*

Decile	A:1988	A:1993
First	4.05	3.07
Second	5.42	4.42
Third	6.46	5.60
Fourth	7.47	6.72
Fifth	8.51	7.84
Sixth	9.63	9.06
Seventh	10.90	10.50
Eighth	12.43	12.39
Ninth	14.56	15.45
Tenth	20.57	24.94

Table A2.7. *Kyrgyz Republic*

Decile	A:1988	M:10-11/1993
First	5.14	0.80
Second	5.43	1.89
Third	6.14	3.20
Fourth	7.02	4.23
Fifth	8.05	5.58
Sixth	9.23	7.16
Seventh	10.62	9.17
Eighth	12.35	12.01
Ninth	14.76	16.96
Tenth	21.26	39.18

Table A2.8. *Latvia*

Decile	A:1988	Q:4/1995
First	4.46	3.18
Second	5.98	4.86
Third	6.99	6.09
Fourth	7.92	7.14
Fifth	8.86	8.12
Sixth	9.85	9.14
Seventh	10.95	10.30
Eighth	12.24	11.81
Ninth	14.00	14.26
Tenth	18.73	25.09

Table A2.9. *Lithuania*

Decile	A:1988	A:1994
First	4.59	2.38
Second	6.05	3.83
Third	7.01	5.08
Fourth	7.91	6.25
Fifth	8.81	7.43
Sixth	9.77	8.70
Seventh	10.85	10.21
Eighth	12.13	12.20
Ninth	13.91	15.51
Tenth	18.96	28.41

Table A2.10. *Moldova*

Decile	A:1988	A:1993
First	4.27	2.58
Second	5.69	3.80
Third	6.80	4.97
Fourth	7.77	6.15
Fifth	8.70	7.40
Sixth	9.67	8.80
Seventh	10.77	10.49
Eighth	12.17	12.75
Ninth	14.32	16.42
Tenth	19.86	26.65

Table A2.11. *Poland*

Decile	A:1987	SA:I/1993
First	4.08	3.20
Second	5.63	5.17
Third	6.63	6.33
Fourth	7.56	7.37
Fifth	8.50	8.40
Sixth	9.52	9.49
Seventh	10.69	10.78
Eighth	12.12	12.38
Ninth	14.21	14.87
Tenth	21.06	22.00

Table A2.11. *Romania*

Decile	A:1989	M:3/1994
First	4.08	3.52
Second	5.89	5.22
Third	6.96	6.25
Fourth	7.99	7.21
Fifth	8.91	8.17
Sixth	9.84	9.27
Seventh	10.82	10.59
Eighth	12.13	12.32
Ninth	14.22	14.95
Tenth	19.16	22.51

Table A2.13. *Russia*

Decile	A:1988	Q:3/1993
First	4.14	1.64
Second	5.77	3.22
Third	6.82	4.19
Fourth	7.79	5.05
Fifth	8.77	5.99
Sixth	9.80	7.09
Seventh	10.95	8.49
Eighth	12.31	10.66
Ninth	14.19	14.14
Tenth	19.45	39.52

Table A2.14. *Slovak Republic*

Decile	A:1988	A:1993
First	5.34	5.70
Second	6.55	6.85
Third	7.37	7.58
Fourth	8.14	8.27
Fifth	8.92	8.96
Sixth	9.76	9.70
Seventh	10.69	10.54
Eighth	11.82	11.57
Ninth	13.40	13.06
Tenth	17.99	17.78

Table A2.15. *Slovenia*

Decile	A:1987	A:1993
First	4.55	4.34
Second	5.94	5.76
Third	6.87	6.69
Fourth	7.74	7.57
Fifth	8.63	8.47
Sixth	9.59	9.44
Seventh	10.68	10.57
Eighth	12.02	11.97
Ninth	13.94	14.04
Tenth	20.05	21.16

Table A2.16. *Turkmenistan*

Decile	A:1988	A:1993
First	5.12	2.72
Second	5.38	3.98
Third	6.08	5.15
Fourth	6.96	6.29
Fifth	7.99	7.48
Sixth	9.19	8.79
Seventh	10.60	10.36
Eighth	12.36	12.47
Ninth	14.82	15.91
Tenth	21.51	26.85

Table A2.17. *Ukraine*

Decile	A:1988	M:6-7/1995
First	4.38	1.51
Second	5.93	2.76
Third	6.92	3.92
Fourth	7.83	5.07
Fifth	8.75	6.27
Sixth	9.73	7.62
Seventh	10.82	9.24
Eighth	12.14	11.45
Ninth	13.99	15.20
Tenth	19.51	32.74

Table A2.18. *Uzbekistan*

Decile	A:1989	A:1993
First	3.83	2.99
Second	5.14	4.29
Third	6.24	5.47
Fourth	7.26	6.61
Fifth	8.26	7.77
Sixth	9.33	9.04
Seventh	10.58	10.55
Eighth	12.21	12.54
Ninth	14.80	15.74
Tenth	22.35	25.00

Appendix 3

Change in the Poverty Deficit Due to a Uniform Slide in Income

The poverty deficit is, by definition, equal to

$$PD = \int_0^z (z-y)\, f(y)\, dy$$

which is shown in Figure A3.1 as the sum of rectangles such as ABEz and CDFz. Obviously, the poverty deficit will be equal to the summation of all such rectangles for all values of $y<z$. Now, if the poverty line z increases infinitesimally, each rectangle expands slightly to the right by the amount $f(y)$. These "expansions" are shown by cross-hatched areas in Figure A3.1. For all the existing rectangles, the increase will be equal to

$$\frac{dPD}{dz} = \int_0^z f(y)\, dy$$

which is exactly the same result as given by equation 5.3.

Figure A3.1. *The Effect of a Higher Poverty Line on the Poverty Deficit*

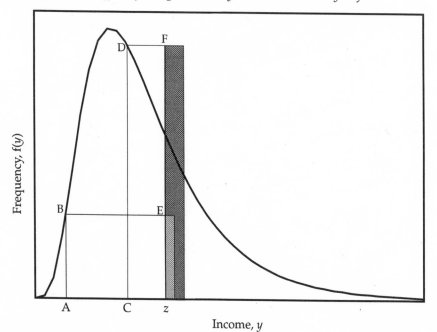

Appendix 4

The Original Income Distribution Statistics

Definitions: Gross income = earnings from labor + cash social transfers + self-employment income + other income (from property, entrepreneurial income, gifts) + consumption-in-kind.

Disposable income = gross income – direct personal taxes.

Money income does not include consumption-in-kind.

Note: All average income values refer to average income per capita.

Cost of living (COL) deflator is always between the two survey dates.

Table A4.1. *Bulgaria*

1989		1993	
Number of people (in 000)	*Average per capita gross income (leva per capita per year)*	*Population percentages*	*Average per capita gross income (leva per capita per year)*
334	914	7.1	5,326
367	1,329	12.7	10,127
726	1,547	16.1	14,009
885	1,791	16.2	17,872
952	2,023	12.5	21,893
924	2,265	9.3	25,880
710	2,506	6.8	29,746
605	2,745	4.4	33,763
526	2,990	3.5	37,732
1,971	4,157	11.4	60,279
Gini	23.3	Gini	34.3
Mean income	2,591	Mean income	23,659
Real mean income	100	Real mean income	54.4
Mean income in $	1,178	Mean income in $	857

Source: 1989: Bulgarian HBS.
   1993: Bulgarian HBS reported in *Biudzeti na domakinstvata v Republika B'lgariya*, National Statistical Institute, Sofia, 1994, page 68. [Non-income items deducted in both surveys.]
   Exchange rate: 1989: $1 = 2.2 leva.
                  1993: $1 = 27.6 leva.
   COL deflator: 16.8

Table A4.2. *Czech Republic*

1988		January 1993	
Population deciles	Average per capita disposable income (crowns per capita per month)	Population deciles	Average per capita disposable income (crowns per capita per month)
10	1,004	10	1,611
10	1,208	10	2,066
10	1,376	10	2,311
10	1,506	10	2,556
10	1,655	10	2,802
10	1,840	10	3,117
10	2,045	10	3,467
10	2,063	10	3,992
10	2,621	10	4,868
10	3,253	10	8,230
Gini	19.4	Gini	26.6
Mean income	1,857	Mean income	3,502
Real mean income	100	Real mean income	87.7
Mean income in $	130	Mean income in $	122

Source: 1988: *Microcensus.*
January 1993: *Economic Expectations and Attitudes.*
Both reported in Večernik et al., (1994).
Exchange rate: 1988: $1 = 14.26 crowns.
　　　　　January 1993: $1 = 28.8 crowns.
COL deflator = 2.15.

Table A4.3. *Hungary*

1987		1993	
Number of people	*Average per capita disposable income (forints per capita per year)*	*Percentage of population*	*Average per capita disposable income (forints per capita per year)*
2,685	25,556	5	50,871
6,487	36,517	5	72,592
7,863	45,583	5	83,253
5,647	54,904	5	91,253
3,717	64,444	5	98,185
2,217	74,117	5	104,321
3,247	100,885	5	109,882
		5	115,485
		5	120,649
		5	126,021
		5	131,499
		5	137,660
		5	143,554
		5	151,284
		5	160,493
		5	170,285
		5	182,769
		5	199,991
		5	231,400
		5	323,619
Gini	21.0	Gini	22.6
Mean income	53,523	Mean income	140,253
Real mean income	100	Real mean income	74.1
Mean income in $	1,139	Mean income in $	1,524

Source: 1987: *Household Budget Survey* reported in *Családi Költségvetés* 1987, Budapest: Central Statistical Office, 1989, pp. 126-7
1993: *Household Budget Survey* (individual data)
Exchange rate: 1987: $1 = 47 forints.
        1993: $1 = 92 forints.
COL deflator: 3.53

Table A4.4. Slovakia

1988		1993	
Number of people	Average per capita disposable income (crowns per capita per year)	Number of people	Average per capita disposable income (crowns per capita per year)
176,693	8,776	539	21,472
237,593	10,854	900	26,594
472,822	11,985	836	31,398
640,711	13,080	831	36,429
800,156	14,290	640	40,671
1,003,174	15,508	401	45,126
1,161,046	16,730	263	49,714
1,257,160	17,971	501	65,838
1,277,633	19,178		
1,104,486	20,397		
974,158	21,617		
871,625	22,848		
738,219	24,069		
665,506	25,274		
579,495	26,553		
490,502	27,720		
434,651	28,968		
367,593	30,226		
15,519	31,401		
280,371	32,625		
45,630	33,811		
206,727	34,954		
163,851	36,348		
257,475	38,024		
605,074	47,184		
Gini	19.5	Gini	18.3
Mean income	22,269	Mean income	37,103
Real mean income	100	Real mean income	71.2
Mean income in $	1,562	Mean income in $	1,201

Source: 1988: *Microcensus.* Data for Czechoslovakia used as approximation for Slovakia.
1993: *Family Budget Surveys* reported in *Príjmy, výdavky a spotreba domacností za rok 1993,* vol.1-3, Bratislava: Slovak Statistics, 1994.
Exchange rate: 1988: $1 = 14.26 crowns.
                        1993: $1 = 30.9 crowns.
COL deflator: 2.34.

Table A4.5. *Slovenia*

1987		1993	
Number of people	Average per capita gross income (000 dinars per capita per year)	Number of people	Average per capita disposable income (tolars per capita per year)
6,329	427.9	15	52,421
51,084	704.4	141	115,138
132,829	926.7	664	176,929
269,561	1,140.3	1,566	238,303
316,854	1,394.5	1,896	296,622
260,982	1,627.4	1,531	358,115
283,689	1,887.7	1,137	414,344
160,472	2,119.7	786	472,635
439,256	2,808.7	526	521,310
		1,603	740,262
Gini	21.5	Gini	25.1
Mean income	1,793.4	Mean income	397,547
Real mean income	100	Real mean income	108.4
Mean income in $	4,808	Mean income in $	3,512

Source: 1987 Yugoslav HBS, published in *Ankete o potrošnji domaćinstava u 1987*, SZS, Belgrade 1988.

1993 Slovenian *HBS*. Computer spreadsheets supplied by Irena Krizman (Slovenian Office of Statistics). [Non-income items deducted in both surveys.]

Exchange rate: 1987: $1 = 373 YUD.

1993: $1 = 113.2 tolars.

COL deflator = 0.2045 (excluding a factor of 1000 due to the 1990 Dinar denomination).

Table A4.6. *Romania*

1989		March 1994	
Population deciles	*Average per capita gross income (lei per capita per month)*	*Population deciles*	*Average per capita income (lei per capita per month)*
10	737	10	16,676
10	1,065	10	24,683
10	1,259	10	29,750
10	1,444	10	34,069
10	1,611	10	38,626
10	1,780	10	43,335
10	1,957	10	49,122
10	2,194	10	56,797
10	2,571	10	68,679
10	3,464	10	105,505
Gini	23.3	Gini	28.6
Mean income	1,808	Mean income	46,563
Real mean income	100	Real mean income	56.4
Mean income in $	25	Mean income in $	29

Source: 1989: Romanian *HBS*. Computer spreadsheets supplied by Mansoora Rashid (World Bank).

March 1994: *Integrated household survey* (individual data available).

Exchange rate: 1989: $1 = 73 lei (blend between the official and parallel rate).

March 1994: $1 = 1601 lei.

COL deflator = 45.7.

Table A4.7. Poland

	1987		1st half of 1993 (June prices)	
Number of people	Average per capita gross income (zloty per capita per month)	Percentage of population	Average per capita disposable (000 zloty per capita per month)	
8,074	6,462	5	367.32	
9,785	9,038	5	622.84	
24,235	12,056	5	748.86	
21,419	15,880	5	850.51	
12,798	19,792	5	937.38	
7,499	23,841	5	1,018.40	
4,133	27,815	5	1,099.93	
5,305	39,768	5	1,178.03	
		5	1,255.24	
		5	1,340.70	
		5	1,423.07	
		5	1,511.75	
		5	1,611.45	
		5	1,720.73	
		5	1,841.38	
		5	1,986.75	
		5	2,170.09	
		5	2,425.09	
		5	2,823.10	
		5	3,978.22	
Gini	25.6	Gini	28.4	
Mean income	16,418	Mean income	1,545.54	
Real mean income	100	Real mean income	73.5	
Mean income in $	62	Mean income in $	89	

Source: 1987: HBS published in *Budżeti Gospodarstw Domowych 1987*, GUS, Warsaw, 1988.
I half of 1993: HBS (individual data available). [Non-income items deducted in both surveys.]
Exchange rate: 1987: $1 = 265 zloty.
        June 1993: $1 = 17,300 zloty.
COL deflator = 128.

Table A4.8. *Estonia*

1988		3rd quarter of 1995 (July prices)	
Upper bound of gross income (Rs. per capita per month)	*Percentage of population*	*Population deciles*	*Average per capita disposable income (EEK per capita per month)*
75	3.9	10	196.39
100	9.0	10	387.37
150	28.0	10	515.64
200	25.5	10	636.65
Open	33.6	10	746.32
		10	860.79
		10	998.96
		10	1,191.17
		10	1,527.56
		10	2,468.20
Gini	23.0	Gini	35.4
Mean income	177.2	Mean income	949.84
Real mean income	100	Real mean income	63.1
Mean income in $	81	Mean income in $	86

Source: 1988: Soviet *HBS* published in *Narodnoe khozyaystvo SSSR 1988*, p. 94.
July-September 1993: *HBS* (individual data available).
Exchange rate: 1988: $1 = 2.2 roubles (blend between the official and parallel rate).
        July 1995: $1 = 11.1 Estonian kroons.
COL deflator = 8.495 (excluding a factor of 10 due to the conversion from roubles to kroons).

Table A4.9. *Lithuania*

1988			1994
Upper bound of gross income (Rs. per capita per month)	*Percentage of population*	*Shares[a]*	*Average per capita money income (in litai per capita per year)*
75	3.6	36	561
100	10.7	36	1,012
150	34.6	24	1,292
200	27.1	24	1,494
Open	24.0	27	1,741
		28	2,043
		27	2,419
		25	2,920
		26	3,715
		22	6,847
Gini	22.5	Gini	37.3
Mean income	164.6	Mean income	2,230
Real mean income	100	Real mean income	58.2
Mean income in $	75	Mean income in $	558

Source: 1988: Soviet *HBS* published in *Narodnoe khozyaystvo SSSR 1988,* p. 94.
1994: Lithuanian HBS reported in *Statistical Yearbook of Lithuania 1994-95,* Vilnius: Lithuanian Department of Statistics, p. 188, and in Cornelius (1995, Table 3).
Exchange rate: 1988: $1 = 2.2 roubles (blend between the official and parallel rate).
1994: $1 = 4 litai.
COL deflator = 1.94 (excluding a factor of 100 due to the conversion from roubles to lita).

a. The data were given in terms of household deciles and average number of individuals per household (per decile). They are converted here in terms of individuals.

Table A4.10. *Latvia*

1988		4th quarter of 1995	
Upper bound of gross income (Rs. per capita per month)	Percentage of population	Percentage of population	Average per capita disposable income (lats per capita per month)
75	3.2	10	15.634
100	9.5	10	27.620
150	31.8	10	34.254
200	27.2	10	38.564
Open	28.3	10	43.436
		10	48.705
		10	54.776
		10	65.068
		10	80.033
		10	113.420
Gini	22.5	Gini	31.0
Mean income	171.16	Mean income	54.15
Real mean income	100	Real mean income	55.3
Mean income in $	78	Mean income in $	101

Source: 1988: Soviet *HBS* published in *Narodnoe khozyaystvo SSSR 1988,* p. 94.
4th quarter of 1995: New Latvian *HBS.* Data provided by the Latvian Committee on Statistics.
Exchange rate: 1988: $1 = 2.2 roubles (blend between the official and parallel rate).
              4th quarter of 1995: $1 = 0.536 lats.
COL deflator = 0.572 (excluding a factor of 200 due to the conversion from roubles to lats).

Table A4.11. Russia

1988		June-September 1993 (July prices)	
Upper bound of gross income (Rs. per capita per month)	Percentage of population	Average per capita gross income (000 Rs. per capita per month)	Percentage of population
75	6.3	5.272	10.0
100	13.1	10.441	10.0
150	34.0	13.654	10.0
200	24.6	16.503	10.0
Open	22.0	19.523	10.0
		23.042	10.0
		27.689	10.0
		34.795	10.0
		46.125	10.0
		126.323	10.0
Gini	23.8	Gini	48.0
Mean income	158.0	Mean income	32.337
Real mean income	100	Real mean income	58.0
Mean income in $	72	Mean income in $	32

Source: 1988: Soviet *HBS* published in *Narodnoe khozyaystvo SSSR 1988,* p. 94.
1993: *Russian Longitudinal Monitoring Survey* Round 3 (individual data available).
Exchange rate: 1988: $1 = 2.2 roubles (blend between the official and parallel rate).
        July 1993: $1 = 1025 roubles.
COL deflator = 353.5.

Table A4.12. *Belarus*

1988		1st quarter 1995 (March prices)	
Upper bound of gross income (Rs. per capita per month)	Percentage of population	Average per capita net income (Bel. rubles per capita per month)	Percentage of population
75	5.0	122,752	10
100	12.9	193,148	10
150	36.8	231,371	10
200	25.8	265,346	10
Open	19.5	301,228	10
		339,073	10
		384,033	10
		486,706	10
		524,828	10
		830,398	10
Gini	22.8	Gini	28.4
Mean income	156.1	Mean income	362,888
Real mean income	100	Real mean income	56.2
Mean income in $	71	Mean income in $	32

Source: 1988: Soviet *HBS* published in *Narodnoe khozyaystvo SSSR 1988,* p. 94.
1 quarter 1995: *New Household Budget Survey* (data provided by Anna Ivanova).
Exchange rate: 1988: $1 = 2.2 roubles (blend between the official and parallel rate).
          March 1995: $1 = 11,525 Belarussian roubles.
GDP deflator = 4131 (excluding a factor of 10 due to denomination change 10 Russian roubles = 1 Belorussian rouble). GDP deflator used because more reliable than COL.

Table A4.13. *Ukraine*

1988		June and July 1995 (June prices)	
Upper bound of gross income (Rs. per capita per month)	*Percentage of population*	*Average per capita gross income (000 karbovanets per capita per month)*	*Percentage of population*
75	8.1	458.8	10.0
100	16.8	979.7	10.0
150	38.5	1,338.5	10.0
200	22.4	1,713.4	10.0
Open	14.2	2,143.2	10.0
		2,555.9	10.0
		3,066.2	10.0
		3,855.8	10.0
		5,291.6	10.0
		12,404.1	10.0
Gini	23.3	Gini	47.4
Mean income	143.8	Mean income	3,380.7
Real mean income	100	Real mean income	37.6
Mean income in $	65	Mean income in $	24

Source: 1988: Soviet *HBS* published in *Narodnoe khozyaystvo SSSR 1988*, p. 94.
June-July 1995: *Ukraina 1995 survey.*
Exchange rate: 1988: $1 = 2.2 roubles (blend between the official and parallel rate).
　　　　　June 1995: $1 = 142,000 karbovanets.
COL deflator = 62,464.

Table A4.14. Moldova

1988		1993	
Upper bound of gross income (Rs. per capita per month)	Percentage of population	Upper bound of gross income (lei per capita per month)	Estimated 000 of people
75	13.0	3	28.4
100	19.8	4	65.5
150	37.3	6	247.0
200	18.9	8	355.5
Open	11.0	10	399.8
		12	398.8
		14	372.7
		16	335.6
		18	295.4
		20	256.4
		22	220.8
		24	189.2
		26	161.7
		28	138.1
		30	117.9
		32	100.8
		34	86.2
		36	73.9
		38	63.4
		40	54.6
		42	47.1
		44	40.7
		46	35.2
		Open	260.9
Gini	24.1	Gini	36.5
Mean income	133.4	Mean income	19.76
Real mean income	100	Real mean income	32.7
Mean income in $	61	Mean income in $	12

Source: 1988: Soviet *HBS* published in *Narodnoe khozyaystvo SSSR 1988,* p. 94.

1993: *Annuarul Statistic al Republica Moldova 1993,* Chisineu: Moldovan Department of Statistics, p.139.

Exchange rate: 1988: $1 = 2.2 roubles (blend between the official and parallel rate).

1993: $1 = 1.6 lei.

COL deflator = 0.453 (excluding a factor of 1000 due to conversion).

Table A4.15. *Turkmenistan*

1988		1993	
Upper bound of gross income (Rs. per capita per month)	Percentage of population	Upper bound of gross income (000 Rs. per capita per month)	Percentage of population
75	36.6	7.5	3.0
100	23.0	10.0	5.3
150	25.8	15.0	14.5
200	9.4	20.0	15.4
Open	5.2	25.0	13.5
		30.0	10.9
		35.0	8.5
		40.0	6.5
		45.0	5.0
		50.0	3.8
		60.0	5.1
		70.0	3.1
		80.0	1.9
		90.0	1.2
		100.0	0.7
		110.0	0.5
		Open	1.1
Gini	26.4	Gini	35.8
Mean income	104.3	Mean income	30.34
Real mean income	100	Real mean income	53.6
Mean income in $	47	Mean income in $	34

Source: 1988: Soviet *HBS* published in *Narodnoe khozyaystvo SSSR 1988*, p. 94.
1993: *Statistical Bulletin CIS*, August 1994, pp. 73ff.
Exchange rate: 1988: $1 = 2.2 roubles (blend between the official and parallel rate).
1993: $1 = 892 roubles.
COL deflator = 543.

Table A4.16. *Kyrgyz Republic*

1988		October-November 1993 (October prices)	
Upper bound of gross income (Rs. per capita per month)	*Percentage of population*	*Average disposable income (som per capita per month)*	*Decile of population*
75	37.1	3.2793	10
100	23.1	10.1726	10
150	26.0	15.8309	10
200	9.2	21.9331	10
Open	4.6	29.2737	10
		38.5805	10
		50.6507	10
		68.6812	10
		97.3894	10
		239.2659	10
Gini	26.0	Gini	55.3
Mean income	103	Mean income	69.3
Real mean income	100	Real mean income	33.8
Mean income in $	47	Mean income in $	9

Source: 1988: Soviet *HBS* published in *Narodnoe khozyaystvo SSSR 1988*, p. 94.
October-November 1993: *Kyrgyz Multipurpose Poverty Survey* (individual data available).
Exchange rate: 1988: $1 = 2.2 roubles (blend between the official and parallel rate).
                    October 1993: $1 = 7 soms.
COL deflator = 2.05 (excluding a factor of 230 due to conversion).

Table A4.17. *Kazakhstan*

1988		1993	
Upper bound of gross income (Rs. per capita per month)	Percentage of population	Upper bound of gross income (000 Rs. per capita per month)	Percentage of population
75	15.9	7.5	3.4
100	19.3	10.0	6.5
150	33.7	15.0	18.2
200	18.1	20.0	18.3
Open	13.0	25.0	14.9
		30.0	11.1
		35.0	8.0
		40.0	5.6
		45.0	3.9
		50.0	2.8
		60.0	3.4
		70.0	1.7
		80.0	0.9
		90.0	0.5
		100.0	0.3
		110.0	0.2
		Open	0.3
Gini	25.7	Gini	32.7
Mean income	134	Mean income	25.34
Real mean income	100	Real mean income	38.5
Mean income in $	61	Mean income in $	22

Source: 1988: Soviet *HBS* published in *Narodnoe khozyaystvo SSSR 1988,* p. 94.
1993: *Statistical Bulletin CIS,* August 1994, pp. 73 ff.
Exchange rate: 1988: $1 = 2.2 roubles (blend between the official and parallel rate).
          1993: $1 = 1168 roubles.
COL deflator = 491.

Table A4.18. Uzbekistan

1989		1993	
Upper bound of gross income (Rs. per capita per month)	Percentage of population	Upper bound of gross income (000 Rs. per capita per month)	Percentage of population
50	16.0	1.5	0.02
75	27.7	2.0	0x.07
100	22.7	3.0	3.7
125	14.1	4.0	6.8
150	8.3	5.0	8.7
175	4.7	6.0	9.4
200	2.7	7.0	9.3
225	1.6	8.0	8.6
250	0.9	9.0	7.7
Open	1.4	10.0	6.7
		11.0	5.8
		12.0	5.0
		13.0	4.2
		14.0	3.5
		15.0	3.0
		16.0	2.5
		17.0	2.1
		18.0	1.8
		19.0	1.5
		20.0	1.3
		22.0	2.0
		24.0	1.4
		Open	4.1
Gini	28.2	Gini	33.3
Mean income	93.5	Mean income	10.0
Real mean income	100	Real mean income	56.9
Mean income in $	28	Mean income in $	11

Source: 1989: Soviet *HBS* reported in Marnie and Micklewright (1993, Table 1).
1993: *Statistical Bulletin CIS*, August 1994, pp. 73 ff.
Exchange rate: 1989: $1 = 3.4 roubles (blend between the official and parallel rate).
              1993: $1 = 951 roubles.
COL deflator = 188.

Appendix 5

Poverty Headcount Calculations Based on the Original Income Distribution Statistics Given in Appendix 4

Note: Poverty line is shown in square brackets next to the country name, in domestic currency, in nominal amounts at the time of survey (e.g., Poland [7265]). It is always equal to $PPP120 (at 1990 international prices). *A* indicates annual survey; *Q*, quarterly; *M*, monthly. Average shortfall shows by how much (in percent), the average income of the poor is less than the poverty line. Elasticity shows by how many percentage points the poverty headcount will increase (fall) if real income declines (rises) by 1 percent. Exchange rate is the average dollar exchange rate at the time of survey.

Table A5. Poverty Headcount Calculations Based on the Original Income Distribution Statistics Given in Appendix 4
All in per capita terms

Country [Poverty line]	Survey period	Poverty headcount (in %)	Average shortfall	Elasticity	Gini	Exchange rate	Poverty line ($ pm)	Average per capita income ($ pm)
Income-based Measures								
Poland [7,265]	1987 A	5.7	19.5	0.25	25.6	265	27	62
Poland [880,650]	1993 6 months	19.9	26.9	0.45	28.4	17,300	51	89
Hungary [17,256]	1987 A	0.5	32.1	0.02	21.0	47.0	31	95
Hungary [63,384]	1993 A	4.0	25.2	0.16	22.6	92.0	57	127
Czech [501]	1988 A	0.02	13.0	0.00	19.4	14.3	35	130
Czech [931]	January 1993 M	0.1	24.2	0.005	26.6	28.8	32	122

Country [Poverty line]	Survey period	Poverty headcount (in %)	Average shortfall	Elasticity	Gini	Exchange rate	Poverty line ($ pm)	Average per capita income ($ pm)
CSSR [501]	1988 A	0.05	26.3	0.0	19.5	14.3	35	129
Slovakia [13,428]	1993 A	0.12	19.6	0.01	18.3	30.9	36	100
Bulgaria [900]	1989 A	1.4	31.7	0.05	23.3	2.2	34	98
Bulgaria [10,080]	1993 A	14.6	25.8	0.32	34.3	27.6	30	71
Romania [783]	1989A	5.8	15.0	0.22	23.3	73	11	25
Romania [45,504]	March 1994 M	59	32	0.7	28.6	1601	28	29

(Continued on the following page)

Table A5. (Continued)

Country [Poverty line]	Survey period	Poverty headcount (in %)	Average shortfall	Elasticity	Gini	Exchange rate	Poverty line ($ pm)	Average per capita income ($ pm)
Slovenia [351,000]	1987A	0.07	46.3	0.00	21.5	373	78	401
Slovenia [99,096]	1993 A	0.3	30.8	0.01	25.1	113.2	73	293
Russia [54]	1988 A	1.5	22.3	0.07	23.8	2.2	25	72
Russia [21,496]	3Q/1993 (July prices)	49.7	39.6	0.57	48.0	1,025	21	32
Ukraine [54]	1988 A	1.9	21.7	0.09	23.3	2.2	25	65
Ukraine [2.988 million]	June and 1 week of July 1995; (June prices)	62.9	46.7	0.51	47.4	142,000	21	24

Country [Poverty line]	Survey period	Poverty headcount (in %)	Average shortfall	Elasticity	Gini	Exchange rate	Poverty line ($ pm)	Average per capita income ($ pm)
Belarus [54]	1988 A	1.1	23.7	0.05	22.8	2.2	25	71
Belarus [219,485]	1Q/1995 (March prices)	22.3	25.6	0.53	28.4	11,525	19	32
Moldova [54]	1988 A	3.5	8.2	0.22	24.1	2.2	25	61
Moldova [21]	1993 A	65.9	43.4	0.55	36.5	1.6	13	12
Estonia [54]	1988 A	0.9	23.5	0.04	23.0	2.2	25	81
Estonia [664]	3Q/1995 (July prices)	37.2	37.1	0.7	35.4	11.1	60	86

(Continued on the following page)

Table A5. (Continued)

Country [Poverty line]	Survey period	Poverty headcount (in %)	Average shortfall	Elasticity	Gini	Exchange rate	Poverty line ($ pm)	Average per capita income ($ pm)
Latvia [54]	1988 A	0.7	22.5	0.03	22.5	2.2	25	78
Latvia [31]	4Q/1995	21.7	27.6	0.49	31.0	0.536	58	101
Lithuania [54]	1988 A	0.8	24.0	0.04	22.5	2.2	25	75
Lithuania [1,260]	1994 A	29.8	33.6	0.48	37.3	4	26	46
Kazakhstan [54]	1988 A	4.6	8.9	0.27	25.7	2.2	25	61
Kazakhstan [26,530]	1993 A	64.9	38.7	0.66	32.7	1,168	23	22

Country [Poverty line]	Survey period	Poverty headcount (in %)	Average shortfall	Elasticity	Gini	Exchange rate	Poverty line ($ pm)	Average per capita income ($ pm)
Uzbekistan [55]	1989 A	23.8	19.8	0.60	28.2	3.4	16	28
Uzbekistan [10,150]	1993 A	62.6	38.9	0.64	33.3	951	11	11
Kyrgyzstan [54]	1988 A	12.0	10.4	0.59	26.0	2.2	25	47
Kyrgyz [111]	Oct-Nov. 1993 (October prices)	88.0	68.0	0.20	55.3	7	16	9
Turkmenistan [54]	1988 A	11.8	10.1	0.60	26.4	2.2	25	47
Turkmenistan [29,329]	1993 A	60.9	40.0	0.61	35.8	892	33	34

(Continued on the following page)

Table A5. (Continued)

Expenditure-based Measures

Country [Poverty line]	Survey period	Poverty headcount (in %)	Average shortfall	Elasticity	Gini	Exchange rate	Poverty line ($ pm)	Average per capita income ($ pm)
Poland [880,650]	1993 6 months	9.8	19.9	0.36	30.6	17,300	51	116
Romania [45,504]	March 1994 M	47.6	33.8	0.72	32.8	1601	28	35
Estonia [664]	Jul-Sept. 95 (July prices)	33.7	28.4		30.7	11.1	60	87
Russia [21,496]	3Q/1993 (July prices)	39.4	43.8	0.44	49.6	1025	21	39
Ukraine [2.988 million]	June and 1 week of July 1995 (June prices)	25.7	37.2	0.35	43.8	142,000	21	50

190

Country [Poverty line]	Survey period	Poverty headcount (in %)	Average shortfall	Elasticity	Gini	Exchange rate	Poverty line ($ pm)	Average per capita income ($ pm)
Hungary [63,384]	1993	6.7	20.1	0.29	27.0	92.0	57	127
Belarus [219,485]	1Q/1995	14.5	22.8	0.37	29.6	11,525	19	39
Kyrgyz [111]	Oct-Nov. 1993 (October prices)	54.9	46.0	0.50	43.3	7	16	19

Appendix 6

Distribution of International Funds Based on Minimization of Deprivation Function

Country	Percentage of funds
Balkans and Poland	*6.1*
Poland	1.2
Bulgaria	0.6
Romania	4.3
Central Europe	*0.1*
Hungary	0.1
Czech Republic	0.0
Slovak Republic	0.0
Slovenia	0
Baltics	*0.8*
Lithuania	0.3
Latvia	0.1
Estonia	0.4
Slavic and Moldova	*76.2*
Russian Federation	46.0
Ukraine	27.7
Belarus	0.9
Moldova	1.6
Central Asia	*16.8*
Kazakhstan	7.7
Kyrgyz Republic	4.3
Turkmenistan	2.1
Uzbekistan	2.8

Note: Total funds = 100. Based on "adjusted" *HBS* data (*INCOME2*).

Appendix 7

Sources for Table 1.2

Privatization: Czech Republic, Hungary, Estonia, and Lithuania (by value of assets): *World Development Report 1996*, first draft, Chapter 3, Table 3.2. Hungary: Prime Minister Gyula Horn's press conference in February 1995 (by value of assets: out of Ft. 2 billion worth of state property, Ft. 0.43 billion privatized). Belarus: G. Lych, "Belrus' na outi k rynochney ekonomike," *Voprosy ekonomiki*, No. 10, 1995, p. 88 (by number of enterprises). Poland: percent of all employed working in newly privatized firms (which used to be SOEs) at the end of 1993 as reported in World Bank Country Assistance Strategy Paper, July 1, 1994. Kazakhstan: *Kazakhstan, The Transition to a Market Economy*, World Bank report 1993, p.80 (in August 1992; by book value of capital). Russia: Minister of Finance Anatoly Chubais' press conference June 30, 1994 as reported by Interfax (percentage of industrial enterprises that have been privatized). Ukraine: *Journal of Commerce*, 14 December 1994. Kyrgyz Republic: presentation by Cevdet Denizer at the World Bank, Policy Research Department, June 1995.

Non-state sector employment: Hungary: *Statistical Yearbook 1995*, p. 239. Latvia: *Monthly Bulletin of Latvian Statistics*, July 1997, p. 45. Bulgaria: *Statistical Yearbook 1996*, p. 77. Poland: *Statistical Yearbook 1996*, p. 351. Czech Republic: *Statistical Yearbook 1996*, p. 262. Slovakia: *Statistical Yearbook of Slovakia 1993*, p.144 (includes both private and mixed sectors). Russia: *Russia in Figures 1997*, Moscow: Goskomstat, 1997, p. 34. Belarus: *Short Statistical Yearbook 1997*, p. 42 (excludes employment in kolkhozes). Ukraine, Moldova, Turkmenistan, Uzbekistan, and Kyrgyz Republic: *CIS 1995 Statistical Yearbook*, p. 18 (includes both private and mixed sectors: Ukraine 26 and 7, Moldova 60 and 6, Uzbekistan 57 and 6, Turkmenistan 52, Kyrgyzstan 64 and 3). Kazakhstan: *Statistical Yearbook 1995*, p.25. Romania: *Statistical Yearbook 1996*, p.142. Slovenia: IMF, "Slovenia: Recent Economic Developments", August 21, 1995.

Retail trade privatization: Czech Republic: Roundtable: Privatization in Eastern Europe, edited by Ben Slay, *RFE/RL Research Report*, 13 August 1993. Slovakia: *Statistička Revue Slovenskej Republiky*, Bratislava, No.2, 1996, p.19. Romania: *Monthly Bulletin of Statistics*, May 1994, p. 7. Ukraine, Uzbekistan, Kyrgyz republic, Russia, Moldova, Kazakhstan and Belarus: *CIS Statistical Bulletin*, September 1997, No. 18 (178), pp. 88-89 (includes only private sector and consumer cooperatives). Turkmenistan: *OMRI Daily News*, February 6, 1997. Lithuania: *Statistical Yearbook 1996*, p. 416. Latvia: *Monthly Bulletin of Latvian Statistics*, July 1997, p. 124. Estonia: *RFE/RL Daily report*, December 30, 1993. Romania: *Statistical Yearbook 1996*, p. 659. Bulgaria: *Statistical Refer-*

ence Book of the Republic of Bulgaria 1995, National Statistical Institute, Sofia, 1995, p.16.

Current account convertibility: IMF Annual Report 1996, Washington:IMF, 1996, p.12.

Subsidies: Hungary: *Monthly Bulletin of Statistics,* No.5, 1996, p.73. Lithuania: *Statistical Yearbook 1996,* p. 94. Latvia: personal communication by Mansour Farsad, World Bank country economist. Ukraine, Final 1996 budget numbers reported by *IntelNews Daily Dispatch,* Kiev and Baltimore, March 17, 1997. Estonia: *IMF Economic Review,* No.4, p.58. Bulgaria: *An Economic Assessment,* OECD, 1992, p.15. Belarus: personal communication by Chandrashekar Pant, World Bank country economist for Belarus. Poland: *Biuletin Statystyczny,* Warsaw:GUS, July 1996, p. 55. Romania, Russia and Kazakhstan: IMF, Expenditure Policy Division Staff, "Social Safety Nets for Economic Transition: Options and Recent Experience", February 1995, Table 2, p.16, mimeo. Slovenia: personal communication by Milan Vodopivec, Research department, World Bank. Bulgaria and Slovakia: Ke-young Chu and Gerd Schwartz, "Output Decline and Government Expenditures in European Transition Economies," *IMF Working paper,* June 1994, p. 13. Czech Republic: IMF, "Czech republic: Recent Economic Developments," IMF, November 13, 1996, p. 91. Turkmenistan: J. Braithwaite: "Social Welfare and Income Distribution in Four FSU countries", Table 5, processed. Moldova: personal communication by K. Gilbertson, World Bank country economist for Moldova.

Inflation: within-the-year (December-on-December) increase.

Country Data Sheets

The following Country Data Sheets present economic and social data from 1987 to 1996 for four countries: Russia, Ukraine, Poland, and Latvia. The same data have been collected for the other fourteen transition economies covered in this book. They are not included here to save space, but can be obtained from author on request.

Branko Milanovic, World Bank
1818 H Street N.W., Washington, D.C. 20433, USA.
E-mail: bmilanovic@worldbank.org

Abbreviations Used

CPI = Consumer price index
COL = Cost of living index
GDP = Gross domestic product
HH = Household(s)
HBS = Household budget survey
p.m. or pm = per month
p.a. = *per annum*
p.c. or pc = per capita
PL = Poverty line
UEB = Unemployment benefit(s)

Russia

Years	1987	1988	1989	1990	1991	1992	1993	1994	1995	1996
Currency	ruble	ruble	ruble	ruble	ruble	ruble	ruble	ruble	ruble	ruble

NOMINAL TERMS

STANDARD OF LIVING (yearly average)

Household survey data
Average per capita income
by social group (per month) [1]

	1987	1988	1989	1990	1991	1992	1993	1994	1995	1996
Workers (from 94 = urban)	152	164	176	198	400	3,950	38,600	145,600	322,700	454,000
Farmers (from 94 = rural)	127	143	148	175	344	1,900	19,000	78,100	174,200	244,000
Pensioners				117	229	1,862	23,188	88,774	217,345	
Mixed										
Overall	146	164	178	197	397	3,300	35,400	119,800	284,200	397,300

Macro data
Average per capita income
by social group (per month)
Workers
Farmers
Pensioners
Mixed

	1987	1988	1989	1990	1991	1992	1993	1994	1995	1996
Overall	146	184	198	215	466	3,979	43,906	207,785	533,252	779,000
Average wage (pm; incl. soc. benef)	214	233	263	303	557	6,011	59,204	217,886	484,542	802,742
Average pension (pm)	80	83	87	102	266	1,613	20,536	79,162	183,533	302,275
Pension:wage (percent)	37.4	35.6	33.1	33.7	47.8	26.8	34.7	36.3	37.9	37.7

Poverty threshold (per month)

	1987	1988	1989	1990	1991	1992	1993	1994	1995	1996
Minimum wage	70	70	70	70	130	714	5,962	17,560	41,071	72,700
Minimum pension	60	60	60	70	161	1,102	11,328	40,669	89,632	
(A) Per capita PL (all population) [2]	75	75	83	100	220	1,893	20,562	86,431	264,150	369,417
Per capita PL (for a family of 4)			54	61	154	1,895	16,462			
PL for 1 adult (at free market price)	82	84	87	93	190	1,893				

Poverty threshold (A) as % of

	1987	1988	1989	1990	1991	1992	1993	1994	1995	1996
Average wage	35.0	32.2	31.6	33.0	39.5	31.5	34.7	39.7	54.5	46.0
Average pension	93.8	90.4	95.4	98.0	82.7	117.4	100.1	109.2	143.9	122.2
Average income per capita for all HHs (survey data)	51.4	45.7	46.6	50.9	55.4	57.4	58.1	72.1	92.9	93.0

STRUCTURE OF INCOME (absolute nominal values; yearly average)

Household survey data (pc per month)

	1989	1990	1991	1992	1993	1994	1995
Labor income (wages and salaries)	128	149	271	2,737	20,532	55,587	111,691
Social transfers	30	23	63	486	6,089	20,845	47,461
Pensions	14						
Family and child allowances	3						
Other social transfers	3						
Private sector income (incl. agro) [3]	7	9	29	375	2,623	4,672	7,673
Other income (including in-kind)	13	16	34	352	6,156	38,695	49,477
TOTAL INCOME	178	197	397	3,950	35,400	119,800	284,200

Russia (continued)

Years	1987	1988	1989	1990	1991	1992	1993	1994	1995	1996
Currency	ruble	ruble	ruble	ruble	ruble	ruble	ruble	ruble	ruble	ruble

NOMINAL TERMS (continued)

Macro data: all HHs (bn per year)

	1987	1988	1989	1990	1991	1992	1993	1994	1995	1996
Labor income (wages and salaries)	203	221	252	293	519	5,121	48,274	169,152	344,201	573,000
Wages paid by cooperatives		2	12	19	21	71	4,583			
Social benefits	39	42	44	50	129	994	11,845	63,506	116,299	175,830
Pensions				48	125	960	11,595	47,859	85,078	125,346
Family and child allowances										
Other soc. tran. (incl. stipends)	2	2	2	2	5	34	250	810		
Private sector income (incl. agro)	7	8	10	14	34	280	4,151	11,342		
Financial income (interest, insurance)	10	11	11	17	119	185	4,050	30,854		
Other income	5	6	8	9	29	520	11,629	89,283	450,246	597,991
Total money income	264	287	325	383	830	7,100	79,949	364,137	910,746	1,346,821
Income in kind										
TOTAL INCOME	264	287	325	383	830	7,100	79,949	364,137	910,746	1,346,821
TOTAL INCOME P.C. (per month)	151	163	183	215	465	3,980	44,875	204,688	533,267	756,301

UNEMPLOYMENT (thousand persons; yearly average)

	1987	1988	1989	1990	1991	1992	1993	1994	1995	1996
Number of registered unemployed					44	272	728	1,286	2,041	2,832
Structure of the unemployed										
Number of women						196			1,400	
Number of young (15-24 years)						85	221	357		
Number with higher education						29	75	135		
Number of those receiving UEB					7	155	473	1,068	1,737	
Those with UEB in total unemployed (%)					15.7	57.2	64.9	83.1	85.1	

GOVERNMENT SOCIAL EXPENDITURES (absolute nominal values; bn per year)

	1987	1988	1989	1990	1991	1992	1993	1994	1995	1996
Pensions	30.9	32.5	34.6	41.4	67.9	757	10,312	36,848	85,078	125,346
Family allowances	8.4	9.3	11.4	12.3	11.6	54	1,029	4,411	1,199	19,458
Child allowances (paid by SIF)					3.1	2				
Sick leave (paid by SIF) [4/]							1,624	6,630	17,458	18,151
Unemployment benefits [5/]					0.2	8	141	908	3,519	3,708
Other: scholarships, bread subsidies, social assistance					1.5	211	1,887	9,326		
Education	16.8	18.4	19.7	22.3	50	679	6,918	27,453	56,400	
Health	10.1	11.2	12.6	14.7	34	468	5,415	19,707	40,400	
Estimate of enterprise-financed benefits			7.9		68	472				

GENERAL MACRO DATA

	1987	1988	1989	1990	1991	1992	1993	1994	1995	1996
Cost of living index (1987=100) [6/]	100.0	101.0	107.0	114.0	233	4,050	40,384	171,385	497,493	738,078
GDP or GNP nominal (bn)	496	531	573	644	1,399	19,201	171,510	630,111	1,658,900	2,256,000
GDP or GNP real in 1987 (bn)	496	523	537	526	500	427	390	341	326	307
Real growth rate (%)		5.6	2.5	-2.0	-5.0	-14.5	-8.7	-12.6	-4.3	-6.0
Exchange rate (per US$1)										
Official rate	0.6	0.6	0.6	0.6	30.0	190.0	928	2,204	4,562	5,152
Market rate	4.2	5.5	8.9	18.8	58.7	222	928	2,131	4,562	5,152
"Actual" rate	1.8	2.2	3.4	6.7	30.0	190	928	2,131	4,562	5,152
Number of persons receiving pensions (thousands)	32,224	32,637	33,155	33,813	35,043	36,395	37,138	36,300	37,000	37,500
Total population (thousands)	145,908	146,857	147,621	148,255	148,704	148,673	148,465	148,249	148,306	148,400
Pensioners as % of total population	22.1	22.2	22.5	22.8	23.6	24.5	25.0	24.5	25.0	25.3

Russia (continued)

Years	1987	1988	1989	1990	1991	1992	1993	1994	1995	1996
Currency	ruble	ruble	ruble	ruble	ruble	ruble	ruble	ruble	ruble	ruble

REAL TERMS (deflated by the cost of living index)

STANDARD OF LIVING (1987 rubles; yearly average)

	1987	1988	1989	1990	1991	1992	1993	1994	1995	1996
Household survey data										
Average per capita income										
by social group (per month) [1]										
Workers	152	162	164	174	172	98	96	85	65	62
Farmers	127	142	138	154	148	47	47	46	35	33
Pensioners				103	98	46	57	52	44	
Mixed										
Overall	146	162	166	172	170	81	88	70	57	54
Macro data										
Average per capita income										
by social group (per month)										
Workers										
Farmers										
Pensioners										
Mixed										
Overall	146	182	185	189	200	98	109	121	107	106
Average wage (per month)	214	231	246	266	239	148	147	127	97	109
Average pension (per month)	80	82	81	89	114	40	51	46	37	41
Poverty threshold (per month)										
Minimum wage	70	69	65	61	56	18	15	10	8	
Minimum pension	60	59	56	61	69	27	28	24	18	
(A) Per capita PL (all population) [2]	75	74	78	88	94	47	51	50	53	50
Per capita PL (for a family of 4)			50	54	66	47	41			
PL for 1 adult (at free market prices)	82	83	81	82	82	47				

STRUCTURE OF INCOME (1987 rubles; yearly average)

	1987	1988	1989	1990	1991	1992	1993	1994	1995	1996
Household survey data (pc per month)										
Labor income (wages and salaries)			120	131	116	68	51	32	22	
Social transfers			28	20	27	12	15	12	10	
Pensions			13							
Family and child allowances			2							
Other social transfers			3							
Private sector income (incl. agro) [3]			6	8	12	9	6	3	2	
Other income (including in-kind)			12	14	14	9	15	23	10	
Total private			19	21	27	18	22	25	11	
TOTAL INCOME			166	172	170	98	88	70	43	
Macro data: all HHs (bn per year)										
Labor income (wages and salaries)	203	218	235	257	223	126	120	99	69	78
Wages paid by cooperatives		2	11	17	9	2	11			
Social benefits	39	41	41	44	55	25	29	37	23	24
Pensions				42	54	24	29	28	17	17
Family and child allowances										
Other soc. tran. (incl. stipends)	2	2	1	1	2	1	1	0		
Private sector income (incl. agro)	7	8	9	13	15	7	10	7		
Financial income (interest, insurance)	10	11	11	15	51	5	10	18		
Other income	5	6	7	8	12	13	29	52	91	81
Total money income	264	284	303	336	356	175	198	212	183	182
Income in kind										
TOTAL INCOME	264	284	303	336	356	175	198	212	183	182
TOTAL INCOME P.C. (per month)	151	161	171	189	200	98	111	119	107	102

Russia (continued)

Years	1987	1988	1989	1990	1991	1992	1993	1994	1995	1996
Currency	ruble	ruble	ruble	ruble	ruble	ruble	ruble	ruble	ruble	ruble

REAL TERMS (deflated by the cost of living index) (continued)

GOVERNMENT SOCIAL EXPENDITURES (1987 rubles; bn per year)

	1987	1988	1989	1990	1991	1992	1993	1994	1995	1996
Pensions	30.9	32.2	32.3	36.3	29.1	18.7	25.5	21.5	17.1	17.0
Family allowances	8.4	9.2	10.7	10.8	5.0	1.3	2.5	2.6	0.2	2.6
Child allowances (paid by SIF)										
Sick leave (paid by SIF) [4]					1.3	0.1				
Unemployment benefits [5]							4.0	3.9	3.5	2.5
Other: scholarships, bread subsidies,					0.1	0.2	0.3	0.5	0.7	0.5
social assistance					0.6	5.2	4.7	5.4		
TOTAL CASH TRANSFERS	39.3	41.4	43.0	47.1	36.2	25.5	37.1	33.9	21.6	22.6
Education	16.8	18.2	18.4	19.6	21.5	16.8	17.1	16.0	11.3	
Health	10.1	11.1	11.8	12.9	14.5	11.6	13.4	11.5	8.1	
TOTAL IN-KIND TRANSFERS	26.9	29.3	30.2	32.5	36.0	28.3	30.5	27.5	19.5	
Estimate of enterprise-financed benefits				7.4	29.0	11.6				
TOTAL TRANSFERS	66.2	70.7	80.6	79.6	101.2	65.4	67.7	61.4	41.0	

Russia (continued)

Years	1987	1988	1989	1990	1991	1992	1993	1994	1995	1996
Currency	ruble	ruble	ruble	ruble	ruble	ruble	ruble	ruble	ruble	ruble

PERCENT OF GDP

GOVERNMENT SOCIAL EXPENDITURES

	1987	1988	1989	1990	1991	1992	1993	1994	1995	1996
Pensions	6.2	6.1	6.0	6.4	4.8	3.9	6.0	5.8	5.1	5.6
Family allowances	1.7	1.8	2.0	1.9	0.8	0.3	0.6	0.7	0.1	0.9
Child allowances					0.2	0.01				
Sick leave							0.9	1.1	1.1	0.8
Unemployment benefits					0.01	0.04	0.1	0.1	0.2	0.2
Other: scholarships, bread subsidies, social assistance					0.1	1.1	1.1	1.5		
TOTAL CASH TRANSFERS	7.9	7.9	8.0	8.3	6.0	5.4	8.7	9.2	6.5	7.4
Education	3.4	3.5	3.4	3.5	3.6	3.5	4.0	4.4	3.4	
Health	2.0	2.1	2.2	2.3	2.4	2.4	3.2	3.1	2.4	
TOTAL IN-KIND TRANSFERS	5.4	5.6	5.6	5.7	6.0	6.0	7.2	7.5	5.8	
Estimate of enterprise-financed benefits			1.4		4.8	2.5				
TOTAL TRANSFERS	13.4	13.4	15.0	14.1	16.8	13.8	15.9	16.7	12.3	

STRUCTURE OF INCOME (macro)

	1987	1988	1989	1990	1991	1992	1993	1994	1995	1996
Labor income	41.0	41.5	44.0	45.5	37.1	26.7	28.1	26.8	20.7	25.4
Social benefits	7.9	7.9	8.0	8.3	6.0	5.4	8.7	9.2	6.5	7.4
Total private income	4.4	4.7	5.0	6.3	13.0	5.1	11.6	20.9	27.1	26.5
TOTAL PERSONAL INCOME	53.3	54.1	57.0	60.1	56.1	37.2	48.5	56.9	54.4	59.3
Health and education	5.4	5.6	5.6	5.7	6.0	6.0	7.2	7.5	5.8	
TOTAL (inc. health and education)	58.7	59.6	62.7	65.8	62.1	43.1	55.6	64.4	60.2	

Russia (continued)

Years	1987	1988	1989	1990	1991	1992	1993	1994	1995	1996
Currency	$	$	$	$	$	$	$	$	$	$

DOLLARS

STANDARD OF LIVING (nominal values; yearly average)

Household survey data
Average per capita income
by social group (per month)

	1987	1988	1989	1990	1991	1992	1993	1994	1995	1996
Workers	84	73	52	30	13	21	42	68	71	88
Farmers	71	64	44	26	11	10	20	37	38	47
Pensioners				18	8	10	25	42	48	
Mixed										
Overall	81	73	52	30	13	17	38	56	62	77

Macro data
Average per capita income
by social group (per month)

Workers										
Farmers										
Pensioners										
Mixed										
Overall	81	82	58	32	16	21	47	98	117	151
Average wage (per month)	119	104	78	46	19	32	64	102	106	156
Average pension (per month)	44	37	26	15	9	8	22	37	40	59

Poverty threshold (per month)

Minimum wage	39	31	21	11	4	4	6	8	9	
Minimum pension	33	27	18	11	5	6	12	19	20	
(A) Per capita PL (all population) 2/	42	33	24	15	7	10	22	41	58	72
Per capita PL (for a family of 4)				16	9	5	10	18		
PL for 1 adult (at free market price)	46	37	26	14	6	10				
GDP (bn per year)	275	237	169	97	47	101	185	296	364	438
GDP per capita per year	1,887	1,614	1,144	653	314	680	1,245	1,995	2,452	2,950
GDP per capita per month	157	135	95	54	26	57	104	166	204	246

NOTE:
SIF = Social insurance fund.

1/ HBS data for 1985 used instead of data for 1987.
2/ New lower (Ministry of Labor) minimum adopted in November 1992.
3/ 1994 and ff. includes entrepreneurial income.
4/ Years 1993-95 include child allowances too.
5/ UEB + early retirement + financial aid.
6/ Cost of living index = retail price index for consumer goods.

Ukraine

Years	1987	1988	1989	1990	1991	1992	1993	1994	1995	1996
Currency	ruble	ruble	ruble	ruble	ruble	ruble	karbov.	karbov.	karbov.	hryvna

NOMINAL TERMS

STANDARD OF LIVING (yearly average)

Household survey data
  Average per capita income
  by social group (per month)

Workers	154	162	174	196	377					
Farmers	131	136	151	171	323					
Pensioners	99	105	119	136	280					
Mixed										
Overall	148	149	162	182	349	3,722			5,966,000	

Macro data
  Average per capita income
  by social group (per month)
    Workers
    Farmers
    Pensioners
    Mixed

Overall	127	138	153	176	329	3,788	100,860	861,753	3,864,375	63.9
Average wage (pm; incl. soc. benef)	185	200	218	248	476	6,458	163,100	1,437,700	8,184,000	154
Average pension (pm)	73	75	85	104	210	2,119	75,181	500,000	2,350,000	50
Pension:wage (percent)	40	38	39	42	44	33	46	35	29	32

Poverty threshold (per month)

Minimum wage					100	119	967	13,642		
Minimum pension										
(A) Per capita PL (all population) 1/	75	75	83	100	220	2,846		698,892	3,443,250	
Per capita PL (for a family of 4)						2,874				
Minimum consumption basket				96	100	4,038	194,842			

Poverty threshold (A) as % of

Average wage	40.5	37.5	38.1	40.3	46.2	44.1		48.6	42.1	
Average pension	102.6	99.7	97.4	96.5	104.7	134.3		139.8	146.5	
Average income per capita from macro data	58.9	54.3	54.3	56.7	66.8	75.1		81.1	89.1	

STRUCTURE OF INCOME (absolute nominal values; yearly average)

Household survey data (pc per month)

Labor income (wages and salaries)	101	104	109	123	205	2,230			2,547,482	
Social transfers	13	12	21	24	67	387			530,974	
Pensions										
Family and child allowances										
Other social transfers										
Private sector income (incl. agro)	17	16	16	19	40	730			1,903,154	
Other income (including in-kind)	11	11	16	16	37	380			996,322	
TOTAL INCOME	141	143	162	182	349	3,726			5,977,932	

Ukraine (continued)

Years	1987	1988	1989	1990	1991	1992	1993	1994	1995	1996
Currency	ruble	ruble	ruble	ruble	ruble	ruble	karbov.	karbov.	karbov.	hryvna

NOMINAL TERMS (continued)

Macro data: all HHs (bn per year)

	1987	1988	1989	1990	1991	1992	1993	1994	1995	1996
Labor income (wages and salaries)	56	61	68	78	135	1,648	35,956	337,677	1,549,129	23.8
Wages paid by cooperatives	0	0	2	3	3	69	1,566			
Social benefits	13	14	15	16	41	418	13,981	106,772	486,907	8.7
Pensions [2/]	11	11	12	13	29	361	13,684	104,180	477,161	
Family and child allowances	2	2	2	3	11	5				
Other soc. tran. (incl. stipends)	0	1	1	1	1	15	297	2,592	9,746	
Private sector income (incl. agro)	4	4	5	6	12	72	2,523	13,651	66,845	1.4
Financial income (interest, insurance)	3	4	4	5	7	32	1,452	10,355		4.8
Other income	3	3	4	3	14	196	9,320	70,458	266,754	0.2
Total money income	79	86	95	108	208	2,366	63,232	538,913	2,369,635	38.8
Income in kind										
TOTAL INCOME	79	86	95	108	208	2,366	63,232	538,913	2,369,635	38.8
TOTAL INCOME P.C. (per month)	129	139	154	174	334	3,788	100,860	861,753	3,864,375	63.9

UNEMPLOYMENT (thousand persons; yearly average)

	1987	1988	1989	1990	1991	1992	1993	1994	1995	1996
Number of registered unemployed					7.0	70.5	77.9	93.8	114.6	280.2
Structure of the unemployed										
Number of women										
Number of young (15-24 years)										
Number with higher education						16.8	26.0			
Number of those receiving UEB					5.2	52.5	40.0	47.4	57.1	140.8
Those with UEB in total unemployed (%)					74.3	74.5	51.4	50.5	49.8	50.3

GOVERNMENT SOCIAL EXPENDITURES (absolute nominal values; bn per year)

	1987	1988	1989	1990	1991	1992	1993	1994	1995	1996
Pensions	10.6	11.3	12.1	12.6	28.5	361	11,447	81,781	419,727	7.0
Maternity, birth all.	0.1	0.1	0.1	0.4	0.5	5	130	1,180		
Child allowances	0.5	0.5	0.5	0.6	3.7	26	352	2,259		
Sick leave	1.1	1.2	1.3	1.5	2.2	26	1,002	11,003		
Unemployment benefits					0.1	11	241	3,300		
SA, rehab. vouchers, Chernobyl, stipends	0.5	0.5	0.5	0.5	4.4	55	1,217	13,842	33,300	1.5
Education	6.0	6.5	6.8	7.5	18.3	281	7,236	70,199	316,985	
Health	3.1	3.4	3.8	4.4	17.4	199	6,014	58,979	262,498	

Estimate of enterprise-financed benefits

GENERAL MACRO DATA

	1987	1988	1989	1990	1991	1992	1993	1994	1995	1996
Cost of living index (1987=100)	100	100	103	109	246	3,493	182,225	1,769,659	8,415,373	152
GDP or GNP nominal (bn)	136	142	154	167	299	5,033	158,273	1,203,769	5,451,000	80
GDP or GNP real in 1987 (bn)	136	140	146	141	129	116	100	81	72	65
Real growth rate (%)		2.7	4.5	-3.8	-8.4	-9.7	-14.2	-19.0	-11.4	-9.0
Exchange rate (per US$1)										
Official rate	0.6	0.6	0.6	0.6	30.0	163	4,796	31,663		
Market rate	4.2	5.5	8.9	18.8	58.7	319	9,508	62,306	155,319	1.8
"Actual" rate	1.8	2.2	3.4	6.7	30.0	241	7,152	46,984	155,319	1.8
Number of persons receiving pensions (thousands)	12,432	12,853	12,748	13,084	13,568	14,191	14,477	14,515	14,500	14,488
Total population (thousands)	51,293	51,521	51,750	51,860	51,944	52,057	52,244	52,114	51,100	50,600
Pensioners as % of total population	24.2	24.9	24.6	25.2	26.1	27.3	27.7	27.9	28.4	28.6

Ukraine (continued)

Years	1987	1988	1989	1990	1991	1992	1993	1994	1995	1996
Currency	ruble	ruble	ruble	ruble	ruble	ruble	karbov.	karbov.	karbov.	hryvna

REAL TERMS (deflated by the cost of living index)

STANDARD OF LIVING (1987 rubles; yearly average)

Household survey data
Average per capita income
by social group (per month)

	1987	1988	1989	1990	1991	1992	1993	1994	1995	1996
Workers	154	162	168	179	153					
Farmers	131	136	146	156	132					
Pensioners				124	114					
Mixed										
Overall	148	149	157	167	142	107			71	

Macro data
Average per capita income
by social group (per month)

	1987	1988	1989	1990	1991	1992	1993	1994	1995	1996
Workers										
Farmers										
Pensioners										
Mixed										
Overall	127	138	148	161	134	108	55	49	46	42
Average wage (pm; incl. soc. benef.)	185	199	211	227	194	185	90	81	97	102
Average pension (per month)	73	75	82	95	86	61	41	28	28	33

Poverty threshold (per month)

	1987	1988	1989	1990	1991	1992	1993	1994	1995	1996
Minimum wage				91	49	28	7			
Minimum pension										
(A) Per capita PL (all population) 1/	75	75	80	91	90	81		39	41	
Per capita PL (for a family of 4)						82				
Minimum consumption basket			93	92		116	107			

STRUCTURE OF INCOME (1987 rubles; yearly average)

Household survey data (pc per month)

	1987	1988	1989	1990	1991	1992	1993	1994	1995	1996
Labor income (wages and salaries)	101	104	105	112	83	64			30	
Social transfers	13	12	20	22	27	11			6	
Pensions										
Family and child allowances										
Other social transfers										
Private sector income (incl. agro)	17	16	16	17	16	21			23	
Other income (including in-kind)	11	11	16	15	15	11			12	
Total private	28	27	31	32	31	32			34	
TOTAL INCOME	141	143	157	167	142	107			71	

Macro data: all HHs (bn per year)

	1987	1988	1989	1990	1991	1992	1993	1994	1995	1996
Labor income (wages and salaries)	56.4	61.2	66.2	71.2	55.1	47.2	19.7	19.1	18.4	15.7
Wages paid by cooperatives		0.4	2.4	3.1	1.4	2.0	0.9			
Social benefits	13.4	14.2	14.5	14.3	16.6	12.0	7.7	6.0	5.8	5.7
Pensions 2/	10.6	11.3	11.7	11.5	11.6	10.3	7.5	5.9	5.7	
Family and child allowances	2.3	2.4	2.3	2.3	4.4	0.2				
Other soc. tran. (incl. stipends)	0.5	0.5	0.5	0.5	0.6	0.4	0.2	0.1	0.1	
Private sector income (incl. agro)	3.7	3.7	4.4	5.4	4.8	2.1	1.4	0.8	0.8	0.9
Financial income (interest, insurance)	3.3	3.6	3.6	5.0	2.7	0.9	0.8	0.6		3.2
Other income	2.7	3.1	3.5	3.2	5.5	5.6	5.1	4.0	3.2	0.1
Total money income	79.4	85.7	92.3	99.0	84.7	67.8	34.7	30.5	28.2	25.6
Income in kind										
TOTAL INCOME	79.4	85.7	92.3	99.0	84.7	67.8	34.7	30.5	28.2	25.6
TOTAL INCOME P.C. (per month)	129	139	149	159	136	108	55	49	46	42

Ukraine (continued)

Years Currency	1987 ruble	1988 ruble	1989 ruble	1990 ruble	1991 ruble	1992 ruble	1993 karbov.	1994 karbov.	1995 karbov.	1996 hryvna

REAL TERMS (deflated by the cost of living index; continued)

GOVERNMENT SOCIAL EXPENDITURES (1987 rubles; bn per year)

	1987	1988	1989	1990	1991	1992	1993	1994	1995	1996
Pensions	10.6	11.3	11.7	11.5	11.6	10.3	6.3	4.6	5.0	4.6
Maternity, birth all.	0.1	0.1	0.1	0.4	0.2	0.2	0.1	0.1		
Child allowances	0.5	0.5	0.5	0.5	1.5	0.7	0.2	0.1		
Sick leave	1.1	1.2	1.3	1.4	0.9	0.8	0.5	0.6		
Unemployment benefits					0.04	0.3	0.1	0.2		
SA, rehab. vouchers, Chernobyl, stipends	0.5	0.5	0.5	0.5	1.8	1.6	0.7	0.8	0.4	1.0
TOTAL CASH TRANSFERS	12.8	13.6	14.0	14.3	16.1	13.8	7.9	6.4	5.4	5.6
Education	6.0	6.5	6.6	6.9	7.5	8.0	4.0	4.0	3.8	
Health	3.1	3.4	3.7	4.0	7.1	5.7	3.3	3.3	3.1	
TOTAL IN-KIND TRANSFERS	9.1	9.9	10.3	10.9	14.5	13.7	7.3	7.3	6.9	
Estimate of enterprise-financed benefits										
TOTAL TRANSFERS	21.9	23.4	24.3	25.2	30.6	27.6	15.2	13.7	12.3	

Ukraine (continued)

Years	1987	1988	1989	1990	1991	1992	1993	1994	1995	1996
Currency	ruble	ruble	ruble	ruble	ruble	ruble	karbov.	karbov.	karbov.	hryvna

PERCENT OF GDP

GOVERNMENT SOCIAL EXPENDITURES

	1987	1988	1989	1990	1991	1992	1993	1994	1995	1996
Pensions	7.8	7.9	7.9	7.5	9.5	7.2	7.2	6.8	7.7	8.7
Maternity, birth all.	0.1	0.1	0.1	0.2	0.2	0.1	0.1	0.1		
Child allowances	0.4	0.4	0.3	0.4	1.2	0.5	0.2	0.2		
Sick leave	0.8	0.8	0.8	0.9	0.7	0.5	0.6	0.9		
Unemployment benefits					0.03	0.2	0.2	0.3		
SA, rehab. vouchers, Chernobyl, stipends	0.4	0.4	0.3	0.3	1.5	1.1	0.8	1.1	0.6	1.9
TOTAL CASH TRANSFERS	9.4	9.6	9.4	9.3	13.2	9.6	9.1	9.4	8.3	10.6
Education	4.4	4.6	4.4	4.5	6.1	5.6	4.6	5.8	5.8	
Health	2.3	2.4	2.5	2.6	5.8	4.0	3.8	4.9	4.8	
TOTAL IN-KIND TRANSFERS	6.7	7.0	6.9	7.1	11.9	9.5	8.4	10.7	10.6	
Estimate of enterprise-financed benefits										
TOTAL TRANSFERS	16.1	16.5	16.3	16.5	25.1	19.1	17.5	20.1	18.9	

STRUCTURE OF INCOME (macro)

	1987	1988	1989	1990	1991	1992	1993	1994	1995	1996
Labor income	41.4	43.1	44.4	46.6	45.3	32.7	22.7	28.1	28.4	29.5
Social benefits	9.4	9.6	9.4	9.3	13.2	9.6	9.1	9.4	8.3	10.6
Total private income	7.1	7.3	7.8	8.8	10.7	6.0	8.4	7.8	6.1	7.9
TOTAL PERSONAL INCOME	57.9	60.0	61.6	64.8	69.1	48.3	40.2	45.3	42.9	48.1
Health and education	6.7	7.0	6.9	7.1	11.9	9.5	8.4	10.7	10.6	
TOTAL (inc. health and education)	64.5	67.0	68.5	71.9	81.1	57.9	48.6	56.0	53.5	

Ukraine (continued)

Years	1987	1988	1989	1990	1991	1992	1993	1994	1995	1996
Currency	$	$	$	$	$	$	$	$	$	$

DOLLARS

STANDARD OF LIVING (nominal values; yearly average)
Household survey data
  Average per capita income
  by social group (per month)

	1987	1988	1989	1990	1991	1992	1993	1994	1995	1996
Workers	86	72	51	29	13					
Farmers	73	61	45	26	11					
Pensioners	55	47	35	20	9					
Mixed										
Overall	82	66	48	27	12	15			38	

Macro data
  Average per capita income
  by social group (per month)

	1987	1988	1989	1990	1991	1992	1993	1994	1995	1996
Workers										
Farmers										
Pensioners										
Mixed										
Overall	71	62	45	27	11	16	14	18	25	35
Average wage (pm; incl. soc. benef)	103	89	64	37	16	27	23	31	53	84
Average pension (pm)	41	34	25	16	7	9	11	11	15	27

Poverty threshold (per month)

	1987	1988	1989	1990	1991	1992	1993	1994	1995	1996
Minimum wage					15	4	4	2		
Minimum pension										
(A) Per capita PL (all population) 1/	42	33	24	15	7	12		15	22	
Per capita PL (for a family of 4)						12				
Minimum consumption basket				28	15	17	27			
GDP (bn per year)	76	63	45	25	10	21	22	26	35	44
GDP per capita per year	1,476	1,232	878	484	192	402	424	492	687	870
GDP per capita per month	123	103	73	40	16	33	35	41	57	73

NOTE:
Karbovanets from November 1992; 1 karb. = 1 Rs.
Hryvna from June 1996; 1 hr = 100,000 karb.

1/ Russian data for used for 1987-91. From 1993 on, value of 32 essential products.
2/ 1993-95 pension data include family benefits.

Poland

Years	1987	1988	1989	1990	1991	1992	1993	1994	1995	1996
Currency	zloty	zloty	zloty	zloty	zloty	zloty	zloty	zloty	new zl.	new zl.

NOMINAL TERMS

STANDARD OF LIVING (yearly average)

Household survey data
Average per capita income
by social group (per month)

	1987	1988	1989	1990	1991	1992	1993	1994	1995	1996
Workers	16,517	29,756	115,955	563,044	979,023	1,428,300	1,762,679	2,346,900	301	395
Farmers	18,040	34,795	134,398	577,278	823,880	1,173,300	1,547,510	2,051,800	282	343
Pensioners	15,425	25,160	84,472	493,384	945,899	1,265,800	1,844,934	2,458,600	320	402
Mixed	16,942	31,974	124,517	596,258	930,171	1,293,600	1,409,101	1,945,600	261	321
Self-employed							2,188,500	2,976,800	386	488
Social transfer recipients							953,300	1,258,700	156	200
Overall	16,491	29,435	124,560	558,215	923,040	1,340,310	1,724,041	2,309,300	301	383

Macro data
Average per capita income
by social group (per month)
Workers
Farmers
Pensioners
Mixed
Self-employed
Social transfer recipients

	1987	1988	1989	1990	1991	1992	1993	1994	1995	1996
Overall	21,458	39,300	149,650	803,942	1,461,883	2,104,217	2,430,833	3,813,910	524	
Average wage (net; per month)	31,180	57,543	217,999	1,029,600	1,756,300	2,438,600	3,201,300	4,250,408	570	710
Average pension (net; per month)	15,807	25,667	93,806	584,800	1,147,600	1,548,400	2,039,700	2,792,200	369	447
Pension:wage (percent)	51	45	43	57	65	63	64	66	65	63

Poverty threshold (per month)

	1987	1988	1989	1990	1991	1992	1993	1994	1995	1996
Per capita (for family of 4) [2/]	11,800	18,200	60,100	395,900	722,000	1,129,000	1,641,000	1,837,000	245	298

Poverty threshold as % of

	1987	1988	1989	1990	1991	1992	1993	1994	1995	1996
Average wage	37.8	31.6	27.6	38.5	41.1	46.3	51.3	43.2	42.9	41.9
Average pension	74.7	70.9	64.1	67.7	62.9	72.9	80.5	65.8	66.3	66.6
Average income per capita from macro data	55.0	46.3	40.2	49.2	49.4	53.7	67.5	48.2	46.7	

STRUCTURE OF INCOME (absolute nominal values; yearly average)

Household survey data (pc per month)

	1987	1988	1989	1990	1991	1992	1993	1994	1995	1996
Labor income/ wages and salaries	8,943	15,975	64,611	287,571	467,975	684,899	759,110	1,027,639	133	174
Social transfers	3,555	6,534	24,755	135,424	304,566	467,743	559,944	743,595	98	123
Pensions			17,164	103,678			434,759	591,181	80	
Family and child allowances			6,094	23,184			65,800			
Other social transfers			1,497	8,562			59,385			
Private income (agriculture)	4,004	9,570	22,131	120,936	159,524	173,427	183,214	247,095	34	39
Other income (incl. self-employed)	156	281	1,262	6,265	10,816	14,271	221,771	290,972	35	47
TOTAL INCOME	16,658	32,360	112,759	550,196	942,881	1,340,341	1,724,039	2,309,300	301	383

Poland (continued)

Years	1987	1988	1989	1990	1991	1992	1993	1994	1995	1996
Currency	zloty	zloty	zloty	zloty	zloty	zloty	zloty	zloty	new zl.	new zl.

NOMINAL TERMS (continued)

Macro data: all HHs (bn per year)

	1987	1988	1989	1990	1991	1992	1993	1994	1995	1996
Labor income (gross) 1/	4,551	8,169	31,181	140,467	249,159	389,650	492,576	669,797	92.7	119.6
Social benefits	1,557	2,766	10,820	63,573	145,034	232,352	308,003	433,420	57.4	
Pensions (gross)	1,220	2,038	7,669	47,879	101,825	167,838	231,941	332,293	44.7	55.0
Family and child allowances	199	492	2,401	9,012	17,028	22,665	23,707	24,376	3.2	
Other social transfers/scholarships	12	30	107	784	876	897	1,235	138	3.6	
Private income (agriculture)	1,096	2,319	9,174	24,760	28,516	54,300	79,658	100,951	14.5	
Private income besides agriculture	506	1,047	4,694	47,466	78,592	200,929	296,380	377,348	51.5	
Other income (as residual)	1,989	3,553	12,305	91,478	40,118	62,564	107,802	183,531	26.9	
Total money income	9,700	17,854	68,175	367,744	541,419	939,795	1,284,419	1,765,047	242.8	
Income in kind										
TOTAL INCOME 1/	9,700	17,854	68,175	367,744	541,419	939,795	1,284,419	1,765,047	243	
TOTAL INCOME P.C. (per month)	21,404	39,273	149,356	802,591	1,177,745	2,038,583	2,779,767	3,813,910	524	

UNEMPLOYMENT (thousand persons; yearly average)

	1987	1988	1989	1990	1991	1992	1993	1994	1995	1996
Number of registered unemployed			9.6	721.8	1,669.5	2,354.9	2,733.7	2,909.6	2,694.3	2,507.2
Structure of the unemployed										
Number of women				357.1	870.7	1,251.5	1,435.6	1,443.7		1,454.2
Number of young (15-24 years)				386.3	398.3	733.1	958.7			
Number with higher education				45.1	64.1	55.6	52.3			7.5
Number of those receiving UEB						1,311.6	1,394.3	1,422.8	1,549.0	1,300.0
Those with UEB in total unemployed (%)						55.7	51.0	48.9	57.5	51.9

GOVERNMENT SOCIAL EXPENDITURES (absolute nominal values; bn per year)

	1987	1988	1989	1990	1991	1992	1993	1994	1995	1996
Pensions (gross)	1,229	2,055	7,685	47,879	101,825	167,838	231,941	332,293	44.37	54.97
Family allowances	187	468	2,370	8,405	15,167	24,145	23,552	28,461	2.81	3.73
Child allowances	13	24	32	607	1,860	2,358	2,828	3,164	0.37	0.43
Sick leave	14	21	54	4,272	9,226	4,392	8,093	14,044	1.72	2.82
Unemployment benefits				1,891	11,145	14,975	18,078	25,337	3.63	4.41
Other: scholarships	12	30	107	801	876	897	1,235	3,430		
Social assistance				1,204	3,384	6,149	8,706	11,900	1.19	1.41
Education	607	1,011	4,342	28,250	34,778	49,805	64,444	93,178	12.48	8.33
Health	541	898	3,773	24,612	38,854	56,734	71,321	95,173	13.13	16.74
Estimate of enterprise-financed benefits	225	356	903							

GENERAL MACRO DATA

	1987	1988	1989	1990	1991	1992	1993	1994	1995	1996
Cost of living index (1987=100)	100	159	572	3,766	6,569	9,394	12,710	16,802	2.1	2.6
GDP or GNP nominal (bn)	16,940	29,629	118,319	591,518	824,330	1,142,430	1,557,800	2,104,073	286.0	363.8
GDP or GNP real in 1987 prices	16,940	17,634	17,670	15,620	14,433	14,577	15,131	15,963	16,841	17,768
Real growth rate		4.1	0.2	-11.6	-7.6	2.6	3.8	5.5	7.0	6.0
Exchange rate (per US$1)										
Official rate	265	431	1,439	9,500	10,576	13,626	18,145	22,727	2.4	2.7
Market rate	1,030	1,979	5,565	9,570	10,731	13,647	17,983	22,727	2.4	2.7
Number of persons receiving pensions (thousands)	6,477	6,669	6,827	7,104	7,944	8,495	8,730	8,919	9,085	9,200
Total population (thousands)	37,764	37,885	38,038	38,183	38,309	38,417	38,505	38,566	38,609	38,618
Pensioners as % of total population	17.2	17.6	17.9	18.6	20.7	22.1	22.7	23.1	23.5	23.8

Poland (continued)

Years	1987	1988	1989	1990	1991	1992	1993	1994	1995	1996
Currency	zloty	zloty	zloty	zloty	zloty	zloty	zloty	zloty	new zl.	new zl.

REAL TERMS (deflated by the cost of living index)

STANDARD OF LIVING (1987 zloty; yearly average)

Household survey data
Average per capita income
by social group (per month)

	1987	1988	1989	1990	1991	1992	1993	1994	1995	1996
Workers	16,517	18,714	20,286	14,949	14,903	15,205	13,869	13,968	14,029	15,364
Farmers	18,040	21,884	23,513	15,327	12,542	12,490	12,176	12,211	13,149	13,339
Pensioners	15,425	15,824	14,778	13,100	14,399	13,475	14,516	14,632	14,887	15,641
Mixed	16,942	20,109	21,784	15,831	14,160	13,771	11,087	11,579	12,145	12,494
Self-employed							17,219	17,717	17,982	18,962
Social transfer recipients							7,501	7,491	7,260	7,789
Overall	16,491	18,513	21,791	14,821	14,051	14,268	13,565	13,744	13,997	14,905

Macro data
Average per capita income
by social group (per month)

	1987	1988	1989	1990	1991	1992	1993	1994	1995	1996
Workers										
Farmers										
Pensioners										
Mixed										
Overall	21,458	24,717	26,181	21,345	22,254	22,400	19,126	22,699	24,404	
Average wage (per month)	31,180	36,190	38,138	27,336	26,736	25,960	25,188	25,296	26,531	27,608
Average pension (per month)	15,807	16,143	16,411	15,527	17,470	16,483	16,048	16,618	17,169	17,376

Poverty threshold (per month)

	1987	1988	1989	1990	1991	1992	1993	1994	1995	1996
Per capita (for family of 4) [2/]	11,800	11,447	10,514	10,511	10,991	12,019	12,911	10,933	11,391	11,568

STRUCTURE OF INCOME (1987 zloty; yearly average)

Household survey data (pc per month)

	1987	1988	1989	1990	1991	1992	1993	1994	1995	1996
Labor income/ wages and salaries	8,943	10,047	11,304	7,635	7,124	7,291	5,973	6,116	6,201	6,751
Social transfers	3,555	4,109	4,331	3,596	4,636	4,979	4,406	4,426	4,549	4,788
Pensions			3,003	2,753			3,421	3,518	3,723	
Family and child allowances			1,066	616			518			
Other social transfers			262	227			467			
Private income (agriculture)	4,004	6,019	3,872	3,211	2,428	1,846	1,442	1,471	1,596	1,517
Other income (incl. self-employed)	156	177	221	166	165	152	1,745	1,732	1,652	1,827
TOTAL INCOME	16,658	20,352	19,727	14,608	14,353	14,268	13,565	13,744	13,997	14,882

Macro data: all HHs (bn per year)

	1987	1988	1989	1990	1991	1992	1993	1994	1995	1996
Labor income (gross) [1/]	4,551	5,138	5,455	3,729	3,793	4,148	3,876	3,986	4,315	4,651
Social benefits	1,557	1,740	1,893	1,688	2,208	2,473	2,423	2,580	2,671	
Pensions (gross)	1,220	1,282	1,342	1,271	1,550	1,787	1,825	1,978	2,084	2,137
Family and child allowances	199	309	420	239	259	241	187	145	148	
Other social transfers/scholarships	12	19	19	21	13	10	10	1	169	
Private income (agriculture)	1,096	1,459	1,605	657	434	578	627	601	673	
Private income besides agriculture	506	658	821	1,260	1,196	2,139	2,332	2,246	2,396	
Other income (as residual)	1,989	2,234	2,153	2,429	611	666	848	1,092	1,251	
Total money income	9,700	11,229	11,927	9,764	8,242	10,004	10,106	10,505	11,306	
Income in kind										
TOTAL INCOME [1/]	9,700	11,229	11,927	9,764	8,242	10,004	10,106	10,505	11,306	
TOTAL INCOME P.C. (per month)	21,404	24,700	26,129	21,309	17,929	21,701	21,871	22,699	24,404	

Poland (continued)

Years	1987	1988	1989	1990	1991	1992	1993	1994	1995	1996
Currency	zloty	zloty	zloty	zloty	zloty	zloty	zloty	zloty	new zl.	new zl.

REAL TERMS (deflated by the cost of living index; continued)

GOVERNMENT SOCIAL EXPENDITURES (1987 zloty; bn per year)

	1987	1988	1989	1990	1991	1992	1993	1994	1995	1996
Pensions (gross)	1,228.6	1,292.5	1,344.4	1,271.2	1,550.1	1,786.7	1,824.9	1,977.7	2,066.1	2,136.9
Family allowances	186.7	294.4	414.6	223.1	230.9	257.0	185.3	169.4	130.7	144.9
Child allowances	12.6	14.8	5.5	16.1	28.3	25.1	22.3	18.8	17.4	16.8
Sick leave	13.7	13.1	9.4	113.4	140.4	46.8	63.7	83.6	80.2	109.5
Unemployment benefits				50.2	169.7	159.4	142.2	150.8	169.0	171.3
Other: scholarships	11.8	18.7	18.7	21.3	13.3	9.5	9.7	20.4		
Social assistance				32.0	51.5	65.5	68.5	70.8	55.4	54.7
TOTAL CASH TRANSFERS	1,453	1,634	1,793	1,727	2,184	2,350	2,317	2,491	2,519	2,634
Education	607	636	760	750	529	530	507	555	581	324
Health	541	564	660	653	591	604	561	566	612	651
TOTAL IN-KIND TRANSFERS	1,149	1,200	1,420	1,404	1,121	1,134	1,068	1,121	1,193	974
Estimate of enterprise-financed benefits	225	224	158							
TOTAL TRANSFERS	2,828	3,057	3,370	3,131	3,305	3,484	3,385	3,612	3,712	3,609

Poland (continued)

Years	1987	1988	1989	1990	1991	1992	1993	1994	1995	1996
Currency	zloty	zloty	zloty	zloty	zloty	zloty	zloty	zloty	new zl.	new zl.

PERCENT OF GDP

GOVERNMENT SOCIAL EXPENDITURES

	1987	1988	1989	1990	1991	1992	1993	1994	1995	1996
Pensions (gross)	7.3	6.9	6.5	8.1	12.4	14.7	14.9	15.8	15.5	15.1
Family allowances	1.1	1.6	2.0	1.4	1.8	2.1	1.5	1.4	1.0	1.0
Child allowances	0.1	0.1	0.03	0.1	0.2	0.2	0.2	0.2	0.1	0.1
Sick leave	0.1	0.1	0.05	0.7	1.1	0.4	0.5	0.7	0.6	0.8
Unemployment benefits				0.3	1.4	1.3	1.2	1.2	1.3	1.2
Other: scholarships	0.1	0.1	0.1	0.1	0.1	0.1	0.1	0.2		
Social assistance				0.2	0.4	0.5	0.6	0.6	0.4	0.4
TOTAL CASH TRANSFERS	8.6	8.8	8.7	11.0	17.4	19.3	18.9	19.9	18.9	18.6
Education	3.6	3.4	3.7	4.8	4.2	4.4	4.1	4.4	4.4	2.3
Health	3.2	3.0	3.2	4.2	4.7	5.0	4.6	4.5	4.6	4.6
TOTAL IN-KIND TRANSFERS	6.8	6.4	6.9	8.9	8.9	9.3	8.7	9.0	9.0	6.9
Estimate of enterprise-financed benefits	1.3	1.2	0.8							
TOTAL TRANSFERS	16.7	16.4	16.3	19.9	26.3	28.6	27.6	28.8	27.9	25.5

STRUCTURE OF INCOME (macro)

	1987	1988	1989	1990	1991	1992	1993	1994	1995	1996
Labor income	26.9	27.6	26.4	23.7	30.2	34.1	31.6	31.8	32.4	32.9
Social benefits	9.2	9.3	9.1	10.7	17.6	20.3	19.8	20.6	18.9	18.6
Total private income	21.2	23.4	22.1	27.7	17.9	27.8	31.1	31.5	32.4	
TOTAL PERSONAL INCOME	57.3	60.3	57.6	62.2	65.7	82.3	82.5	83.9	83.7	
Health and education	6.8	6.4	6.9	8.9	8.9	9.3	8.7	9.0	9.0	6.9
TOTAL (inc. health and education)	64.0	66.7	64.5	71.1	74.6	91.6	91.2	92.8	92.7	

Poland (continued)

Years	1987	1988	1989	1990	1991	1992	1993	1994	1995	1996
Currency	$	$	$	$	$	$	$	$	$	$

DOLLARS

STANDARD OF LIVING (nominal values; yearly average)

Household survey data
Average per capita income
by social group (per month)

	1987	1988	1989	1990	1991	1992	1993	1994	1995	1996
Workers	62	69	81	59	93	105	97	103	124	147
Farmers	68	81	93	61	78	86	85	90	116	127
Pensioners	58	58	59	52	89	93	102	108	132	149
Mixed	64	74	87	63	88	95	78	86	107	119
Self-employed							121	131	159	181
Social transfer recipients							53	55	64	74
Overall	62	68	87	59	87	98	95	102	124	142

Macro data
Average per capita income
by social group (per month)
Workers
Farmers
Pensioners
Mixed

	1987	1988	1989	1990	1991	1992	1993	1994	1995	1996
Overall	81	91	104	85	138	154	134	168	216	
Average wage (net; per month)	118	134	151	108	166	179	176	187	235	263
Average pension (net; per month)	60	60	65	62	109	114	112	123	152	166

Poverty threshold (per month)

	1987	1988	1989	1990	1991	1992	1993	1994	1995	1996
Per capita (for family of 4) 2/	45	42	42	42	68	83	90	81	101	110
GDP (bn per year)	64	69	82	62	78	84	86	93	118	135
GDP per capita per year	1,692	1,816	2,162	1,631	2,035	2,182	2,230	2,401	3,050	3,495
GDP per capita per month	141	151	180	136	170	182	186	200	254	291

NOTE:
From January 1, 1995 new zloty =10,000 old zloty.

1/ From 1992 onward, gross values.
2/ Social minimum. Revised social minimum from 1994 onwards.

Latvia

Years	1987	1988	1989	1990	1991	1992	1993	1994	1995	1996
Currency	ruble	ruble	ruble	ruble	ruble	ruble	lat	lat	lat	lat

NOMINAL TERMS

STANDARD OF LIVING (yearly average)

Household survey data
Average per capita income
by social group (per month) 1/

	1987	1988	1989	1990	1991	1992	1993	1994	1995	1996
Workers	168	177	193	223	430	2,944	30.0			55.9
Farmers	176	168	182	205	373	2,457	22.4			47.5
Pensioners		102	105	112	282	1,811				45.8
Mixed										
Overall	163	170	186	215	414	2,775	27.4	40.3	49.3	51.5

Macro data
Average per capita income
by social group (per month)

	1987	1988	1989	1990	1991	1992	1993	1994	1995	1996
Workers	196	198								
Farmers	214	230								
Pensioners										
Mixed										
Overall	169	184	213	237	482	3,445	27.9	29.1	33.0	
Average wage (gross per month) 2/	209	227	250	322	600	4,300	47.2	74.3	89.4	98.7
Average pension (per month)	83.1	85.4	92.3	94.7	162	1,582	14.8	27.9	30.2	44.0
Pension:wage (percent)	39.8	37.6	36.9	29.4	27.0	36.8	31.3	37.6	33.8	44.6

Poverty threshold (per month)

	1987	1988	1989	1990	1991	1992	1993	1994	1995	1996
Minimum wage	70	70	70	100	140	876	15.0	22.0	28.0	
Minimum level of living				100	153	1,436				
Per capita PL (for a family of 4)				83		764				
(A) Per capita PL (all population)	75	75	83	100	348	3,714	37.6	51.5	63.8	73.4
Minimum consumption basket 3/							30.3	38.4	47.2	52.2

Poverty threshold (A) as % of

	1987	1988	1989	1990	1991	1992	1993	1994	1995	1996
Average wage	35.9	33.0	33.2	31.1	58.0	86.4	79.6	69.3	71.4	74.3
Average pension	90.3	87.8	89.9	105.6	214.8	234.8	254.7	184.5	211.1	166.8
Average income per capita from macro data	44.4	40.7	39.0	42.2	72.1	107.8	134.5	176.7	193.1	

STRUCTURE OF INCOME (absolute nominal values; yearly average)

Household survey data (pc per month)

	1987	1988	1989	1990	1991	1992	1993	1994	1995	1996
Labor income/ wages and salaries	119	127	138	156	258	1,782	17.2	27.0	25.7	25.8
Social transfers	21	22	23	24	87	496	5.6	7.0	11.6	14.0
Pensions	13	13	14	15	32	271	2.8		7.8	9.4
Family and child allowances	0.3	0.3	0.3	0.3	1	127	2.3		1.0	1.1
Other social transfers	8	8	9	9	54	98	0.5		2.8	3.5
Private sector income (agriculture)	10	12	9	14	25	219	1.5	2.2		
Other income (including in-kind)	13	11	17	22	45	278	3.1	4.1	12.0	11.8
TOTAL INCOME	163	170	186	215	414	2,775	27.4	40.3	49.3	51.6

Latvia (continued)

Years Currency	1987 ruble	1988 ruble	1989 ruble	1990 ruble	1991 ruble	1992 ruble	1993 lat	1994 lat	1995 lat	1996 lat

NOMINAL TERMS (continued)

Macro data: all HHs (bn per year)

Labor income/wages and salaries	3.3	3.6	4.2	5.8	9.6	54.8	0.5	0.7	0.8	
Social benefits	0.7	0.8	0.8	0.9	3.2	22.6	0.2	0.2	0.2	
Pensions	0.6	0.6	0.7	0.7			0.1	0.2	0.2	
Family and child allowances	0.1	0.1	0.2	0.2						
Other social transfers/scholarships	0.02	0.03	0.03	0.03						
Private sector income (self-employed)	0.5	0.6	0.8	0.7	2.1	31.0	0.1			
Other income	0.8	0.9	1.1	0.2	0.5	0.4	0.004			
Total money income	5.4	5.9	6.8	7.6	15.4	108.8	0.9	0.9	1.0	
Income in kind										
TOTAL INCOME	5.4	5.9	6.8	7.6	15.4	108.8	0.9	0.9	1.0	
TOTAL INCOME P.C. (per month)	169	184	213	237	482	3,445	27.9	29.1	33.0	

UNEMPLOYMENT (thousand persons; yearly average)

Number of registered unemployed							14.9	62.5	83.8	86.6	95.4
Structure of the unemployed										
Number of women							7.2	33.9			46.0
Number of young (15-24 years)							4.4	10.8			
Number with higher education							2.3	4.8			
Number of those receiving UEB							12.2	44.3	37.5	37.1	38.7
Those with UEB in total unemployed (%)							81.9	70.9	44.8	42.8	40.6

GOVERNMENT SOCIAL EXPENDITURES (absolute nominal values; bn per year)

Pensions	0.6	0.6	0.6	0.7	2.2	12.4	0.1	0.2	0.2	0.3
Family allowances	0.001	0.001	0.001	0.002	0.5	3.0	0.03		0.02	0.02
Child allowances	0.04	0.04	0.04	0.004	0.2	1.3	0.01			
Sick leave	0.04	0.04	0.03	0.04	0.03	0.2				0.01
Unemployment benefits						0.2		0.01	0.01	0.01
Other: social assistance	0.1	0.1	0.1	0.1	0.2	2.3		0.02		
Education	0.5	0.4	0.5	0.6	1.2	9.1	0.1	0.1	0.2	0.2
Health	0.3	0.3	0.3	0.4	0.7	5.7	0.04	0.1	0.1	0.1
Estimate of enterprise-financed benefits	0.7	0.7	0.7	0.7						0.001

GENERAL MACRO DATA

Cost of living index (1987=100)	100	104	109	119	299	3,148	33	45	56	66
GDP or GNP nominal (bn)	8.9	9.3	10.3	12.5	28.7	200.9	1.5	2.0	2.0	2.8
GDP or GNP real in 1987 (bn)	9.5	10.0	10.6	10.9	9.8	6.4	5.4	5.5	5.5	5.7
Real growth rate (%)		5.2	6.8	2.9	-10.4	-34.9	-14.9	2.0	0.0	2.8
Exchange rate (per US$1)										
Official rate	0.6	0.6	0.6	0.6	0.6	134				
Market rate	1.6	1.5	1.6		46.2	142	0.7	0.6	0.5	0.6
"Actual" rate	1.8	2.2	3.4	6.7	30.0	142	0.7	0.6	0.5	0.6
Number of persons receiving										
pensions (thousands)	575	585	592	605	628	654	662	663	660	661
Total population (thousands)	2,641	2,666	2,674	2,671	2,662	2,632	2,586	2,550	2,529	2,501
Pensioners as % of total population	21.8	21.9	22.1	22.6	23.6	24.9	25.6	26.0	26.1	26.4

Latvia (continued)

Years	1987	1988	1989	1990	1991	1992	1993	1994	1995	1996
Currency	ruble	ruble	ruble	ruble	ruble	ruble	lat	lat	lat	lat

REAL TERMS (deflated by the cost of living index)

STANDARD OF LIVING (1987 rubles; yearly average)

	1987	1988	1989	1990	1991	1992	1993	1994	1995	1996
Household survey data										
Average per capita income										
by social group (per month) 1/										
Workers	168	171	178	187	143	94	91			85
Farmers	176	162	168	172	124	78	68			72
Pensioners				94	94	58				70
Mixed										
Overall	163	164	171	181	138	88	83	90	88	78
Macro data										
Average per capita income										
by social group (per month)										
Workers	196	191								
Farmers	214	222								
Pensioners										
Mixed										
Overall	169	178	196	199	161	109	85	65	59	
Average wage (per month; gross) 2/	209	219	230	271	200	137	144	166	160	150
Average pension (per month)	83	82	85	80	54	50	45	62	54	67
Poverty threshold (per month)										
Minimum wage	70	68	65	84	47	28	46	49	50	
Minimum level of living					84	51	46			
Per capita PL (for a family of 4)					70		24			
(A) Per capita PL (all population)	75	72	76	84	116	118	114	115	114	112
Minimum consumption basket 3/							92	86	85	80

STRUCTURE OF INCOME (1987 rubles; yearly average)

	1987	1988	1989	1990	1991	1992	1993	1994	1995	1996
Household survey data (pc per month)										
Labor income/ wages and salaries	119	122	127	131	86	57	52	60	46	39
Social transfers	21	21	21	20	29	16	17	16	21	21
Pensions	13	13	13	13	11	9	8		14	14
Family and child allowances	0.3	0.3	0.3	0.3	0.5	4	7		2	2
Other social transfers	8	8	8	7	18	3	2		5	5
Private sector income (agriculture)	10	11	8	11	8	7	5	5		
Other income (including in-kind)	13	10	15	18	15	9	9	9	22	18
Total private	23	22	24	30	23	16	14	14	22	18
TOTAL INCOME	163	164	171	181	138	88	83	90	88	79
Macro data: all HHs (bn per year)										
Labor income/ wages and salaries	3.3	3.5	3.8	4.9	3.2	1.7	1.5	1.5	1.4	
Social benefits	0.7	0.7	0.7	0.8	1.1	0.7	0.7	0.5	0.4	
Pensions	0.6	0.6	0.6	0.6			0.4	0.5	0.4	
Family and child allowances	0.1	0.1	0.1	0.2						
Other social transfers /scholarships	0.02	0.03	0.02	0.03						
Private sector income (selfemployed)	0.5	0.6	0.7	0.6	0.7	1.0	0.4			
Other income	0.8	0.8	1.0	0.2	0.2	0.01	0.01			
Total money income	5.4	5.7	6.3	6.4	5.1	3.5	2.6	2.0	1.8	
Income in kind										
TOTAL INCOME	5.4	5.7	6.3	6.4	5.1	3.5	2.6	2.0	1.8	
TOTAL INCOME P.C. (per month)	169	178	196	199	161	109	85	65	59	

Latvia (continued)

Years Currency	1987 ruble	1988 ruble	1989 ruble	1990 ruble	1991 ruble	1992 ruble	1993 lat	1994 lat	1995 lat	1996 lat

REAL TERMS (deflated by the cost of living index; continued)

GOVERNMENT SOCIAL EXPENDITURES (1987 rubles; bn per year)

	1987	1988	1989	1990	1991	1992	1993	1994	1995	1996
Pensions	0.6	0.6	0.6	0.6	0.7	0.4	0.4	0.5	0.4	0.5
Family allowances	0.001	0.001	0.001	0.001	0.2	0.1	0.1		0.03	0.03
Child allowances	0.04	0.03	0.03	0.004	0.1	0.04	0.03			
Sick leave	0.04	0.03	0.03	0.04	0.01	0.01				0.02
Unemployment benefits						0.01		0.02	0.02	0.02
Other: social assistance	0.1	0.1	0.1	0.1	0.1	0.1		0.05		
TOTAL CASH TRANSFERS	0.7	0.7	0.7	0.7	1.1	0.6	0.5	0.6	0.5	0.5
Education	0.5	0.4	0.5	0.5	0.4	0.3	0.3	0.3	0.3	0.2
Health	0.3	0.3	0.3	0.3	0.2	0.2	0.1	0.2	0.2	0.2
TOTAL IN-KIND TRANSFERS	0.7	0.7	0.8	0.8	0.6	0.5	0.4	0.5	0.5	0.4
Estimate of enterprise-financed benefits	0.7	0.7	0.6	0.6						0.001
TOTAL TRANSFERS	2.2	2.2	2.1	2.1	1.7	1.1	0.9	1.1	0.9	0.9

Latvia (continued)

Years	1987	1988	1989	1990	1991	1992	1993	1994	1995	1996
Currency	ruble	ruble	ruble	ruble	ruble	ruble	lat	lat	lat	lat

PERCENT OF GDP

GOVERNMENT SOCIAL EXPENDITURES

	1987	1988	1989	1990	1991	1992	1993	1994	1995	1996
Pensions	6.3	6.4	5.9	5.5	7.8	6.2	9.6	11.7	10.3	10.8
Family allowances	0.01	0.01	0.01	0.01	1.8	1.5	1.9		0.8	0.7
Child allowances	0.4	0.4	0.4	0.03	0.7	0.6	0.8			
Sick leave	0.4	0.4	0.3	0.4	0.1					0.5
Unemployment benefits						0.1		0.4	0.4	0.4
Other: social assistance	0.8	0.8	0.7	0.7	0.7	1.1		1.1		
TOTAL CASH TRANSFERS	7.9	7.9	7.3	6.6	11.2	9.7	12.3	13.2	11.6	12.3
Education	5.3	4.8	4.9	4.5	4.1	4.5	6.5	6.1	6.7	5.9
Health	3.2	3.5	3.4	3.3	2.6	2.8	2.4	3.9	4.2	4.1
TOTAL IN-KIND TRANSFERS	8.4	8.3	8.2	7.8	6.7	7.4	8.9	10.0	10.8	10.0
Estimate of enterprise-financed benefits	8.2	7.8	6.6	5.8						0.04
TOTAL TRANSFERS	24.5	24.0	22.2	20.2	17.9	17.1	21.2	23.3	22.4	22.3

STRUCTURE OF INCOME (macro)

	1987	1988	1989	1990	1991	1992	1993	1994	1995	1996
Labor income	37.1	38.7	40.5	46.3	33.5	27.3	33.7	32.8	32.3	
Social benefits	7.9	7.9	7.3	6.6	11.2	9.7	12.3	13.2	11.6	12.3
Total private income	8.2	7.7	8.0	9.0	7.8	7.8	9.7	9.4	15.5	12.8
TOTAL PERSONAL INCOME	53.2	54.3	55.9	61.9	52.5	44.8	55.7	55.4	59.4	
Health and education	8.4	8.3	8.2	7.8	6.7	7.4	8.9	10.0	10.8	10.0
TOTAL (inc. health and education)	61.6	62.6	64.1	69.7	59.2	52.1	64.6	65.5	70.2	

Latvia (continued)

Years	1987	1988	1989	1990	1991	1992	1993	1994	1995	1996
Currency	$	$	$	$	$	$	$	$	$	$

DOLLARS

STANDARD OF LIVING (nominal values; yearly average)

Household survey data
Average per capita income
by social group (per month) 1/

	1987	1988	1989	1990	1991	1992	1993	1994	1995	1996
Workers	93	79	57	34	14	21	45			102
Farmers	98	75	54	31	12	17	33			86
Pensioners		45	31	17	9	13				83
Mixed										
Overall	91	76	55	32	14	20	41	72	94	94

Macro data
Average per capita income
by social group (per month)

Workers	109	88								
Farmers	119	103								
Pensioners										
Mixed										
Overall	94	82	63	36	16	24	41	52	63	

Average wage (per month; gross) 2/	116	101	74	48	20	30	70	133	169	179
Average pension (per month)	46	38	27	14	5	11	22	50	57	80

Poverty threshold (per month)

Minimum wage	39	31	21	15	5	6	22	39	53	
Minimum level of living				15	5	10				
Per capita PL (for a family of 4)				12		5				
(A) Per capita PL (all population)	42	33	24	15	12	26	56	92	121	133
Minimum consumption basket 3/							45	69	89	95

GDP (bn per year)	4.9	4.2	3.0	1.9	1.0	1.4	2.2	3.7	4.5	5.0
GDP per capita per year	1,862	1,560	1,135	702	359	537	841	1,432	1,769	2,010
GDP per capita per month	155	130	95	59	30	45	70	119	147	168

NOTE:
Lat from 1993; 1 lat = 200 rubles.

1/ 1993 and 1994, money income alone.
2/ From 1993, gross wages.
3/ Officially called "crisis minimum basket."

References

The word "processed" indicates that the work may not be commonly available through the library system.

Ahluwalia, Montek S. (1976), "Inequality, Poverty and Development," *Journal of Development Economics*, no. 3.

Ahuja, Vinod (1997), "Growth with Redistribution? Inequality and Poverty in Malaysia," Poverty Reduction and Economic Management Department, World Bank, Washington, November 26, processed.

Akchurin, Marat (1995), "Another Bosnia in the Making?," *Central Asian Monitor*, no. 3, p. 9.

Andorka, Rudolf, and Zsolt Spéder (1994), "Poverty in Hungary: Some Results of the First Two Waves of the Hungarian Panel Survey in 1992 and 1993," TARKI, Budapest, processed.

Árvay, János, and András Vértes (1994), "Impact of the Hidden Economy on Growth Rates in Hungary," paper prepared for the 23rd General Conference of International Association for Research in Income and Wealth, St. Andrew's, Canada, August 21-27, 1994, processed.

Asselain, Jean-Charles (1987), "The Distribution of Income in East-Central Europe" in Pierre Kende and Zdenek Strmiska (eds.), *Equality and Inequality in Eastern Europe*, Lemington Spa, Hamburg, New York:BERG.

Atkinson, Anthony B. (1995), "On Targeting Social Security: Theory and Western Experience with Family Benefits," in Dominique van de Walle and Kim Nead, (eds.), *Public Spending and the Poor: Theory and Evidence*, Washington, D.C. and Baltimore: World Bank and Johns Hopkins University Press.

Atkinson, Anthony B., and John Micklewright (1992), *Economic Transformation in Eastern Europe and the Distribution of Income*, Cambridge and New York: Cambridge University Press.

Atkinson, Anthony B., Lee Rainwater, and Timothy Smeeding (1995), "Income Distribution in Advanced Economies: Evidence from the Luxembourg Income Study," Luxembourg Income Study (LIS) Working Paper no. 12, LIS, Luxembourg, processed.

Bain, George S., and Farouk Elsheikh (1976), *Union Growth and the Business Cycle: An Econometric Analysis*, Oxford:Basil Blackwell.

Bairoch, Paul (1993), *Economics and World History: Myths and Paradoxes*, New York and London:Harvester Wheatsheaf.

Banks, James and Paul Johnson (1994), "Equivalence Scale Relativities Revisited," *Economic Journal*, vol. 104, July, pp. 883–890.

Bergson, Abram (1961), *The Real National Income of Soviet Russia since 1928*, Cambridge, Mass.:Harvard University Press.

_____ (1984), "Income Inequality under Soviet Socialism," *Journal of Economic Literature*, vol. 22, September, pp. 1052–1099.

Bird, Edward J., Joachim R. Frick, and Gert G. Wagner (1995), "The Income of Socialist Elite during the Transition to Capitalism: Credible Evidence from Longitudinal East German Data," W. Allen Wallis Institute of Political Economy, Working Paper no. 6, University of Rochester, processed.

Block, H. (1976), "Soviet Economic Power Growth: Achievements and Handicaps" in Joint Economic Committee, *Soviet Economy in a New Perspective*, Washington, D.C.:Congress of the United States, December.

Bloem, Adriaan M., Paul Cotterell, and Terry Gigantes (1996), "National Accounts in Transition Countries: Distortions and Biases," IMF Working Paper no. 96/130, International Monetary Fund, Washington, D.C., November, processed.

Boateng, E. Oti, Kodwo Ewusi, Ravi Kanbur, and Andrew McKay (1992), "Un profil de pauvreté au Ghana 1987–88," Social Dimension of Adjustment, World Bank, Washington, D.C., processed.

Braithwaite, Jeanine D. (1990), "Poverty Differentials in the USSR: Implications for Social Stability," Center for International Research, Bureau of the Census, July, processed.

_____ (1994), "The Old and the New Poor in Russia: Trends in Poverty," European II Department, International Monetary Fund, Washington, D.C., January, processed.

_____ (1997), "The Old and the New Poor in Russia" in Jeni Klugman (ed.), *Poverty in Russia: Public Policy and Private Responses*, Washington, D.C.:World Bank.

Browning, Edgar K. (1993), "The Marginal Cost of Redistribution," *Public Finance Quarterly*, January, vol. 48, no. 1, January, pp. 3–32.

Canceill, Geneviève (1989), "Les révenus fiscaux des ménages en 1989," no. 605, Collections de l'INSEE, Serie M, no.139. INSEE, Paris, processed.

Center for Economic Conjuncture (1994), *Osnovnie pokazateli...*, Moscow, June.

Chase, Robert (1995), "Returns to Education and Experience in Transition Czech Republic and Slovakia," Yale University, New Haven, Conn., January, processed.

Commander, Simon, Andrei Tolstopiatenko, and Ruslan Yemtsov (1997), "Channels of Redistribution: Inequality and Poverty in the Russian Transition," paper prepared for the conference on inequality and poverty in transition economies, EBRD, London, 23–24 May 1997, processed.

Cornelius, Peter K. (1995), "Cash Benefits and Poverty Alleviation in an Economy in Transition: The Case of Lithuania," *Comparative Economic Studies*, vol. 37, no. 2, pp. 49–69.

Cornelius, Peter K., and Beatrice S. Weder (1996), "Economic Transformation and Income Distribution: Some Evidence from the Baltic Countries," IMF Working Paper, International Monetary Fund, Washington, D.C., February, processed.

Cornia, Giovanni Andrea (1991), "Economic Reforms and Child Welfare: In Pursuit of Adequate Safety Net for Children" in Giovanni Andrea Cornia and Sandor Sipos (eds.), *Children and the Transition to the Market Economy*, Aldershot:Avebury, and UNICEF.

_____ (1994), "Income Distribution, Poverty, and Welfare in Transitional Economies: A Comparison between Eastern Europe and China," Innocenti Occasional Paper, Economic Policy Series no. 44, UNICEF, Florence, Italy, October, processed.

Coulter, Fionna A.E., Frank A. Cowell, and Stephen P. Jenkins (1992), "Equivalence Scale Relativities and the Extent of Inequality and Poverty," *Economic Journal*, vol. 102, September, pp.1067–1082.

Czech Statistical Office (1994), *Statistika rodinných účtů: příjmy, vidáný, a spotřeba domácnosti za rok 1993*, vol. 1, Prague: Czech Statistical Office.

d'Agostino, Serge, and Gabriel Trombert (1992), *Les Inegalités des Revenus*, Paris:Vuibert.

Debroy, B. (1986), "Income Inequality in East Europe," *Artha Vinana*, vol. 28, September, pp. 253–316.

Deininger, Klaus, and Lyn Squire (1995), "Measuring Income Inequality: A New Data Base," Policy Research Department, World Bank, Washington, D.C., December 1, processed.

de Melo, Martha, Cevdet Denizer, and Alan Gelb (1996), "From Plan to Market: Patterns of Transition," World Bank Policy Research Working Paper no. 1564, World Bank, Washington, D.C., processed.

Fijalkowski, Tadeusz (1992), *O zatrudnieniu i bezrabociu oraz pomocy spolecznej: ustawi, akty wykonawcze, objaśnienia*, Warsaw:K. Krajewski.

Flakierski, Henryk (1986), *Economic Reform and Income Distribution: A Case Study of Hungary and Poland*, Armonk, N.Y. and London:M.E. Sharpe.

_____ (1989), *The Economic System and Income Distribution in Yugoslavia*, Armonk, N.Y. and London:M.E. Sharpe.

_____ (1993), *Income Inequalities in the Former Soviet Union and Its Republics*, Armonk, N.Y. and London:M.E. Sharpe.

Foley, Mark C., and Jeni Klugman (1997), "The Impact of Social Support:Errors of Leakage and Exclusion" in Jeni Klugman (ed.), *Poverty in Russia: Public Policy and Private Responses*, Washington, D.C.:World Bank.

Förster, Michael F. (1993), "Comparing Poverty in 13 OECD Countries: Traditional and Synthetic Approaches," Luxembourg Income Study (LIS) Working Paper no. 103, LIS, Luxembourg, processed.

Fozouni, Shirin, Alan Gelb, and Martin Schrenk (1992), "Economic Crashes and Recovery Prospects in Eastern Europe: Some Comparable Lessons," Policy Research Department, Transition Economics, World Bank, Washington, D.C., processed.

Gazier, Bernard (1983), *La Crise de 1929*. Paris:Que sais-je?

Goldenberg, Suzanne (1994), *Pride of Small Nations: The Caucasus and Post-Soviet Disorder*, London and New Jersey:Zed Books Ltd.

Gontmakher, Evgeny, I. Gritz, V. Kosmarsky, and S. Smirnov (1995), "The Poverty Line in Russia," Center for Institutional Reform and the Informal Sector (IRIS) Research Project, University of Maryland, Virginia, and Moscow, Russia, April, processed.

Graham, Carol (1994), *Safety Nets, Politics, and the Poor: Transitions to Market Economies*, Washington D.C.:Brookings Institution.

Gramlich, Edward M. (1996), "Different Approaches for Dealing with Social Security," *Journal of Economic Perspectives*, vol. 10, Summer, pp. 55–66.

Grosh, Margaret E. (1994), *Administering Targeted Social Programs in Latin America: From Platitudes to Practice*, Washington, D.C.:World Bank.

Gurr, Ted Robert (1994), "Peoples against States: Ethnopolitical Conflicts and the Changing World System," *International Studies Quarterly*, vol. 38, no. 3, pp. 347–78.

Heimerl, Daniela (1993), "La situation sociale dans les Länder orientaux de la RFA," *Le Courrier des pays de l'est*, October, pp. 75–85.

Heleniak, Timothy (1995), "Dramatic Population Trends in the Countries of the FSU," *Transition Newsletter*, vol. 6, September-October, Policy Research Department, World Bank, Washington, D.C.

_____ (1997), "Mass Migration in Post-Soviet Space," *Transition Newsletter*, vol. 8, October, Development Research Group, World Bank, Washington, D.C.

Hiršl, Miroslav, Jiří Rusnok, and Martin Fassman (1995), "Market Reforms and Social Welfare in the Czech Republic: A True Success Story?," Innocenti Occasional Paper no. 50, UNICEF, Florence, Italy, processed.

INE (Instituto Nacional de Estadística) (1989), *Encuesta Contínua de Presupuestos Familiares*, Madrid:INE.

Jackman, Richard, and Michal Rutkowski (1994), "Labor Markets: Wages and Employment" in Nicholas Barr (ed.), *Labor Markets and Social Policy in Central and Eastern Europe: The Transition and Beyond*, Washington and London:World Bank and London School of Economics.

James, Harold (1986), *The German Slump, Politics and Economics 1924–1936*, Oxford: Clarendon Press.

Kadera, Vladimir (1995), "The Importance and Role of the Shadow Economy in the Transformation Period of the Czech Republic," processed.

Kaelble, Hartmut, and Mark Thomas (1991), "Introduction," in Y.S. Brenner, Hartmut Kaelble, and Mark Thomas (eds.), *Income Distribution in Historical Perspective*, Cambridge and Paris:Cambridge University Press and Editions de la Maison des Sciences de l'Homme.

Kakwani, Nanak (1995), "Income Inequality, Welfare and Poverty: An Illustration Using Ukrainian Data," World Bank Policy Research Department Working Paper no. 1411, World Bank, Washington, D.C., processed.

Kakwani, Nanak, and Kalanidhi Subbarao (1990), "Rural Poverty and Its Alleviation in India: A Discussion," *Economic and Political Weekly*, vol. 25, March, processed.

Kanbur, Ravi (1987), "Measurement and Alleviation of Poverty," *IMF Staff Papers*, vol. 34, pp. 60–85.

Kanbur, Ravi, Michael Keen, and Matti Tuomala (1995), "Labor Supply and Targeting in Poverty-Alleviation Programs" in Dominique van de Walle and Kim Nead, (eds.), *Public Spending and the Poor: Theory and Evidence*, Washington and Baltimore: World Bank and Johns Hopkins University Press.

Kazlauskas, Arturas, and Helen Jensen (1993), "Household Expenditures and Income: Lithuania, March 1992–January 1993: Preliminary Analysis," Center for Agricultural and Rural Development, Department of Economics, University of Iowa, Ames, Iowa, May, processed.

Kende, Pierre (1987), "The Division of Resources in the Area of Consumption," in Pierre Kende and Zdenek Strmiska (eds.), *Equality and Inequality in Eastern Europe*, Lemington Spa, Hamburg, New York:BERG.

Khanin, Gregory (1992), "Economic Growth in the 1980s" in M. Ellman and V. Kontorovich (eds.), *The Disintegration of the Soviet Economic System*, London:Routledge & Kegan Paul.

Klugman, Jeni (1995), "Poverty in Russia: An Assessment," *Transition Newsletter*, vol. 6, September–October, Policy Research Department, World Bank, Washington, D.C.

Koen, Vincent (1996), "Russian Macroeconomic Data: Existence, Access, Interpretation," *Communist Economies and Economic Transformation*, vol. 8, September, pp. 321–333.

Kordos, Jan (1994), "Outline of the Current Budget Surveys in Poland," Polish Central Statistical Office, Warsaw, processed.

Kozel, Valerie (1991), "The Composition and Distribution of Income in Côte d'Ivoire," Living Standards Measurement Survey (LSMS) Study no. 68, Policy Research Department, World Bank, Washington, processed.

Krause, Peter (1992), "Einkommensarmut in der Bundesrepublik Deutschland," *Aus Politik und Zeitgeschichte*, 27 November, pp. 4–9.

Kritsman, Lev (1926), *Geroicheskii period velikoi russkoi revoliutsii*, Moscow and Leningrad, 1926.

Kudrov, Valentin B., (1995), "Sovietskiy ekonomicheskiy rost: offitsialn'yie dannyie i al'ternativnye otsenki," *Voprosy Ekonomiki*, no. 10, pp.100–112.

_____ (1996), "On the Alternative Statistics of G. Khanin," *Europe-Asia Studies*, vol. 48, no. 7, November, pp. 1203–1218.

Lapins, Janis, and Edmunds Vaskis (1996), "The New Household Budget Survey in Latvia," *Statistics in Transition*, vol. 2, no. 7, pp. 1085–1102.

Latvia (1994), "Law on Social Assistance and State Budget Benefits," Ministry of Social Protection, Riga, Latvia, processed.

Lydall, Harold (1968), *The Structure of Earnings*, Oxford:Clarendon Press.

Madžarević, Sanja, and Davor Mikulić (1997), "Mjerenje neslužbenog gospodarstva sustavom nacionalnih racuna," *Financijska praksa*, vol. 21, nos. 1–2, pp. 141–156.

Magocsi, Paul R. (1993), *Historical Atlas of East Central Europe*, Seattle and London: University of Washington Press.

Marer, Paul (1985), *Dollar GNPs of the USSR and Eastern Europe*, Washington D.C. and Baltimore: World Bank and Johns Hopkins University Press.

Marnie, Sheila, and John Micklewright (1993), "Poverty in Pre-reform Uzbekistan: What Do Official Data Really Reveal," European University Institute, Florence, Italy, processed.

Martini, Alberto, Anna Ivanova, and Svetlana Novosyolova (1996), "The Income and Expenditures Survey of Belarus: Design and Implementation," *Statistics in Transition*, vol. 2, no. 7, pp. 1063–1084.

McAuley, Alastair (1994), "What Happened during the Transition in Russia?," Policy Research Department, Transition Economics Research Paper no. 6, World Bank, Washington, D.C., processed.

McIntyre, Robert J. (1988), *Bulgaria: Politics, Economics, and Society*, Marxist regimes series, London and New York: Pinter Publishers.

Michel, Richard C. (1991), "Economic Growth and Income Equality since the 1982 Recession," *Journal of Policy Analysis and Management*, vol. 6, no. 2, pp. 181–203.

Milanovic, Branko (1992), "Poverty in Poland, 1978-88," *Review of Income and Wealth*, vol. 38, no. 3, September, pp. 329–340.

_____ (1994), "Cash Social Transfers, Direct Taxes, and Income Distribution," *Journal of Comparative Economics*, vol. 18, no. 2, April, pp. 175–197.

_____ (1994a), "Determinants of Cross-country Income Inequality: An Augmented Kuznets' Hypothesis," World Bank Policy Research Department Working Paper no. 1246, World Bank, Washington, D.C., processed.

_____ (1995), "Distributional Incidence of Cash and in-Kind Transfers in Eastern Europe and Russia," in Dominique van de Walle and Kim Nead, (eds.), *Public Spending and the Poor: Theory and Evidence*, Washington, D.C. and Baltimore: World Bank and Johns Hopkins University Press, pp. 489–520.

_____ (1995a), "Poverty, Inequality, and Social Policy in Transition Economies," World Bank Policy Research Department Working Paper no. 1530, World Bank Washington, D.C., processed.

_____ (1996), "Income, Inequality, and Poverty during the Transition in Eastern Europe: A Survey of the Evidence," *MOCT-MOST*, vol. 6, no. 1, pp. 131–147.

Morley, Samuel (1994), "Changes in Poverty and the Distribution of Income in Latin America during the 1980's," Inter-American Development Bank, Washington, D.C., processed.

Morrisson, Christian (1984), "Income Distribution in East European and Western Countries," *Journal of Comparative Economics*, vol. 8, no. 2, June, pp. 121–138.

Muller, Klaus, Gert G. Wagner, Richard Hauser, and Joachim Frick (1991), "Income Transition in East Germany: Measurement by Means of Objective and Subjective Indicators," Working Papers of the ESF Network on Household Panel Studies, Paper no. 30, processed.

Narodna Banka Slovenska (1996), *Annual Report 1996*, Bratislava:Central Bank of Slovakia.

O'Higgins, Michael, and Guenther Schmaus, and Geoffrey Stevenson (1989), "Income Distribution and Redistribution: A Microdata Analysis for Seven Countries," *Review of Income and Wealth*, vol. 35, June, pp. 107–131.

Okrasa, Wlodimierz (1988), "Redistribution and the Two Dimensions of Inequality: An East-West Comparison," *European Economic Review*, vol. 32, pp. 633–643.

Phelps-Brown, Henry (1988), *Egalitarianism and the Generation of Inequality*, Oxford: Clarendon Press.

Pierenkemper, Toni (1987), "The Standard of Living and Employment in Germany, 1850–1980: An Overview," *Journal of European Economic History*, vol. 16, Spring.

Pipes, Richard (1990), *The Russian Revolution*, New York:Alfred A. Knopf.

Polish Central Statistical Office (1993), "Pomoc spoleczna w Polsce 1993," Warsaw.

_____ (1994), *Budżety gospodarstw domowych w 1993. roku*, Warsaw.

_____ (1995), *Budżety gospodarstw domowych w 1994. roku*, Warsaw.

Polonsky, Antony (1975), _The Little Dictators: The History of Eastern Europe since 1918_, London and Boston: Routledge & Kegan Paul.

Psacharopoulos, George, Samuel Morley, Ariel Fiszbein, Haeduck Lee, and Bill Wood (1992), "Poverty and Income Distribution in Latin America: The Story of the 1980s," Latin American and the Caribbean Technical Department, Regional Studies Program, Report no. 27, World Bank, Washington, D.C., processed.

Rashid, Mansoora (1994), "Household Welfare in a Transition Economy: Growth, Equity, and Poverty in Romania," 1989–92, Europe and Central Asia Department, Human Resources, World Bank, Washington, D.C., processed.

Ravallion, Martin (1993), "Growth, Inequality and Poverty: New Evidence on Old Questions," Policy Research Department, World Bank, Washington, D.C., processed.

Redor, Dominique (1992), _Wage Inequalities in East and West_, Cambridge: Cambridge University Press.

Roberti, Paolo (1994), "Poverty in Belarus: Before and During the Transition," Europe and Central Asia Department, World Bank, Washington, D.C, January, processed.

Romer, Christina D. (1993), "The Nation in Depression," _The Journal of Economic Perspectives_, vol. 7, no. 3, Spring, pp. 19–39.

Rutkowski, Jan (1995), "Labor Markets and Poverty in Bulgaria," Europe and Central Asia Department, Human Resources, World Bank, Washington, D.C, October, processed.

_____ (1996), "High Skills Pay Off: The Changing Wage Structure during Economic Transition in Poland," _Economics of Transition_, vol. 4, May, pp. 89–112.

Sadowski, Wieslaw, and W. Herer (1996), _Szara gospodarka w Polsce-rozmiary, przyczyny, konsekwencje_, Warsaw: Central Statistical Office (GUS) Zaspol Badania Statystyczno Ekonomycznich.

Saunders, Peter, Helen Stott, and Garry Hobbes (1991), "Income Inequality in Australia and New Zealand: International Comparisons and Recent Trends," _Review of Income and Wealth_, vol. 37, no. 1, March, pp. 63–79.

Sawhill, Isabel (1988), "Poverty in the U.S.: Why Is It So Persistent?," _Journal of Economic Literature_, vol. 26, September, pp. 1073–1119.

Schkolnik, Mariana, and Paulina Aguero (1993), "Composición de las Transferencias Monetarias" in _Programas Sociales: Su Impacto en los Hogares Chilenos, Casen 1990_, Santiago:Ministerio de Planificación y Cooperación.

Schwartz, Gerd, and Teresa Ter-Minassian (1995). "The Distributional Effects of Public Expenditures: Update and Overview," Fiscal Affairs Department, International Monetary Fund, Washington, D.C., August, processed.

Sipos, Sándor (1992), "Poverty Measurement in Central and Eastern Europe before the Transition to the Market Economy," Innocenti Occasional Papers no. 29, UNICEF International Child Development Centre, Florence, Italy (unpublished addition on Russia), processed.

———— (1994), "Income Transfers: Family Support and Poverty Relief" in Nicholas Barr (ed.), *Labor Markets and Social Policy in Central and Eastern Europe: The Transition and Beyond*, Washington D.C. and London: World Bank and London School of Economics.

———— (1995), "Hungary Public Sector Adjustment Loan: Social Assistance," Europe and Central Asia Department, Human Resources, World Bank, Washington, D.C, September, processed.

Slovak Statistics (1994), *Príjmy, výdavky a spotreba domacností za rok 1993*, vol. 1–3, Bratislava:Slovak Statistics.

Slovenian Statistics (1994), "Statistične informacije," Slovenian Statistics, Ljubljana.

Sologoub, Michel (1988), "L'inegalité des révenus primaires en France de 1962 à 1979," *Revue Économique*, no. 3, pp. 545–572.

Sokoloff, Georges (1993), "La croissance économique dans l'Empire Russe et en URSS," *Économie Internationale*, vol. 54, no. 2, pp. 185–193.

Spéder, Zsolt (1995), "Some Aspects of the Social Transition Processes in Hungary and East Germany: Income Inequality and Poverty," German Institute for Economic Research (DIW) Discussion Paper no. 104, Berlin, processed.

Statistics Canada (1991), *Income Distribution by Size in Canada 1990*, Ottawa: Statistics Canada, December.

Statistical Office of Estonia (1995), "Monthly Statistical Indicators," September, Tallinn, processed.

Sugar, Peter F., Peter Hanak, and Tibor Frank (eds.) (1990), *A History of Hungary*, Bloomington and Indianapolis: Indiana University Press.

Tóth, István György, Rudolf Andorka, Michael Förster, and Zsolt Spéder (1994), "Poverty, Inequality, and the Incidence of Social Transfers in Hungary," Europe and Central Asia Department, World Bank, Budapest Regional Office, June 26, processed.

Tóth, István György, and Michael F. Förster (1994), "Income Poverty and Households' Income Composition in Hungary," paper presented at the Third Prague International Workshop on Social Responses to Transformations in East-Central Europe, March, processed.

Turkish Central Statistical Office (1990), *Statistical Yearbook 1990*, Ankara: Central Statistical Office.

Ukrainian Committee for Statistics (1996), *Statistical Yearbook 1995*, Kiev: Ukrainian Committee for Statistics.

UNICEF (1995), *Poverty, Children and Policy: Responses for a Brighter Future,* Economies in Transition Studies, Regional Monitoring Report no. 3, Florence, Italy:United Nations Children's Fund.

United Kingdom Central Statistical Office (1991), "Economic Trends," London, March.

_____ (1994), "Economic Trends," London, January.

_____ (1994), *Social Trends,* London: Central Statistical Office.

United Nations Economic Commission for Europe (1994), "International Purchasing Power Comparison of GDPs in Europe," Conference of European Statisticians, Statistical Standards and Studies Working Paper no. 45, processed.

Večernik, Jiří (1991), "Poverty in Czechoslovakia: A Brief Report Based on Two Surveys," Institute of Sociology, Prague, processed.

_____ (1994), "Changes in the Rate and Types of Poverty: The Czech and Slovak Republics 1990–1993," Institute of Sociology, Prague, processed.

_____ (1994a), "Changing Earnings Inequality under the Economic Transformation. The Czech and Slovak Republics in 1984–92," Institute of Sociology, Prague, processed.

Večernik, Jiří, et al. (1994), "Czech and Slovak Republics in 1990–93: Tables and Figures on Income, Labor Market, Poverty and Attitudes of the Population," Institute of Sociology, Prague, January, processed.

Veit-Wilson, John (1996), "Aktualne problemy ubóstwa w krajach Europy zachodniej" in Stanislawa Galinowska (ed.), *Polityka spoleczna wobec ubóstwa:ujecie porównawcze,* Warsaw:Instytut Praci i Spraw Socjalnych.

Vietnam State Planning Committee-General Statistical Office (1994), *Vietnam Living Standards Survey 1992–93,* Hanoi:General Statistical Office.

von Rauch, Georg (1974), *The Baltic States: The Years of Independence 1917–40,* Berkeley and Los Angeles: The University of California Press.

Walters, Garrison E. (1988), *The Other Europe: Eastern Europe to 1945,* Syracuse, N.Y.:Syracuse University Press.

Winiecki, Jan (1991), "The Inevitability of a Fall in Output in the Early Stages of Transition to the Market: Theoretical Underpinnings," *Soviet Studies,* vol. 43, no. 4, pp.669–667.

World Bank (1993), "Jordan Poverty Assessment," vol. 1, Middle East Department, Washington, D.C., September, processed.

_____ (1994), "Peru Living Standards Measurement Survey 1994: Means Tables," Policy Research Department, Poverty and Human Resources Division, Washington, D.C., processed.

———— (1994a), "Russia: Poverty, Policy, and Responses: A Preliminary Assessment," vol. 1, Europe and Central Asia Department, Human Resources Division, Washington, D.C., September, processed.

———— (1994b), "Colombia Poverty Assessment," Latin America and Caribbean Department, Washington, D.C., August, processed.

———— (1995), *Understanding Poverty in Poland*, A World Bank Country Study, Washington, D.C.

———— (1995a), "Romania Poverty Assessment," Europe and Central Asia Department, Washington, D.C., June, processed.

———— (1995b), "Poverty and Social Transfers in Hungary," Europe and Central Asia Department, Washington, D.C., May, processed.

———— (1995c), "Economic Decline, Living Standards, and Equity in Belarus," Europe and Central Asia Department, Washington, D.C., December, processed.

———— (1995d), "Ecuador: Poverty Report," Latin America and Caribbean Department, Washington, D.C., November, processed.

———— (1995e), "Poverty in Russia: An Asssessment," Europe and Central Asia Department, Human Resources Division, Washington, D.C., March, processed.

———— (1995f) "Brazil: A Poverty Assessment," Latin America and Caribbean Department, Washington, D.C., June, processed.

———— (1996), "Estonia: Living Standards Assessment," Europe and Central Asia Department, Washington, D.C., June, processed.

———— (1996a), "Belarus: Poverty in Belarus," Europe and Central Asia Department, Washington, D.C., January, processed.

———— (1996b), "Poverty in Ukraine," Europe and Central Asia Department, Washington, D.C., June, processed.

———— (1996c), "Madagascar: Poverty Assessment," East Africa Department, Washington, D.C., processed.

———— (1997), "Romania: Poverty and Social Policy," Europe and Central Asia Department, Washington, D.C., processed.

World Bank and Government of the Russian Federation (1995), *Russian Federation: Report on the National Accounts*, Washington D.C. and Moscow, Russia: World Bank and Government of the Russian Federation.

World Bank Socio-economic Data Division (1992), "Measuring the Incomes of Economies of the Former Soviet Union," World Bank Policy Research Department Working Paper no. 1057, Washington, D.C., processed.

Yugoslav Federal Government (1995), "Causes of Black Economy and Factors Promoting its Expansion," *Yugoslav Survey*, no.1, pp. 85–94.

Zaborkas, K., (1996), "The Results of the First Quarter Household Budget Survey in 1996," Lithuanian Central Statistical Office, processed.

Zimonjic-Peric, Vesna (1995), "Former Yugoslavia: The Grim Statistics," Interpress Service, IGP News Desk, 24 November, processed.

Subject Index

Albania, 2, 5, 25, 58
Armenia, 1n, 3, 5, 25, 27n, 31
Azerbaijan, 1n, 3, 5, 27n

Balkans, 72; inequality in, 42; poverty in, 74, 76 (*see also* individual countries)
Baltic republics, 3, 58, 71; income decline, 33; income shares, 37, 38; inequality in, 42, 132; non-pension transfers, 111; poverty in, 74, 76, 79, 80; unemployment benefits, 110 (*see also* individual countries)
Belarus, 3, 27, 58, 74, 80, 134; income shares, 38; poor in, 105, 106, 117; poverty in, 79, 92, 93, 94
Besarabia, 3n
Bosnia and Herzegovina, 2n, 3
Bulgaria, 2, 3n, 7, 12, 13, 23n, 58, 80, 124, 134; family benefits, 110; income shares, 38; inequality in, 44ff, 49, 54; poor in, 92, 96, 107, 117; poverty in, 79; private sector in, 39; returns to education, 104n

Central Asian republics, 34, 65n, 71, 118; inequality in, 40, 132; poverty in, 74, 76, 79 (*see also* individual countries)
Central Europe, 71, 118; inequality in, 41, 132; poverty in, 67, 79, 80 (*see also* individual countries)
Communism: and attitude toward private sector, 20; and attitude toward wealth, 21; and composition of income, 13ff; consumer subsidies, 15n; family benefits in, 15, 20; inequality in, 15; *nomenklatura*, 15, 21; pensions in, 17; and private sector income, 18; social transfers in, 16; state employment in, 12; taxation in, 15, 19; and wage distribution, 18, 20;
Croatia, 3, 27n, 31n
Czech republic, 3, 7, 29, 31, 71; income shares, 38; inequality in, 45; poverty in, 85, 86; poverty line in, 98; poor in, 102, 103; private sector in, 39; returns to education, 104n; social assistance system, 116

Czechoslovakia, 2, 13, 16, 17, 58; poverty line in, 86n

Eastern Europe 49; income decline, 33; income shares, 37; non-pension transfers, 111; private sector in, 39; unemployment in, 29; unemployment benefits, 110; wage decline, 29;
Eastern Germany: poor in, 104
Estonia, 27, 37n, 38, 58, 81, 124; inequality in, 45; poor in, 117; poverty in, 92, 93; social assistance system, 116

Georgia, 3, 5, 25
German Democratic Republic, 2; poor in, 103
Great Depression, 26ff

Habsburg Empire, 2n
Health and education expenditures: during transition, 38
Hungary, 1n, 2, 3n, 7, 12, 13, 16, 17, 27, 31, 35, 65n, 71, 124; income shares, 38, 39; inequality in, 44ff, 54; poor in, 95, 102, 106, 117; poverty in, 93; poverty line in, 98; social assistance system, 116

Income during transition: changing income shares, 37ff; compared to expenditures 32, 33; consumption-in-kind 32n; decline, 30ff; measurement, 32 (*see also* Output during transition)
Inequality during transition, 40ff; and differences among social groups, 54; and distribution of income sources, 47ff; income vs. expenditure distribution, 42; regressive redistribution, 45; and type of adjustment, 46
International Comparison Project (ICP), 65

Kazakhstan, 1n, 71, 83
Kuznets curve, 15n
Kyrgyz Republic, 33n, 41, 74, 83

Latvia, 25, 134; income shares, 38; inequality in, 45, 49

Name Index